T0279802

The Bravest Pets of Gotham

The Bravest Pets *of* Gotham

TALES OF FOUR-LEGGED FIREFIGHTERS OF OLD NEW YORK

❧— Peggy Gavan —❧

RUTGERS UNIVERSITY PRESS

New Brunswick, Camden, and Newark, New Jersey
London and Oxford

Rutgers University Press is a department of Rutgers, The State University of New Jersey, one of the leading public research universities in the nation. By publishing worldwide, it furthers the University's mission of dedication to excellence in teaching, scholarship, research, and clinical care.

Library of Congress Cataloging-in-Publication Data
Names: Gavan, Peggy, author.
Title: The bravest pets of Gotham : tales of four-legged firefighters of Old New York / Peggy Gavan.
Description: New Brunswick, New Jersey : Rutgers University Press, [2024] | Includes bibliographical references and index.
Identifiers: LCCN 2023055473 | ISBN 9781978839892 (cloth) | ISBN 9781978839908 (epub) | ISBN 9781978839915 (pdf)
Subjects: LCSH: Fire departments—New York (State)—New York—Juvenile literature. | Firehouse dogs—New York (State)—New York—Juvenile literature. | Mascots—New York (State)—New York—Juvenile literature.
Classification: LCC TH9148 .G38 2024 | DDC 636.7/088609747—dc23/eng/20240325
LC record available at https://lccn.loc.gov/2023055473

A British Cataloging-in-Publication record for this book is available from the British Library.

References to internet websites (URLs) were accurate at the time of writing. Neither the author nor Rutgers University Press is responsible for URLs that may have expired or changed since the manuscript was prepared.

∞ The paper used in this publication meets the requirements of the American National Standard for Information Sciences—Permanence of Paper for Printed Library Materials, ANSI Z39.48-1992.

rutgersuniversitypress.org

Dedicated to all human and animal firefighters—past, present, and future—and especially to those who have made the supreme sacrifice in the performance of their duties

CONTENTS

The Bravest Pets of Gotham

Introduction

Everybody knows that a mascot is as necessary wherever men who wear blue coats are gathered as the very coats themselves, for how else is good luck going to attend the wearers of those coats in their daily hazardous duties?

—"Animal Mascots of Police and Firemen
Aid to Stop Thieves and Save Lives,"
New York Evening Telegram, December 3, 1911

In twentieth-century Gotham, the Fire Department of the City of New York (FDNY) permitted firemen to keep one dog, one cat, or multiple singing birds in their firehouse. Most, if not all, fire companies broke these rules, keeping multiple pets that served as good-luck mascots and companions. In 1911, a reporter for the *New York Evening Telegram* observed that if the city's firemen and policemen were to have a parade of mascots, "it would probably be such a procession of dogs and cats that it would take hours to pass a given point." These pets, along with the horses that pulled the apparatus, provided companionship for the men, who were required to live at their firehouses for extended periods of time with only a few hours off for dinner breaks. As FDNY Secretary Alfred Michael Downes wrote in 1907, "A gentler phase of the fireman's life is shown in their devotion to their horses and pets. Dogs, cats, and even monkeys are adopted in the fire-houses, and share the affections of the men with the horses."

Although the FDNY permitted firemen to keep one dog, one cat, or multiple singing birds in the firehouse, most companies had two or more pets. (Photograph provided courtesy of the Municipal Archives, City of New York)

In addition to friendship, many firemen believed their mascots would bring good luck; they regarded their pets as much as a guard against evil in dangerous situations as a source of happiness in the firehouse—a purring kitten or a puppy wagging his tail was sometimes all a man needed to steady his nerves following a tough call. Some remarkable animals also took on the role of hero, performing daring or ingenious feats to save the lives of firemen, civilians, or other animals in distress.

Unlike the horses, which, under the city's paid fire department, received official assignments to each company, most animal mascots intentionally claimed a particular firehouse as their own, recognizing a good thing when they had it. Some mascots, however—especially the full-bred Dalmatian fire dogs—were gifts from grateful benefactors who wanted to offer the men a token of their appreciation. Others earned a spot in the firehouse following their dramatic rescue from a burning building. There was also no shortage of gifts from neighborhood children who wanted to share every stray dog or cat they found with their local firehouse. At one time, there were indications that firehouses might become private zoos, with so many contributions "from hero worshipping small boys." Thus, the department had to limit the number of mascots permitted, giving preference to dogs, cats, and singing birds. These rules technically banned mascots such as Jake, the parrot of Ladder 111, who didn't sing but rather squawked angrily when left alone; Nosey, the turtle of Engine 8, who slowed the men down by napping under apparatus wheels; Foxy, the fox of Engine 40; or Mrs. Herman of Engine 31, one of the department's many monkey mascots in the early twentieth century. For the most part, though, the rules didn't stop the men from having more animals than allowed.

Always a source of pride to the firemen, the horses were working partners rather than mascots, but they were also the men's friends. In 1930, several years after the last remaining fire horses had retired, a veteran explained the bond to the *New York Sun*: "There were pets among them, of course, for almost anyone loves a horse, and you can't be with them every day most of your life without getting to like them even if you were not gaited that way to begin with." Dr. Harry Mortimer Archer, a fire buff who spent sixty years responding to fires and attending to the injured firemen, told the *New-York Tribune* in 1920, "Loyalty and courage were two of the predominant qualities among the beasts, and they rarely flinched when called to the test. Because of these and other qualities, the animals invariably became great pets, loved alike by the firemen and by the children in the neighborhood."

According to a report in the *New York Press*, there were about 90 dogs and 120 cats among the 200 fire companies in Manhattan and Brooklyn in 1903, a number that no doubt excluded dozens, if not hundreds, of unreported firemen's pets throughout these two boroughs alone. During this period, there were also about 1,500 horses in the FDNY across all five boroughs. These reports provide but a small snapshot in time and do not include the thousands of horses and animal mascots that made their marks in the history of the FDNY before and after this era. The following accounts of friendship, dedication, and bravery represent only a sampling of amazing FDNY animal tales, but together they honor the legacy of every horse, dog, cat, monkey, and other animal who ever served the FDNY as a working partner, good-luck charm, comforting companion, or lifesaving hero.

1

Fire Horses

Short of your mother, your wife, and your sister, the finest thing living is the fire horse, from training stable to hospital.
—Chief Joseph Shea, FDNY veterinarian, "Making a Brain for a Gallant Fire Horse," *New York Times*, March 6, 1904

Until 1865, the year New York's political leaders pushed through state legislation to create a paid fire department for the City of New York (Manhattan), the city's volunteer fire companies primarily used manpower to pull and operate the apparatus. Young boys called runners, who were too young to join a company, would also run with the volunteers, clearing the streets and using ropes to help pull the heavy engines.

Although fire horses are most associated with the steam-engine era of the paid department, a few horses served the volunteer fire service in the early nineteenth century. For example, Eagle Fire Engine Company 13 used a horse and cart on January 8, 1808, following a major snowstorm. The volunteers also used horsepower on May 18, 1827, during a fire involving multiple buildings. The first officially reported volunteer company to employ a horse in New York City was Mutual Hook and Ladder 1 on Beaver Street, courtesy of Foreman John W. Towt, an Old Slip merchant who purchased the horse in 1830. According to Abraham B. Purdy, a member of Oceanus Engine Company 11, "the introduction of horsepower was owing to a squabble in the company, which resulted in the resignation of so many members that not enough remained to draw the truck to a fire." The horse became winded, and after losing a race with the men of Oceanus while going up a hill on Canal Street, he was "no good after that." Apparently, the squabble was related to an outbreak of cholera; only a handful of Mutual volunteers were willing to enter the plague-ridden district and expose themselves to the health risk.

Two years later, when another cholera outbreak took out many volunteers in November 1832, Chief Engineer James Gulick billed the city comptroller $863.75 for horses to replace the men who had taken ill. Other reports from the volunteer era mention an aged sorrel horse who achieved local fame by running away from Niagara-Knickerbocker Hose Company 2 on Duane Street and two horses that were attached to Bolivar Engine 9 on Beaver Street. Franklin Waterbury, foreman of Excelsior Engine 2 on Henry Street, also received notoriety for attaching his horse to an engine to pull it through deep snow. This valuable horse died from excessive exertion.

Aside from using richly decorated horses to pull their apparatus on wheeled platform wagons during parades, the volunteer firemen didn't appreciate the true potential of the horse, especially because horses couldn't run the apparatus on sidewalks as they could do. Horsepower eventually caught on, but Ladder 1, which purchased its first horse on November 8, 1832, was the only volunteer company with a full-time horse for many years. Public hearings to address the need for a paid department with horses to draw the engines took place as early as 1840, but it would take twenty-five more years for the full transition to happen.

By 1866, most of Manhattan's volunteer units had been phased out and replaced by the thirty-four engine companies and twelve ladder companies of the new Metropolitan Fire Department. The paid department equipped each company with steam engines, a telegraph system, and horses. By transitioning to horse-drawn

Prior to 1865, the city's volunteer fire companies used manpower to pull and operate the apparatus. (The Miriam and Ira D. Wallach Division of Art, Prints and Photographs: Picture Collection. "The night alarm." *The New York Public Library Digital Collections.* 1881-01)

steam engines and reducing manpower from 3,421 volunteers in 1865 to 599 paid firemen in 1869, the city was able to cut its fire-related losses by almost $4 million, a 60 percent reduction. Talk about horsepower.

Fully recognizing the monetary and functional value of horses, Acting Department Chief Edward Franklin Croker issued the following special order on June 29, 1899:

In the future, when drivers and others have occasion to be around the horses, the practice of shouting and talking in a loud and boisterous manner must not be tolerated. They will speak to the animals in a kind and gentle manner, and in that way find that the horses will become more gentle and intelligent, and quicker to obey. The whip, stable broom, or fork must not be used to punish the horses. The drivers and other members of Companies cannot pay too much attention to this important branch of the service, and Company Commanders will see that the provisions of the above sections are enforced to the letter. Attention is also called to the trimming of the horses' fetlocks and manes, and the care of harness. The practice of washing the harness in hot water will be discontinued, and water of a medium temperature used. The harness will then be thoroughly dried, and a small quantity of harness oil, or dressing, applied. The dressing can be obtained from the Supply Clerk on requisition. In all cases, Officers will see that the harness fits the horse properly, and that the bit is in its proper place, and not hanging down in the mouth. Stalls must also be kept neat and clean, and in as healthful a condition as possible, and properly bedded down.

When it came to responding to fires, the job of a fire horse was equally as demanding as the job of a fireman, if not more so. The horses had to gallop up hills on hot summer days and dash down icy cobblestone streets in the winter. They had to be fast learners, full of spirit, and courageous and to always exert themselves. With guidance from their drivers (also called whips), they had to quickly maneuver through the giant obstacle course that was Old New York, avoiding trolley cars and horse-drawn vehicles, pedestrians, stray animals, and the dreaded "L" pillars of the elevated railway structures. Nothing they saw or heard could intimidate them, be it flashing lights, surging crowds, trolley bells, human screams, burning buildings, or falling walls. And while fire horses were a cut above the rest, they were not unlike the apparatus in that they were also prone to accidents, breaking down, or just running out of steam at inopportune times. The following true accounts illustrate just a few of the hazards these horses and their drivers faced every day and provide insight on the love and pride the firemen had for their loyal and courageous equine partners.

While responding to an afternoon alarm in the Bronx in July 1898, Engine 46 at 451 East 176th Street almost lost its favorite horse to a freak strangulation accident. The company was going to a fire in West Farms when Tom, drawing the tender, fell into an open cellar grate in the sidewalk. Tom hung suspended by his harness and collar and slowly began choking to death as the men tried in vain to unhitch him. Fortunately, the building had an elevator for lowering supplies, and the men were able to raise the elevator under Tom until it supported the horse, allowing them to unhitch him and lower him into the cellar. Now the problem was getting the horse out of the cellar. Chief Hugh Bonner ordered that "no expense should be spared to save Tom," and thus, workmen cut an opening through the brick wall in the rear of the building.

Another fluke accident took place in August 1901, when two of the three horses of Engine 74 at 207 West Seventy-Seventh Street became impaled on an iron fence at the foot of a steep hill on West Sixty-Ninth Street. According to news reports, Driver John Biggers was making a turn and heading toward a fire plug (hydrant) when a group of children blocked his way. Due to the weight of the heavy truck and the steepness of the hill, he couldn't hold back, so he sent the team of black horses smashing into a brick wall and iron fence on the other side of the street. Baby, the lead horse, took the wall at a bound and leaped sixty feet down onto the railroad tracks of the New York Central. A large chunk of the wall fell onto the tracks, followed by the other two horses. As the horses hung suspended by the fence, a train approached. One of the firemen flagged down the train, thus preventing what could have been a fatal accident if the fence had given way. Baby was unscathed, but one of the other horses died. The third horse survived, but he would never work as a fire horse again. The driver and crew narrowly escaped severe injuries.

In July 1907, Dan of Brooklyn's Engine 101 at 5113 Fourth Avenue became temporarily blinded after the engine collided with a trolley car. Dan slipped under the engine, and the hot cinders landed over his eyes. A veterinary surgeon told Driver Cornelius Nolan that Dan would never see again, but Nolan told the press he'd never give up on Dan, even if two hundred veterinarians confirmed the diagnosis. He bought all the borax he could carry, placed it in warm water, and bathed Dan's eyes. One by one—to the surprise of the veterinarian—the cinders came out. It took a few days, but eventually Dan began to blink his eyes. The veterinarian said the horse would be "as good as ever after a week or so."

In addition to facing dangerous conditions on the street, some horses created havoc by running away from the firehouse unhitched to the apparatus. New horses (called green horses) still on probation often ran away due to their lack of experience, such as Jerry

With guidance from the drivers, fire horses such as this team running through the heart of Times Square had to maneuver around trolley cars, horse-drawn vehicles, "L" pillars, and pedestrians. (Library of Congress, Prints & Photographs Division [LC-DIG-ggbain-15067])

of Brooklyn's Engine 124, who ran from the firehouse at 274 Hicks Street in May 1905—even breaking the chain stretched across the door—instead of waiting for the harness to drop. His mates Tom and Dick, a dynamic duo who pulled a lighter engine, decided to follow Jerry, who had just been recruited to help pull the big new engine. The three horses galloped down Hicks Street with a crowd of hundreds following. Eventually all three horses were retrieved about a mile from the firehouse, but the episode created much excitement and put many human lives in danger.

Three horses running unharnessed and abreast for three miles without a driver from Bushwick to Williamsburg created an impressive picture on the morning of June 28, 1910. According to the *Brooklyn Daily Eagle*, an early-morning alarm had come into Brooklyn's Engine 137 at 43 Morgan Avenue. As the front doors of the engine quarters opened, and the men began sliding down the pole and scrambling for their gear, the three gray horses dashed from their stalls to their positions in front of the engine. Before the men could stop them, the horses rushed out of the building. The clattering of hoofs sent several policemen into the streets, "but they might just as well have tried to stop a whirlwind as to head off the galloping grays." Eventually, Policeman Frank Wrightman of the Bedford Avenue station was able to grip the mane of one of the horses. The team dragged him off his feet, but he got another good grip and was able to stop the horses and secure them with a rope. The members of Engine 137 received notification of the capture, and the horses, now quite docile after their long run, returned to the firehouse.

Runaways were quite common among those horses on active duty, but retired fire horses still working on the city streets were also apt to make a run for it when they heard a clanging bell or saw their old pals sweeping past. With instincts kicking in, they'd heed the imaginary alarm, dashing off to follow their original calling. As FDNY Secretary Alfred Downes noted in 1907, "A fire-horse . . . never forgets that he was a fire-horse. He never forgets the clang of the gong, the sharp snap of the electric signal, or the sound of the engine whistle and bell. If one of these old horses who has fallen into the hands of the huckster happens to be near an engine-house when the alarm rings in, he will dash after the engine, no matter what kind of load he may be drawing. These instances are often-times pathetic rather than funny."

One such story of a runaway retired horse that was both pathetic and comical involved an ambulance horse who mistook a trolley bell for an alarm. Pete, a former fire horse in Brooklyn, was working as an Eastern District Hospital ambulance horse in February 1911 when he heard the clanging bell of a trolley car. The ambulance driver and doctor had just placed an injured man into the ambu-lance when Pete heeded his old calling and took off up Greenpoint Avenue. The driver and doctor stood watching in disbelief as their horse and patient headed east toward Manhattan Avenue. Three policemen from the Bedford Avenue station tried to stop him, but Pete was determined to do his job. He eventually made it back to the hospital on South Third Street, where the driver and doctor were waiting for him. The injured man was treated and expected to recover from both his injuries and the unexpected joy ride.

Many times, the opposite of a runaway incident happened, when the horses simply refused to budge. On February 6, 1901, for example, the three horses of Brooklyn's Ladder 56 refused to leave the warm firehouse at 124 Greenpoint Avenue when an alarm sounded at two in the morning. The horses set up and dashed outside, but as soon as they reached the icy roadway, they stopped short and refused to go further. Despite coaxing and prodding, they stayed put. The men sent word to headquarters, which detailed Ladder 54 to the fire. Fortunately, the blaze was minor, so the delay did not cost loss of life or property. That was not the case in January 1913, when a fire destroyed two frame dwellings in Staten Island and threatened a dozen more buildings. There was a long delay in getting apparatus to the blaze because the firemen had to allow their horses to stop and rest a few times on the steep hills—it took about thirty minutes for the men to finally arrive on the scene and start attacking the flames.

Fire horses also created comical and chaotic scenes that resulted in property damage while preventing the apparatus from reaching the fire. In January 1896, the large bay horse who pulled the buggy of Battalion Chief Joseph P. Byrne broke loose from his halter and plunged toward the glass doors of Nathaniel Levy's butcher shop at 238 West Twentieth Street. The horse landed in the store, with the upper part of the door frame hanging from his neck. He kicked over whatever he could reach until firemen and policemen finally lassoed him with a clothesline. A few years later, in November 1903, the big grays of Engine 55 at 363 Broome Street slid into a group of children playing in front of Isaac Schrieber's saloon at Broome and Orchard Streets when Driver John Wakely attempted to avoid a collision with Ladder 6 by pulling up hard on the left. The harness of the nigh (left) horse burst, sending the other two horses plunging ahead. One of them crashed into a plate-glass window, knocking wine and whisky bottles to the floor. Somehow, Schrieber's three-year-old son landed on top of the horse's hind legs. There were no injuries, and fortunately, it was a false alarm.

By 1920, with only a few hundred horses still in service, news stories of the gallant fire horses were few and far between. As the *New-York Tribune* noted in January 1920, "The city had grown great; the distances to be covered are long; speed is an essential factor in saving lives and properties and fire horses no longer are equal to the task. But the tradition and custom die hard, no matter how closely pressed by progress, and there isn't a firehouse in the city but retains with jealous pride its quota of stories of the services that were performed by the courageous old quadrupeds." Following are just a few of thousands of such stories.

Engine 33: Jim, Jack, and Jerry

Under the rules of the FDNY, when horses were no longer fit for the hard service of pulling engines, hose reels, or ladder trucks, the department would sell them at auction to any huckster who needed an old horse to pull his cart or do his dirty work. But no such fate was to come to Jim—at least not if Chief Bonner or Engine 33 Captain William H. Nash had any say in the matter.

Jim was a large strawberry roan of thoroughbred pedigree, born in Kentucky and thought to be related to Norman, the famous racehorse of the American financier August Belmont Jr. Officially known as Registered Horse No. 60, Jim began his FDNY career with Engine 33 at 220 Mercer Street on January 14, 1879, when he was about seven years old. He remained on active and reserve duty for nearly nineteen years until November 4, 1897. For eleven of those years, Jim and his mate drew a heavy first-class engine—the type that in later years was drawn by three horses. Jim was always the offside horse, meaning he took the right side of the engine.

During his long FDNY tenure, Jim wore out several mates that couldn't keep up with him. Should the nigh horse loaf around, Jim would turn toward him—even while in full gallop—and nip at the other's neck to admonish him for slacking on the job. One of the few horses that worked well with Jim was another strawberry roan named Jack. Sadly, Jack died while responding to an alarm in May 1881 when the team collided with the Engine 13 tender. A pole plunged twelve inches into the horse's body, fatally wounding him. The company replaced Jack with Horse No. 350, whom they also named Jack. Jim and his new partner pulled the engine, and a horse named Jerry drew the tender. The men called them "the three Jays."

Jim of Engine 33 served as an FDNY fire horse for eighteen years. (The Miriam and Ira D. Wallach Division of Art, Prints and Photographs: Picture Collection. "'Jim' of Engine 33." *The New York Public Library Digital Collections.* 1887)

Jim and Jack achieved fame and publicity on October 26, 1883, when they took first prize in the hitch-up drill at the inaugural National Horse Show at Madison Square Garden. The pair beat the competition by hitching into a swinging harness in just under two seconds. During the show, high-society ladies stroked Jim's neck, and millionaires pointed to his muscular flanks and powerful legs while commenting on his massive proportions. Following the event, Engine 33 became popular with visitors who had read about the horses and wanted to reward them with sugar cubes. Sometimes Jim would perform tricks for the visitors, such as "shaking hands," bowing for candy, carrying a bucket of water, and kneeling in a prayer position.

Jerry was also a massive horse, at seventeen hundred pounds. The coal-black horse began his FDNY career with Ladder 7 on East Twenty-Eighth Street in 1876, when he was four years old. In 1881, he transferred to Engine 33, where he earned recognition for his "pluck, strength and ambition." One of his greatest feats took place on the first night of the Great Blizzard of 1888. On that night, he pulled the seventy-two-hundred-pound tender for one and a half miles, keeping up with the two-horse engine and passing four-horse tenders stuck in the snow. At times during the storm, Jerry pulled the tender through drifts that were higher than his head. When the engine got so far ahead that it was out of his view, he grew frantic and strained every muscle to catch up with Jim and Jack.

On December 22, 1889, Engine 33 responded to a small kitchen fire at the New York Hotel. There was no urging required from Driver William E. Wise as Jerry pulled the tender with ten men aboard down Great Jones Street and up Broadway. But as Jerry reached Fourth Street, Fire Patrol 2 came racing down the street, whereupon the two large pieces of apparatus collided. The iron tip of the patrol wagon's pole plunged six inches into Jerry's chest. The driver for the patrol wagon backed up his team to extract the pole from Jerry, who continued to the fire as blood streamed from the hole. The tender was the first to reach the fire; Jerry was immediately unhitched and led to the department's horse hospital, then located at 199 Chrystie Street. The veterinarian told the men he expected Jerry to fully recover following a brief respite.

The final fates of Jerry and Jack were not reported, but Jim continued his storied career with Engine 33 for a few more years, under the care of Driver Charley Specht. Although Jim retired from active duty in 1891, he remained on reserve duty with the double company's second-section engine until 1897. Calls for the second section were relatively rare, so Jim reportedly acquired a taste for beer and chewing tobacco during his twilight years. His last day of duty was November 3, 1897, when he helped pull the engine down to Chambers Street. The horse alongside him was a spare horse known to loaf, and Jim—who was nearly blind by this time—began biting the horse's neck while galloping in style down the street.

Following this last run, Captain Nash sent Jim to the horse hospital. There, he grew restive and depressed from being away from the action and the sound of the fire gong. When he refused to take his feed, the captain sent Driver Specht to the hospital two or three times a day. Jim would always welcome Specht and eat whatever food he offered.

In a letter that Captain Nash penned to the Fire Board requesting Jim be allowed to retire with dignity, he wrote extensively of Jim's intelligence. All the officers and members connected with the company, as well as many distinguished guests who visited the quarters, had expressed the belief that no other horse showed more intelligence than Jim. At the sound of the gong, Nash wrote, Jim would bound from his stall at full speed and slide along the floor as much as eight feet before stopping directly under his harness. Whenever the men turned him loose on the street for exercise, he'd immediately return to his proper place under the harness should the gong sound. He never missed a day of work, and even when showered with broken glass or other falling objects or drenched with water from a broken hose, he kept on working undisturbed. "There was never a horse connected with this department who performed so much hard service as faithfully as poor old Jim, to say nothing of the pleasure he gave the many visitors at these quarters by his actions, which showed almost human intelligence," Nash concluded.

Chief Bonner also wrote a letter to the board, stating that he fully endorsed the captain's letter while reiterating the opinion that Jim was one of the most intelligent horses in the department. "I appeal to the board on behalf of this faithful animal that he be retained in the service of the department and assigned to some company where the duties will be light, and that the Superintendent of Horses be directed to not include in his sale registered No. 60, which is the number assigned to this faithful animal."

Engineer Hugh Burns, who had been in his position since 1869, didn't write a letter about Jim, but he did wax sentimental about the beloved horse at the board's meeting on November 19, 1897. With "an affection for the horse as deep and great as the friendship which exists between man and man," Burns bragged about all the tricks Jim could do, noting that the horse was "like a little child at school" when he was a youngster. Jim could turn the faucet on when he wanted water and pull the alarm gong before the attendant could reach it (before the days of electricity, when the gong was rung by hand). He could also distinguish between the men he liked and those he disliked.

The letters and speeches worked. The fate that met other equine firefighters was not to be Jim's. Instead of sending him to the auction block, Fire Board President James Rockwell Sheffield ordered that Jim be saved from the milk or grocery wagon. He sent Jim to one of the new firehouses in the Bronx—reportedly Engine 52 at 4550 Riverdale Avenue—where he'd spend his remaining days in green pastures and his nights in the comfort of the quiet firehouse.

"He will feel strange up there in the country, so far from his old engine-house," Nash told a reporter from the *New York World*. "You know, an old horse like that, when he finds himself put away, is like an old man retired from business. He potters around for a while and then breaks down altogether, because he has nothing to keep him interested in life." Nash said he was sure the horse would receive proper care, but he felt certain Jim's heart would eventually break if he couldn't answer any more fire alarms.

As of 1902, Jim was the only FDNY fire horse to receive a pension. According to the *New York Sun*, he lived at the Bronx firehouse for the rest of his life, nibbling the grass along the country lanes and doing tricks for the firemen. One day the men found him in a heap near the firehouse, stricken with paralysis. An officer from the Society for the Prevention of Cruelty to Animals (SPCA) humanely dispatched Old Jim, who would have been about thirty years old at the time of his death.

HISTORICAL HOOK

On May 30, 1907, the remarkable horses of Engine 33 made the headlines again. On this day, close to two thousand workhorses that carted produce and lumber and garbage and firefighting equipment finally had their day in the sun—and a chance to shine for the people of New York City. For on this Decoration Day, these everyday heroes were all invited to participate in the first annual New York City Workhorse Parade. The parade, organized by the Women's Auxiliary of the SPCA, was based on the successful workhorse parades in London and Boston, in which horses and their drivers won cash prizes and ribbons. The main purpose of the event was to incentivize owners and drivers to provide their horses with quality care and treatment—in other words, as Mrs. Minnie Cadwalader Rawles Jones noted, "to show men that it pays to treat their horses well."

Mrs. Jones, then president of the auxiliary, explained that although all workhorses were invited to participate—including the teams of horses used in the fire, police, correction, and sanitation departments—the intent of the parade was to showcase the horses of expressmen, junkmen, small market men, and others who owned only one horse and perhaps drove it themselves. She acknowledged that these workhorses were apt to be older horses that were often poorly treated and neglected. Some of these horses may have even been retired FDNY horses.

Following a parade up Fifth Avenue from the Washington Square Arch to the Worth Monument at Madison Square, the horses separated into forty-seven classes, including milk wagons, ambulances, grocers, florists, fire, corrections, charity, police, street cleaning, and aged equine veterans. The judges, led by Mrs. Ellin Prince Speyer, spent four hours doling out ribbons, medals, diplomas, and gold-piece prizes to the more than one hundred horses and their drivers. For the fire department teams, first prize went to the two-horse tender team driven by Michael V. Corbett of Engine

In 1907, Engine 33 Driver John Roth and his three-horse team took second place at the New York City Workhorse Parade, winning this medal made by Tiffany & Co. (Photograph provided courtesy of Lt. Ed Sere, Ret., FDNY)

Engine 14 Driver Charles F. Gilbride and horses Lightfoot, Reporter, and Evade at the New York City Workhorse Parade in May 1914. (Library of Congress, Prints & Photographs Division [LC-DIG-ggbain-16149])

33, second prize went to a three-horse engine team driven by John Roth of Engine 33, and third prize went to Captain James J. Caberly for the three-horse team of Ladder 8.

The last workhorse parade in Manhattan took place in 1914. That year, the blue-ribbon award in the fire-horse class went to Engine 14 Driver Charles F. Gilbride and the engine's big white horses, Lightfoot, Reporter, and Evade. Driver Louis Lubcker, also of Engine 14, earned a red ribbon for the tender horses, Ranger and Bushmill. Ben Hur, Brenham, and Medford—three black horses driven by William S. Carney of Ladder 12—took home a ribbon and a Speyer silver medal.

Engine 7, Ladder 23, and Engine 18:
Joe Hoss, Old Charley, Big Jim, and Dick

There was no shortage of intelligent fire horses in the FDNY, but department favorites earned publicity by performing those tricks that their human companions considered worthy of a bold headline.

Joe Hoss, Old Charley, Big Jim, and Dick were just a few of the many horses who stood out during the late nineteenth century.

Joe Hoss began working as an FDNY fire horse in 1890, joining Engine 7 at 22 Chambers Street about two years later. Like Jim of Engine 33, Joe also won a prize at the National Horse Show and once held the department record for getting himself into his harness faster than any other horse. Joe Hoss had a repertoire of tricks, such as "shaking hands" with his right foreleg and putting wood under the engine boiler when told to do so. He could stick out his tongue and bare his teeth on command to make the children laugh and pick up his own collar from the floor when the alarm bell rang by going down on his knees and wriggling into it. Best of all, when told to pick out "the most glorious flag on earth" from a dozen flags laid out before him, he'd pick up the US flag with his teeth every time.

Joe's partner was Old Charley, a large bay horse who joined Engine 7 around 1893. He was a fast and high-spirited horse, and Joe could barely keep up with him when the company raced to fires. As the engine began pumping water on the flames, Charley would stomp and whinny excitedly, but when the fire was over, he'd hang his head mournfully and take his sweet time returning to the firehouse. Charley could raise his right foreleg and shake hands, but his most famous trick was getting his own water when he was thirsty. He'd simply walk to the faucet near his stall, give it a turn, and drink from the attached hose. When he had enough, he'd drop the hose and turn off the water.

Big Jim, the pure white horse of Ladder 23 at 504 West 140th Street, also figured out how to get water when he was thirsty. Jim's stall, like all those in the old firehouses, had a single chain across the front and rear. The front chain released when the electric alarm acted on a trip wire connected to the shank of the halter. Early in his career, Jim discovered that by dropping his hoof gently on the trip wire, he could release himself without having to wait for the electric signal. Whenever he wanted a drink, he'd touch the trip, release himself, walk slowly to the faucet at the rear of the firehouse, and turn on the faucet with his teeth. Eventually, he learned to perform the same routine for his mate, Jerry, and the horses would take turns drinking from the faucet.

Dick, the pride of Engine 18 and a favorite with the children in Greenwich Village, figured out how to satiate his addiction to sugar by stamping his foot as the children gathered around the chain in front of the firehouse at 132 West Tenth Street. As soon as he got the sugar, he'd reward the child by "shaking hands." (If he didn't get sugar from someone standing next to him, he'd give a little nip on the forgetful person's shoulder; if reproved for this action, he'd immediately offer his foot as a token of his apology.) Dick didn't figure out the faucet trick, but he did learn to strike the iron stall-post with his forward shoe to call attention to his desire for water. Even better, he learned how to count the alarm signals, so he always knew when it was time for his company to respond. Dick was also a joker who loved to trip the harnesses on the other horses; he'd slyly stretch his head into a neighboring stall and grasp the reins in his teeth, pulling on it until the harness dropped down onto his teammate; he'd then meekly back into his stall "and assume an expression of absolute innocence."

In August 1900, Charley fell ill with colic. When his last alarm sounded, he didn't run and stick his head into his harness but instead tried to lie down on the floor. Unfortunately, Joe Hoss was not available, so the men had to hitch Charley to the engine and respond to the fire. The horse spent the rest of the night lying in pain in his stall, where he died the next day.

Joe was condemned to the auction block in September 1902. The old horse had been slowing down ever since Charley died, and his driver finally had to admit he wasn't pulling as hard as he did before. The men of Engine 7 vehemently protested to save Joe from a peddler's cart, which led to a temporary compromise: Joe would replace an even older gray horse who drew the fuel wagon. Since the wagon only went out on large fire calls to carry fresh loads of coal for the engines, neither speed nor great strength was required.

As for Big Jim, he continued performing his tricks until he retired around 1906. Dick was still up to his tricks in 1907, which is the year the city finally enacted a new law giving the FDNY the option to turn over its old fire horses to the SPCA, which would send eligible horses to farms to live out their lives.

HISTORICAL HOOK

While some horses like Charley and Dick taught themselves to get their own water or perform other tricks, many horses learned their tricks from their human companions, who'd spend hours during their downtime teaching them crowd-pleasing actions such as "shaking hands" or doling out kisses. But in the second decade of the twentieth century, something new arrived at each of the thirty-three fire companies in Queens that changed this horse-human dynamic for these companies. The new arrivals were library books.

To reach the residents of Queens living in outlying villages and isolated farmlands—especially the newly arrived immigrants who were not comfortable exploring a large public library—the Queens Library Board established twelve traveling library stations in grocery stores, social clubs, police stations, firehouses, and the Life Saving Station of the Rockaways. Each station had a collection of five hundred to one thousand books, offering free access to "a treasure house of knowledge and instruction."

When library books first arrived at Queens firehouses in 1912, the men began spending more time reading and less time teaching the horses new tricks. (Unidentified firemen, Jamaica, December 1, 1914. Photographed for the Queens Borough Public Library. William Davis Hassler, PR 083-2106. New-York Historical Society)

The library services for the firemen started in 1912, after a group of fire chaplains urged the Library Board to furnish reading materials to the firemen so they might improve their minds during their leisure hours by reading good fiction and books on science, history, travel, and engineering. The board agreed to send each company a box of fifty books every two months. Much time and thought went into preparing well-balanced collections of books with such topics as aerial navigation, international peace, civil engineering, wireless telegraphy, standard fiction, and other topics carefully chosen to meet the needs of firemen who were perusing studies for their careers. The *Brooklyn Daily Eagle* reported, "The first box aroused keen delight and interest in the fire laddies. They could hardly wait until it was unpacked and crowded around it like children." Although the veterans were not as excited about the books as were the younger laddies (newspapers were more than enough literature for them), they eventually dipped their toes in the literature water. One shy man asked for good love stories because he wasn't finished loving yet, and another requested more books about Abraham Lincoln. No longer did the men have to while away the hours reading the house journal or staring at the wall waiting for that slight click preceding the ring of the joker fire alarm.

According to the *Brooklyn Daily Eagle*, the one downfall of the library services was that the horses no longer received as much attention as they had before. "The men who used to spend hours in teaching the animals tricks do not now forget to caress them as they pass and feed them sugar, but they do pass. That's the rub! And what sensitive horse can bear without a whinny to see his erstwhile playmate's attention taken up by books, mere books? Their horse feelings are hurt, and they show it as best they may."

Engine 14: Tom

Tom, the big white horse who took center stage at Engine 14 at 14 West Eighteenth Street, joined the FDNY in 1894 when he was seven years old. Before joining the engine company, though, he had to receive training and pass an examination proving his fitness for the job. For example, he had to demonstrate that he was able to work hard and make long runs in all kinds of weather. He also had to prove he was sufficiently intelligent to understand his assigned tasks when it was his turn to enter the service. After passing his examination, Tom took his place in a stall on the right side of the

Engine 14 firehouse, where he continued his training with Captain Charles Shay. The captain trained him specifically for the center position of the three-horse team. As he explained, once a horse's stall and position were set, this could never change, because the horses were trained to start from a specific spot at the sound of the alarm.

The first thing Captain Shay did was strike the fire gong and lead Tom by his halter to his place in the center. It took several times before Tom realized the captain was rushing him to the engine after the gong sounded. "We use up an awful lot of patience in training a horse," Captain Shay told a reporter from the *New-York Tribune*. "Some horses take a longer time than others to understand what is required of them, but Tom was always bright from the first, and he soon began to learn that there was some connection between the ringing of the gong and that hurried dash to another spot, although he couldn't understand just why all this happened."

Once Tom showed the first inclination to leave his stall at the stroke of the gong, the next step was to leave him unfastened and encourage him to step forward to his spot by himself. When he hesitated to move alone, the captain had to push him out of the stall and toward the engine (by pushing the horse instead of leading him, Captain Shay taught Tom that he was on his own; no one would ever lead him to his position again). The day finally came when Tom understood what it all meant, and as soon as the gong sounded, he dashed to his place under the harness with a look of pride and satisfaction. The men rewarded him with candies and bananas (he preferred the bananas).

Tom shared his duties with Dick, Harry, Louis, and Major. Although Tom was no more affectionate than the other horses, he got more attention from the children and young women who loved to talk to him and bring him boxes of candy. According to Captain Shay, the other horses got jealous when Tom received more treats, and they'd show their displeasure by violently kicking the sides of their stalls and reaching their heads out toward the visitors. Tom loved all the attention, but he also loved the wild dash and excitement of going to a fire. "He's always eager to get away, and he enjoys nothing better than being driven at the highest rate of speed he can command," Captain Shay said. "The wilder the pace is the better he likes it."

HISTORICAL HOOK

During the early twentieth century, about seventy to eighty horses a year received training to take the places of those fire horses killed or maimed in the line of duty, retired, or transferred to newly organized companies in the outlying districts. Captain Joseph Shea—later Battalion Chief Shea—was responsible for examining and overseeing the training of the fire department horses during this era. In early years, experienced horsemen selected horses on the open market, doing business only with those horse dealers who were deemed to be trustworthy or who had furnished numerous horses for the department. Later, the department contracted with the lowest bidder, who provided the FDNY with horses throughout the year at a rate of $250 per horse.

All green horses had to be between five and eight years old to even be considered. After checking each horse for height and weight (about sixteen hands and twelve hundred to fourteen hundred pounds was ideal), Chief Shea would examine their eyes. "An animal with what we call 'pig's eyes' is apt to be near-sighted," he said. "He's the sort of horse that will stumble and fall all over himself and that ought to wear spectacles. A horse with eyes set close together doesn't seem to have enough room for much brain, and, sure as fate, you couldn't teach him anything if you pumped at him for a month of Sundays."

Following the physical exam, each horse underwent a thirty-day trial to examine the horse's disposition, alertness, speed and strength, grit and nerves, common sense, and habits. Horses received training to take the center in a three-abreast engine, so two veteran horses could steady the candidate while he pulled the heaviest of the dead weight of about four and a half tons. Green horses tended to spring away from the engine and carry the entire load on their own; but after a few hours of going up and down the block, exhaustion eventually kicked in, and the horse would submit to the assistance of the veteran horses.

Many tests took place during this period, including maneuverability trials, backing up the engine, getting into the swinging harness, and hard braking to see if the horse would "dig his toes into the asphalt and make fire fly before he gives up" (a horse who balked would not be good when the engine got stuck in a snowbank). Country-born horses also had to become accustomed to "peculiar terrors" of the city, such as trains and streetcars (elevated structures and headlights on the surface cars often terrorized new horses, who would refuse to pass under a structure or run toward headlights). Every battalion had two extra horses on standby to take the immediate place of a horse who died, got sick, or lost a shoe; that way, the green horses could get adequate training time before joining a company.

Once the green horses passed every test at the stables, they were ready for their real-world training. Captains and drivers would pick out the horse of their choice and take it for another thirty-day trial at their firehouse. The men had to get the new horses up and running as soon as possible, which is why training them to run in answer to the gong was the first step, as Captain Shay did with Tom. Typically, it took six to eight days to break a horse into running before the engine. If a horse didn't pass muster after the thirty days had passed—even if it were because the horse had an annoying habit such as stamping at night or champing at the bit—the captain had the option of exchanging the horse, and the horse would go back to the dealer. "You see," Chief Shea said, "a fire horse needs to be a pretty perfect and well-behaved sort of an animal if he wants to work for this city, and when you get a horse that answers all our requirements you are apt to have a pretty good one, whether he costs you $250 or $1,250."

Engine 4: Dan and Dick

When FDNY veteran Martin Cook received a promotion to captain of Engine 4 in 1886, the company received horses Dan and Dick. At this time, Engine 4 occupied a narrow, four-story brick firehouse at 39 Liberty Street, diagonally across from the old post office building on Nassau Street. This was the heart of the city's financial district, and the little firehouse was dwarfed by large brick and stone buildings housing the United States Treasury, Custom House, New York Stock Exchange, and dozens of banks and insurance firms. The two large horses were up for the challenge of protecting these world-famous institutions. Even as they aged, Dan and Dick did the city and the FDNY proud. Captain Cook often received offers to trade in his team for younger animals, but he always turned them down. According to the veteran, there was not a more dependable, more careful, or faster team of fire horses in the United States.

Directly to the east of Engine 4 was a five-story, brick L-shaped building at 37 Liberty Street, which wrapped around the engine house. When workers demolished the walls of this structure in May 1893, it became evident that the eastern wall of the engine house could not stand on its own without the support of the larger building. The contractor told Captain Cook that he would not be responsible for the safety of the men and their horses should they receive an alarm. The vibration created by the engine, tender, and horses could easily take down the walls. Rather than take any chances, the captain ordered the engine house cleared of everything on the first floor. This task required precision and slow work.

First, the men carefully led the horse whose stall was closest to the threatening wall toward the engine, where his mate later joined him. The men snapped on the collars and lines and gently led the fire engine into the street. After removing all the hose, they took the same steps with the tender. The men threw blankets over Dan and Dick and then lit a fire under the engine boiler to keep up the requisite steam pressure. Then the men and their horses camped out for the night. On May 19, the city condemned the old firehouse, and Engine 4 relocated to Ladder 15 at 73 Water Street, where the company stayed for the next seventeen years.

By 1897, Dan was about eighteen years old and had more than fourteen years of service in the department. In all those years, he was never ill, and he never missed a fire or false alarm below Houston Street. According to Captain Martin, the horse ran with the engine or tender to thirty-six hundred calls. Dan was also a gentleman horse, always "shaking hands" with visitors and displaying a "wonderful masculine instinct in his preference for fair womankind when he [was] asked for a kiss." Dick was younger, but he also had an exceedingly amiable disposition. The neighborhood children loved visiting and playing with the good-natured horses.

One day a little girl entered Dan's stall and sat down on the soft bedding. Within minutes, she had fallen into a deep sleep. Then the alarm sounded, sending every man and horse scurrying to his place. Dick dashed to his engine, but Dan didn't budge. The men looked on in wonder as Dan peered anxiously out of his stall, this being the first time in fourteen years that he had failed to respond. One of the men investigated the stall and discovered the cause of the delay. Dan must have realized that if he moved, he would crush the little girl. The fireman picked up the sleeping child, and the noble Dan dashed to his place, "seemingly pleased with his heroism."

HISTORICAL HOOK

For New York City Comptroller William A. Prendergast, there were just too many fire horses named Dan, Jim, Mike, Jerry, and Patty in the early twentieth century. For Fire Commissioner Rhinelander Waldo, a former army man, the horses' pet names were not official enough for the department. He believed that the horses should have assigned names, just as they did in the army. Tom and Bob might be nice horse names, but they weren't official. Thus, the era of calling out such familiar cries as "Giddyap, Dan!" and "Go it, Mike!" ended on March 23, 1910, when Commissioner Waldo ordered all companies to change the names of their horses to avoid duplication. By having only one Pat or one Dan, Prendergast would no longer have trouble telling which horse needed new shoes or medical care. The assigned names would also allow the department to create an official horse roster and index files with vital information on each equine employee, including the horse's age and first day of service, original company name and subsequent transfers, and the date and cause of death.

Up to this point, fire horses were listed only by consecutive numbers at the department level—the number was stamped on a lead seal and fastened to a narrow strap worn around the horse's neck. When the horse died or retired, its number was dropped. The men of each company gave the horses unofficial pet names—as one veteran noted, "When a fireman gets to know a horse so well that he can carry on a one sided conversation with him he doesn't like to call the horse No. 1345 or something like that. He wants to call the horse Pete or Bill, and the horse appreciates it too." Many horses shared a name with the driver or captain of the company, which meant that every battalion could have half a dozen or more horses with the same popular names. Other horses received unique names to match their personality or traits. In 1885, for example, Ladder 15 had a horse named Dan O'Leary, who had a habit of walking in circles five or six miles a day. The horse was named for Daniel O'Leary, a competitive pedestrian who broke American records by walking more than five hundred miles in six days straight. The one problem with pet names was that the name would change every time a horse was transferred, making it difficult for the men to follow their favorite horses throughout their careers.

Under the new orders, not only would the horses receive an official name, but the name would go on the department's permanent roster and stay with that horse for his entire career. Shortly after Commissioner Waldo issued the naming order, every company received a notice like this: "You are respectfully informed that horse No. 170 assigned to your company is officially to be named hereafter Acolian by order of the Commissioner."

When Commissioner Waldo decided to name all fifteen hundred horses in the department, he assigned Deputy Chief William Guerin to coordinate the logistics. Poor Captain George Bauer of Ladder 23 got stuck with the job of providing all the unique names. It took him two months to complete the task. First, he had to find masculine names, as there were very few female horses in the FDNY (in 1905, there were only three mares; they pulled the light wagons of the battalion chiefs). Unlike using "euphonious names," to which no one would be likely to object, Captain Bauer was challenged with finding names that were "horsey to begin with" while also considering the horse's human companions. To achieve this task, he scoured through several almanacs as well as books on trotting horses and geography. When all was said and done, Captain Bauer assigned many odd and fancy names, such as Aleshter, Billiken, Alcedo, Cannon Bell, and Angostura.

Although the firemen didn't seek to appeal this order, they were not afraid to speak their minds about the new names. Some said the names were more fit for the racetrack than the firehouse—one man demanded to know whether the horses would also be provided with calling cards—but they conceded that Captain Bauer's task was not an easy one. Others feared that their horses would receive names better suited for Pullman railroad cars, and so they proactively submitted their own choices. For example, Battalion Chief B. J. Galvin put in a request to name his horse St. Patrick, which the department approved. Chief Patrick A. Maher and the Irish laddies of Brooklyn's Engine 143 and Engine 153 devised a plan to name their horses "after counties of the old sod." At Engine 143, a combination company at 8653 Eighteenth Avenue, all the horses save Frank, the chief's brown gelding, were gray. The three big grays who pulled the engine were Jim, Dan, and Baby. The company's other grays were Lem and Charley, who pulled the tender, and Pat and Mike, who drew the truck. At Engine 153, a combination company at 2429 Eighty-Sixth Street, Lem and Jim pulled the engine, Pat and Bill were on the tender, and Joe and Harry drew the truck. The men devised a scheme to rechristen the horses from both companies after counties in Ireland: Mayo, Cork, Galway, Donegal, Tipperary, Roscommon, Connough, Limerick, Kerry, Antrim, and Meath.

The men at Engine 40 at 153 West Sixty-Eighth Street in Manhattan were also none too pleased with the new names for Jerry, Mike, Bob, Paddy, and Chester: Hanover, Woodbine, Blue Jeans, Alvine, and Arthur. After receiving reprimands for failing to call Paddy by his new name, one fireman cried out, "Oh, consternation! The elite has descended on [the] fire hall. I suppose I will have to call myself Sydney Algernon Harold Smythe or something as sweet."

As a reporter for the *New York Times* surmised, many of the firemen would resent the prospect of losing their pet names for their favorite horses and would no doubt continue calling them by their old names despite the official nomenclature. However, the new index system would help the men stay in touch with their old equine friends as they grew older and moved to quieter firehouses in the Bronx and Staten Island. The system also settled all disputes as to the oldest horse in the department. At the top of the list in 1910 was Abbott, named in honor of former commissioner John J. Scannell, a Tammany Hall man who had paid $26,500 for a horse named The Abbott, a trotting champion who set the world record for the fastest mile in 1900. The FDNY's Abbott entered the department at age five in 1891 and was still running to fires with Engine 45 in the Bronx. Second honors went to Arrowood, who was twenty-two years old and had seventeen years of service. Twenty-one-year-old Brentwood, who hitched up to Manhattan's Engine 30 fuel wagon, also made the top list with nineteen years of service.

Engine 16: Jerry

Horse No. 206 in the records of 1900 was described as a "chunky white horse sixteen hands high" with twenty years of service as the nigh horse of an engine team. The FDNY purchased him on August 16, 1880, when he was about nine years old. Save for a period of three months while he recuperated from an injury at Engine 26, horse No. 206 reported to Engine 16, a double company with two engines at 223 East Twenty-Fifth Street. The men called him Jerry.

Under the watch of Captain Edward Stack and Firemen George Harris, Dennis Murphy, and James J. Oates, Jerry went through the same daily routine as every other fire horse. But Jerry was unique because he was also an equine model for the sculptor and illustrator James Edward Kelly, who specialized in designing commemorative monuments depicting people and events surrounding the Civil War.

In 1886, Kelly received a commission to design two panels for the Battle of Saratoga monument at Saratoga National Historical Park. The bronze panels would be cast at Maurice J. Power's National

Fine Art Foundry, which was located on the same block as Engine 16. The native New York sculptor needed a model for a bas-relief panel. He found one quite suitable for the job at Engine 16.

Although Jerry was a docile horse, the men warned Kelly that should an alarm sound, Jerry wouldn't wait for anything or anyone in front of him. Sure enough, one day while Kelly was making a sketch of Jerry, an alarm came in. At the first stroke of the gong, "Jerry was transformed from an amiable model for a figure to go into a historical sculpture in the Saratoga Monument to a contemporaneous New York fire horse." Kelly jumped out of the way as Jerry bolted for the engine.

In 1900, the thirty-year-old horse was still active in the department. Having pulled the first-section engine for fourteen years, Jerry spent the last five or six years of his career on the second-section engine. This engine answered only those calls that came in while the first section was out, so Jerry worked only half the time he did when he was on the first-section team. He didn't have a youthful spring in his step, but he was still alert and strong, always placing his shoulders against the collar and using his weight to start the engine with his first move. The veteran horse was still good looking in his old age, but everyone who knew him said he had been quite a handsome white horse, "a picture in his day." In other words, he had the looks of a model.

Battalion 3: Dick

Tricky Dick may be a derogatory nickname used to refer to former president Richard Nixon, but the nickname could have been used in a joking way for many FDNY fire horses named Dick. For some reason, horses named Dick were often troublemakers who also did tricks or pulled pranks in the firehouse.

In Battalion 3, quartered with Ladder 20 in the old Firemen's Hall at 155 Mercer Street in Manhattan, Dick was the horse assigned to pull the battalion chief's buggy. By 1909, when he was driving Battalion Chief Edward J. Worth to fires, Dick had fifteen years of service, having started with Chief Croker when he was the battalion chief. (The horse was named for Croker's uncle, Richard "The Boss" Croker, a former alderman, fire commissioner, and leader of the Tammany Hall political machine.)

As a battalion chief horse, Dick had more authority on the roads than the engine or truck horses did, so he fully expected all vehicles but streetcars to yield to him. He had more than one run-in with trucks, but it was on the fire scenes and in the firehouse that Dick caused the most trouble. At fires, he often wandered away to go rummaging in garbage barrels, sometimes traveling many blocks to find something that he liked. He was also known to cross the streets on his own, drawing the wagon along a curb on the Bowery and taking his place behind a pushcart to snatch a banana or two. Inside his stall, he insisted on facing away from the door so he could tease the horse behind him. He also loved to ring the bell on the truck, especially in the middle of the night, when the men were asleep in their bunk room. He'd leave his stall, stick his head through the ladders, and grab the bell rope with his teeth. With a few vigorous tugs, the bell would resound louder than the regular alarm gong, startling new and superstitious firemen alike.

Dick's canine partner was Buster, a Dalmatian who was also attached to the battalion chief. Buster joined the department almost by accident, when a young boy warned Chief Worth that a dog was under the wagon. Worth didn't have a dog at the time, but sure enough, there was Buster under the front axle, "as if he had been following a fire chief all his life." Chief Worth thought he looked like a good recruit who could take a dose of smoke, so when no owner claimed him, the dog was assigned to the chief of Battalion 3. Buster was adept at navigating stairs in burning buildings and even catching rats, but he didn't have much patience with Dick, often biting the horse's legs if he thought Dick was taking too long. Dick had his own trick for Buster, answering the dog's bites with quick, short leg jolts that would just miss his head.

Engine 122: Richard C.

Perhaps Richard C. didn't like his new department-issued name and was jealous that one of his equine teammates got to keep the horsey name Dan. Or maybe, as a reporter for the *Brooklyn Daily Eagle* suggested in 1912, he now felt too aristocratic to pull the old Amoskeag steam fire engine that his company was using while its newer engine was at the repair shop. A horse named Richard C. should never have to break a sweat pulling such an "ugly-looking thing" with those heavy iron tires, "whose rattle and clatter over the pavement make the use of a fire bell unnecessary," especially when he had only recently pulled a "bright and shining engine that bounced over the stones on its soft rubber tires like a chariot."

Richard C. of Brooklyn's Engine 122 at 836 Quincy Street was a massive sorrel horse with "quivering nostrils and fiery eyes." He was born into racing-stock snobbery, but once he joined the FDNY, he seemed to recognize that pulling a fire engine to burning buildings and helping save lives was more important than racing with other highbred steeds. He took his job seriously and was always considerate of Captain Emmet Soden and the other members of the company. But the very first night the ancient steam engine replaced the newer model, his attitude changed. His pride would not allow him to draw the old-fashioned machine. When the first alarm came in that evening, Richard C. got into position with Dan and Hadoline (another victim of Commissioner Waldo's naming initiative). The three started off up Putnam Avenue, but less than one block into the trip, Richard C. stopped dead in his tracks and refused to budge. He was not about to go out in public "drawing an antiquated contrivance with iron tires." And so, the engine tender reached the fire, and the men pulled off the hose; but with no engine to pump water into the hose, it lay idle on the sidewalk.

Three more times, Richard C. stopped in disgust on the way to a fire. Only through coaxing and cajoling was "the bloomin' aristocrat of a horse persuaded to do his duty." His antics provided great amusement for spectators, but it was a serious matter, especially when the engine didn't reach the scene. Captain Soden had to report the matter to headquarters, and Richard C. had to go on temporary leave until the new engine returned. In the meantime, while Richard C. stood in his stall and looked on in disgust, a replacement horse named Bollolot took his place. This horse did his job; apparently Bollolot was not embarrassed by his peculiar name or the old steam engine with iron tires.

HISTORICAL HOOK

When it came to responding to alarms, speed was the name of the game for the horse teams—not just galloping speed but hitching speed. Annual inspection tours, during which the city's fire commissioners visited each company "for the purpose of finding fault" with the conditions of the firehouse, firemen, or horses, featured a trial of speed that allowed each company to compete for the fastest team. The men thoroughly enjoyed the speed drill, as it inspired them to surpass the other companies or at least beat their own record. During the drill, a gong would sound, sending the horses thundering from their stalls. Each horse then took his place under the tackle, and the harnesses dropped onto necks held high in anticipation. The men then deftly snapped the collars together and double-checked that everything was secure before the timekeeper yelled, "Time!"

The average time for a three-horse team was about ten seconds, depending on the distance from the stalls to the harnesses. A two-horse hitch could make it in about eight seconds. In firehouses where the stalls were conveniently located close to the apparatus, the horses could hitch up in three to six seconds. For many years during the late nineteenth century, Engine 24 at 78 Morton Street was the fastest company in the department. In 1881, under Captain William McLaughlin, the two gray horses, each eight years old and fifteen hands high, completed the task in just under two seconds. Engine 4 at 39 Liberty Street, under Captain Crum, was almost as fast, hitching in three seconds. Captain Crum explained that it didn't matter how many seconds it took the men to make it from their beds to the engine at night; the company always had two men on house patrol, so it was their job to get the horses ready while the others made their way downstairs. Fire horses also performed the hitch-up drill at the National Horse Show at Madison Square Garden, which debuted in 1883 (Engine 33 won the drill that year). During the second annual event, Engine 24 took home the blue ribbon for hitching its handsome grays in under two seconds.

In 1881, Fire Commissioner John J. Gorman explained the importance of hitching as fast as possible. "The New York Fire Department doesn't hitch up for boasting, rivalry, or wagers, but for business," he told the *New*

York Sun. "Their ingenuity is taxed to the upmost to get to fires as early as possible. We know, in fighting a fire in a dry goods district, that one second earlier is often worth one million dollars. Our companies are classed and timed, and if they are late, they are reprimanded." The commissioner noted that if an engine arrived late because it ran into a streetcar, encountered a barricade, or ran over a pedestrian, then the tardiness was excusable. But if the company arrived late because the men and their horses were slow, they'd have to train harder to achieve faster times.

Engine 30: Victor

As the personal chauffeur for Chief Croker in the early twentieth century, John Rush earned the nickname Daredevil Rush. Fellow firemen often made bets that Bullet, "the famous black horse who carried Chief Croker to fires with the speed of the wind," would determine the fate of Rush. In later years, only a few people believed he would survive while driving the chief's high-powered automobile, "The Red Devil," fifty miles an hour through the city's congested streets. No one ever dreamed Battalion Chief Rush would lose his life while driving leisurely home for lunch on a buggy harnessed to Victor, one of the horses of Engine 30 at 278 Spring Street (now home to the New York City Fire Museum).

Rush was born in New York City on February 21, 1871, the oldest of four children born to Fireman William Henry Rush and his wife, Sarah. In 1889, when he was only eighteen, police arrested Rush for stealing cash and promissory notes. After serving time in prison for the felony, he received a pardon from Governor Roswell Pettibone Flower in 1892. A year later, he joined the New York Fire Patrol 2, then stationed at 31 Great Jones Street. It was during his service with the Fire Patrol—a paid fire salvage service organized and funded by the New York Board of Fire Underwriters—that several members of the FDNY began taking notice of his daring rescues. One of his most courageous rescues took place on November 5, 1895, during a five-alarm fire that destroyed the Manhattan Savings Institution building and other structures on Broadway and Bleecker Street. At this fire, Rush saved the lives of firemen trapped on a roof by creating a human bridge. He did this by swinging upside down across an alleyway (while other men held his heels) and gripping a windowsill on the bank building. He used his own body to form the lifeline on which the firemen crawled across to safety. Rush joined the FDNY about a year after this incident; he lied on his civil service test about the felony charge. He quickly advanced "from the zone of great danger as a driver to one of more comparative calm and safety as a battalion chief."

On April 25, 1912, Chief Rush was traveling from the head-quarters of Battalion 5, located above Engine 30, to his home on West Eleventh Street. His driver, John Harvey, was in control of the chief's horse-drawn buggy, pulled by Victor. Victor was a large roan—more than sixteen hands high—who had earned a reputation for being skittish ever since his former owner, New York Chief of Police William Stephen Devery, had presented him to Chief Croker. But Harvey was accustomed to handling the troublesome horse.

The men had just passed Christopher Street when the rear wheel of the light buggy struck a truck, causing the horse to get jumpy. The collar snapped under the strain, and Victor plunged half out of his harness as he raced toward a group of children who were crossing Hudson Street. Chief Rush seized the reins from his driver and pulled the horse back on his haunches to prevent a collision with the children. The buggy reared and plunged, and one wheel caught in a car rail, causing the buggy to overturn. The chief and his driver were ejected from the vehicle. Harvey landed on his feet. Chief Rush plunged headfirst into the curb and fractured his skull.

According to news reports, Chief Rush had only time to ask Harvey to send for Chief Croker before he lost consciousness. Father Philip McGrath of the Catholic Mission to Seamen, who happened to be passing by, issued last rites and then helped Harvey carry the chief to a nearby drugstore while they waited for an ambulance from the hospital. Victor took off running, but he halted in front of Ladder 5 on Charles Street, where Chief Rush often stopped during inspection tours. Seeing the driverless buggy, the men went running toward the crowd gathering on Hudson Street. Recognizing the seriousness of the accident, the firemen insisted that Dr. Harry Mortimer Archer and Dr. F. D. Smith respond to the hospital. The physicians hurried to St. Vincent's Hospital, arriving at the same time as the ambulance.

After determining that Chief Rush had a fractured skull, Dr. Archer sent for two other renowned physicians. The four doctors were preparing the operating table at 3:20 p.m. when the chief died, never having regained consciousness. Chief Croker and Chief Rush's seventeen-year-old daughter, Sarah, were at his side. Rush was buried at the New York Bay Cemetery in Jersey City, with services conducted by the FDNY chaplain Father Vincent de Paul McGean. According to Rush's sister, Florence Hannon, at the time of his death, the chief's estate was worth only $200. Although he made $3,300 a year as a battalion chief, he began giving much of his salary to his mother after his father was hurled from a fire engine and killed instantly. Chief Croker, Captain Robert H. Mainzer, and other firemen established a fund to help Rush's mother and daughter.

"It seems a strange irony of fate that a minor accident should have killed Chief Rush," Dr. Archer told the *New York Times*. "I had almost come to think he bore a charmed life. One gets such ideas of men who pass through seemingly impassable dangers unscathed." Dr. Archer recalled a time when he was speeding up Second Avenue with Chief Croker and Rush in the chief's motorized vehicle when the front wheel popped off:

> I didn't see how anybody could save us, going as we were at fifty miles an hour or over. I held to the side of the car, expecting every minute to smash against the curbing and be dashed to the street with a fatal force. But Rush kept his head, and on three wheels he drove the car for one hundred and ninety feet, for we measured them afterward, and it was a marvel to all who knew of the matter that Rush's career was not ended then and there. He was a man without fear or nerves, and so, of course, a splendid, resourceful fireman.

As Chief Croker wiped away his tears, he told the press, "There goes one of the bravest men this country has ever produced. Rush was brave without being foolhardy. This may seem strange to thousands who have seen him driving my car in an apparently reckless manner, but the fact is he had a wonderful eye and a brain that could size up any situation in a flash. I've never known a cooler man under fire. His courage was superb and his loyalty unbounded. . . . I loved him as a friend, and I will always cherish his memory."

Victor got into trouble one more time on August 1, 1912, while Battalion Chief John Spencer was bringing pay envelopes to the men of Engine 30. After a vehicle spooked him on Varick Street, Victor broke into a gallop, causing the driver, John Foote, to lose control. Chief Spencer rang the gong as a warning to get people out of the way. As the horse passed Grand Street, a man tried to jump and catch the bridle, but he fell hard to the street and was severely bruised. Victor eventually ran into a pushcart and fell, breaking his harness and scattering the pay envelopes all over the street. Noting that this was the fifth time Victor had bolted, Chief Spencer told the press he would soon need to strike Victor from the rolls.

HISTORICAL HOOK

On Saturday, December 2, 1899, Chief Croker took a new motorized wagon for the first of many test drives to determine whether the automobile was superior to the horse-drawn buggy that carried him to fires. The vehicle was a Stanhope-Style Locomobile produced by twin brothers Freelan and Francis Stanley at their factory in Bridgeport, Connecticut. It seated two people snugly and got its power from steam generated by gasoline. The engine was under the seat, and the gas tank was inside the front of the wagon. Under favorable conditions, the vehicle could go forty miles an hour, although it could reach sixty miles an hour for a short stretch. It carried enough fuel to travel one hundred miles. The chief kept the vehicle at Engine 33 at 42 Great Jones Street, from where he responded to his first fire in the vehicle that Saturday night.

Over the next five months, the chief experimented with the Locomobile and another vehicle powered by electricity. He considered the steam-powered Locomobile more dependable, although he said he'd prefer a heavier model to handle the workload. (Chief Croker was reportedly rough on the vehicles and would break one "every day or so," according to one Locomobile employee.) During this time, Chief Croker and his aide, Lieutenant Robert Oswald, responded to numerous fires on the East Side. The chief kept his intentions a secret during the experimental phase so rival manufacturers would not swamp him with offers.

Chief Edward Croker and his aide, Lieutenant Robert Oswald, responded to numerous fires in the Locomobile, reaching speeds up to sixty miles an hour. (Photograph provided courtesy of the New York City Fire Museum)

The Locomobile was not the first vehicle ever considered for replacing the horse. According to Chief Croker, the department had experimented with self-propelling engines about ten years earlier, but back then, the propelling power was a huge chain turning a ratchet in the same way a bicycle chain works. "The strain on the chain proved too great," he said, "and the speed of the machine was not as great as when it was drawn by two horses."

In July 1900, Chief Croker received a new Locomobile fire wagon designed for longer runs and higher speeds. The chief used the vehicle for the first time in responding to a fire on July 5, in which he made it from Great Jones Street to the Bronx in fifteen minutes. He reportedly also broke all records on reaching a fire when he drove what the *Boston Globe* called his "Black Ghost" from Great Jones Street to the Clara de Hirsch Home for Working Girls at 225 East Sixty-Third Street in five minutes on December 28, 1901. The chief kept a horse and buggy at the ready, but he never did go back to the old ways. By 1907, he had ditched the small vehicle and was racing through the city in his "Red Devil," a six-cylinder, red-painted vehicle that seated four persons, including his new driver and aide, Captain Rush. As the *New York Sun* reported a few years later, "That red devil wagon of his has sent a shiver down a good many spines as it bounced over car tracks and heeled around corners with [the] big bell clanging constantly and its screecher uttering intermittent warnings that made folks dodge half a block away."

History was made on January 27, 1909, when Chief Croker "demonstrated his title as the greatest firefighter in the world by linking the automobile fire wagon with the high pressure water service" in a demonstration at the foot of Gansevoort Street. On that day, the new Knox Automobile Company apparatus, assigned to Engine 72 at 22 East Twelfth Street, traveled twenty-six miles an hour with twenty men on board from Madison Square Garden to Gansevoort Street. During the test, the wagon threw a stream of water through its swivel nozzle 125 feet at all angles. The successful test was a sure sign the horses' days with the FDNY were numbered.

Engine 21: Roger

Unlike Dick, the horse of Engine 18 who was addicted to sugar, Roger was hooked on soft-shell crabs. The crustacean-loving fire horse was named for Roger Connor, a large first baseman who wore tailor-made uniforms and was one of the reasons his New York baseball team was named the Giants (Connor's other claim to fame was hitting the first recorded grand slam on September 10, 1881). Roger's ball-playing namesake also had an appetite for soft-shell crabs—albeit for Connor, the term "soft-shell crab" was an old baseball term sometimes applied to struggling pitchers.

According to the tale, one day a peddler who often sold his wares to the men of Engine 21 at 216 East Fortieth Street brought crabs to the firehouse and prepared them with salt and pepper for sandwiches. After taking a few bites of his sandwich, one of the firemen was summoned to the rear of the engine house. He laid his unfinished sandwich on the footboard, thinking it was safe with the horse, but when he returned, he saw that Roger had finished his meal. After that, the men discovered that Roger would devour any kind of meat sandwiches. Roger also loved hot tea, onions, scallops, and anything else edible and within reach.

Although Roger earned a great deal of fame because of his gastronomic traits, he also stood out as one of the few horses of the early twentieth century who had no fear of fire. He'd stand quietly as the flames blazed about him and the smoke hid him from view, while his mates reared and plunged until the driver released them and removed them from the scene. To show his appreciation for Roger's heroism, the captain would scrub him with soap and water and then rinse him with water from the fire hydrant. Then he'd let Roger walk up and down the street on his own to dry off. Roger never strayed off the block, and if the alarm sounded while he was taking his constitution, he'd dash back into quarters and take his place as the center horse without any assistance or encouragement (edible or otherwise).

HISTORICAL HOOK

Shortly after the department published its new rations for horse feed in 1910, a few citizens criticized the rations and suggested that the horses who died in the line of duty had received too little to eat to manage the workload. At this time, the daily ration consisted of eleven pounds of oats, twelve pounds of hay, one and a half pounds of bran, one-tenth of a pound of oil meal, and a twenty-fourth of a pound of salt, with three pounds of straw allotted for bedding. The firemen laughed at the allegation that any of the horses had died of starvation—if anything, the drivers and captains said, they had to watch their horses to make sure they weren't overfed. While some industrious fire horses in busy districts would always receive more than the allocated rations, most didn't work too hard. As one fireman told the *New York Times*, "Do you realize that in the one hundred and thirty fire companies in Manhattan, the Bronx, and Richmond [Staten Island], there are not more than twenty-four that answer on the average thirty calls a month, and that in these alarms the haul is generally only half a mile out and home? The horses travel fast while they are going, but the apparatus, heavy as it is, once it is started, runs easily on rubber tires and ball bearings. If we were to feed the horses more than we do they'd be ill."

Another fireman explained that occasionally the horses in northern Manhattan or the Bronx had to make three or four long runs over bad roads on a single night. If the men fed these horses too much food, they wouldn't be able to eat or digest it. In those cases, he explained, it was better to give the horses a few days of rest. Furthermore, another man said, the standard ration was more of a bookkeeping arrangement put in place for budgetary purposes. Before there were regulations, the drivers and captains used their own discretion and fed their horses as they pleased—and this practice would no doubt continue, he said. Apparently, some drivers even gave their horses soft-shell crabs.

Engine 47: Fairfax, Happy, and Democrat

On March 16, 1911—nine days before the Triangle Shirtwaist Factory fire—the FDNY evaluated the first "automobile fire engine" of its kind in the country. Bright red, twenty feet long, with two seats and a 110-horsepower motor, the $20,000 Nott fire engine could pump seven hundred gallons of water a minute at a pressure of 125 pounds. It featured four large, red, solid rubber wheels with chains to prevent skidding as it whizzed up to forty miles an hour through city streets. The explosion from the motor, like that of "a large-bored shotgun, . . . was the death knell of the horses of the Fire Department."

The test began in front of the FDNY repair shops on Fifty-Sixth Street and Twelfth Avenue. Dozens of fire officials from neighboring cities came out to watch Commissioner Rhinelander Waldo and ex-chief Charles O. Shay take the new engine for its first trial spin up to Eighty-Third Street and Central Park West and back—a trip lasting less than eleven minutes. When the men returned with their faces covered in "frozen tears of speedomaniac joy," Waldo told the audience, "The horse is sure gone as far as the fire business is concerned. It'll do for pleasure, but it's out of the business."

Later that day, Herbert Penny, a master mechanic of the Nott Company, and Driver Oliver of Engine 58 (who would take charge of the new engine) took the machine through a more serious forty-minute road test up Broadway to 110th Street, over to Lexington Avenue and up the steep Duffy's Hill at 105th Street, across the Queensboro Bridge, then out to Thomson Avenue in Sunnyside, Queens. Based on the success of the tests, FDNY officials predicted that 50 percent of the fire engines in the city would be gasoline propelled within two years and that there would not be a single horse-drawn engine, tender, truck, or water tower in the city by 1914.

The transition went slower than expected, but on March 12, 1913, two years after the test run took place, Commissioner Joseph H. Johnson Jr. announced that the FDNY would not purchase any more horses. Those fifteen hundred horses still in service, he said, would be retired as fast as possible and replaced with motorized apparatus. Since the average service life of a horse was seven years and the horses died or retired at the rate of forty to seventy a year, Johnson estimated the department would be completely motorized within four or five years. By that time, he thought, all the horses would have been sold or deceased.

Commissioner Johnson's projections were also a bit off the mark. On August 25, 1920, there were still 333 horses in the FDNY: 186 in Brooklyn, 82 in Queens, 39 in the Bronx, 18 in Staten Island, and 8 in Manhattan. The last of the 8 fire horses of Manhattan went out of service that morning at 9:30. Following a brief but silent inspection of the horses of Engine 47 at 502 West 113th Street, Driver Charles Rinschler led them back to their stables while several firemen ran forward and gave them "a final affectionate hug about the neck and put their noses against the friendly noses." When the false alarm sounded, Happy, Fairfax, and Democrat took their places underneath the falling harnesses and dashed out into the street as they had done hundreds of times before. A new seven-ton, motorized combination steam engine and hose truck backed into the station along the grooves set in the cement for the narrower-tired wagons, and the chauffeurs took their seats. At that moment, of the 304 engine companies in the FDNY, 243 had been motorized, including every company in Manhattan. According to the press, the Engine 47 horses went to outlying districts where fire horses were still in use. It would be two more years before the last of the FDNY horses retired.

HISTORICAL HOOK

Although injured and old horses had always been retired and sold, there was little talk about the fate and welfare of these horses in the nineteenth century. Mrs. Ellin Prince Speyer, founder of the Women's League of the SPCA, took an interest in the old horses and even met with Commissioner Waldo in 1910 to share her thoughts on turning them over to other city departments for light duty (the commissioner thought her idea was a good one). But the discussion didn't pick up in earnest until 1911, when Waldo proposed motor-driven fire apparatus for the FDNY, and then again in 1913, when Commissioner Johnson announced plans to replace all those fire horses still in service with motorized vehicles as soon as possible.

Prior to 1907, the law required the fire department to sell its old horses at auction, which took place at the department's training stables on West Ninety-Ninth Street in Manhattan and St. Edwards Street in Brooklyn. Grocers, butchers, peddlers, bakers, and others in need of "cheap horses of proved work" would line up to bid a few bucks on animals that would probably spend the rest of their lives in agony. Months or years following these auctions, it was common for firemen to meet up with their old friends "dragging a truck or a delivery wagon, sad-eyed, broken-spirited, wrecks of their old fiery selves."

In 1907, the city enacted a new law giving the department the option to turn over fire horses who had become unfit for service to the SPCA. Under the Fire Horses' Pension Act, fire commissioners decided whether to sell the horses at auction or surrender them to the SPCA, which would either euthanize them if necessary or send them to a farm to live out their lives in honorable leisure. Unfortunately, the SPCA didn't have enough funds to fully take on this task, so even with the pension act in place, many discharged fire horses were sold or transferred to other agencies in the city that were still using horse-powered vehicles.

A few lucky horses, such as Babe, the horse who pulled Chief John Kenlon's buggy, or Dan, the big bay of Ladder 5, were saved from this fate when a fireman or a sympathetic horse lover placed the highest bid and took them to a family farm. Wealthy benefactors were perhaps influenced by Fire Commissioner Winthrop Gray, who once proposed to buy all the old horses himself and send them to country farms. In 1905, for example, Nicholas F. Brady, the son of a well-to-do railroad man, purchased six horses for $612.50 before anyone else could place a bid. The horses—Tom, Dick, Harry, Dan, Jack, and Selim—lived out their lives in fields of clover. Other fortunate horses were saved through the efforts of the Horse Aid Society, a nonprofit founded in 1911 by Mrs. Jacob Ehrlich, who let the horses retire on her farm in Briarcliff Manor, New York. Injured or frail horses unfit for auction were either humanely dispatched by the SPCA or sent to Blackwell's Island (Roosevelt Island) to do light hauling for the Department of Charities and Correction. (One such blind fire horse, excited by the clanging of car bells on the Queensboro Bridge, charged into the river, dragging with him a Blackwell's Island deadwagon and the body of an inmate.)

During the transition from horsepower to motor power, the city's newspapers often ran stories about the fates of the FDNY horses. Charles Samson, executive secretary of New York City's Board of Inebriety, hated to read about the passing of the fire horses and how the city "rewarded" them for their gallant service. He especially did not like that hero horses, who had spent their strength and shortened lives in the service of the FDNY, were getting auctioned off to anyone who offered the highest bid. And so in September 1913, Samson sent a letter to Commissioner Johnson offering a plan that would allow every fire horse in service to live well into his old age at the agency's Hospital and Industrial Colony in Warwick, New York, also known as the City Farm for Inebriates. He explained that there would be ample forage for the horses on the eight-hundred-acre farm, where the city offered treatment for people addicted to alcohol, heroin, opium, and other drugs. None of the horses, Samson stressed, would have to work, and over the stall of each one would be a plate bearing the horse's name and record of service. Commissioner Johnson eagerly accepted the offer and said he would send three or four horses there the following week.

One of the horses who received a life pension at the Warwick farm was Accident, a large sorrel gelding who joined the department in 1896 when he was just five years old. Accident had partnered with Abbott, a large chestnut gelding, for many years at Engine 46 in the Bronx. When Abbott—then the oldest horse in the FDNY—was sold at auction in 1914, Accident became inconsolable, and his health began to fail rapidly—even more so after his pal Captain John Eagan retired after fifty years of service. Of the twenty-one horses who were retired in January 1915 to make way for motorized apparatus, Accident was the only horse whom Fire Commissioner Robert Adamson saved.

In 1917, the department could no longer sell its horses at auction until an SPCA veterinary surgeon established that they were still fit for further service. If the animal didn't receive a clean bill of health, the SPCA would euthanize it. Auctions continued to take place, but if the SPCA wasn't satisfied with the way the horses were treated, it had the authority to remove them from the bad situation. By 1920, all of Manhattan's last retired horses—including Fairfax, Happy, and Democrat of Engine 47; Carl and Carnot from Engine 53; and Roma, Mouse, and Charlie from Engine 78—were either sent to farms or assigned light duty (such as pulling lawn mowers) for the city's park departments. In 1922, 165 fire horses still working in rural areas outside of Manhattan were retired and provided with good homes where they could do light work and get plenty of rest.

Reminiscing about the last of the FDNY fire horses in September 1920, Clinton McGuffog of Engine 78 asked a reporter from the *New York Herald*, "Do you think they'll even remember that once they were the best fire engine horses New York ever had? And do you think they'll ever miss us fellows? We used to pet them a lot."

Engine 156: Bob

Before Bob got his name in the papers for being one of twelve fire horses slated for the auction block on August 13, 1908, he'd never done anything truly remarkable to receive publicity. He never saved a child's life or caused havoc by running away with a driverless engine. In fact, as a reporter for the *Brooklyn Citizen* noted, news of the auction was "probably the first time his name has appeared in print." What Bob was, though, was the pride and joy of Brooklyn's Engine 156.

Bob joined Engine 156 as a green horse in July 1903, the year the company was first installed at 124 DeKalb Avenue, across from Fort Greene Park. The new company, under the command of Captain Cornelius Cunningham, comprised all Brooklynite firemen who had previously been assigned to Manhattan companies; the first piece of apparatus for Engine 156 was a two-horse engine that had been on reserve at the department's repair shop. Bob was a natural fit for the FDNY—on his second alarm, he automatically stepped forward and lowered his head for the halter "as naturally as if he had been in the service for years." He formed a close bond with Driver Charley McPartland, who treated Bob with the greatest respect. One day while Bob was being shod, the smithy struck Bob with a hammer in a burst of anger. McPartland grabbed the farrier by the throat and shook him until he promised never to mistreat Bob or any other horse again.

By 1908, Bob's health was failing, and no veterinarian could find a cure that would allow him to remain on active duty. One week before the auction, a reporter observed that while Bob would probably end up pulling a peddler's cart, his career had been noble, and he'd been admired more than any famous racehorse, albeit by fewer people. "To fortune and to fame he was unknown. Yet all who were acquainted with Bob in his halcyon days agree that he is entitled to a place in equine history." Here's to you, Bob.

HISTORICAL HOOK

It was alleged that until Commissioner Waldo introduced a novel way to shoe the fire horses, the procedure "was the cause of more picayune bickering and wire pulling than anything else in city government." Prior to January 1911, horseshoeing was tied to politics, with the National Horse-Shoers Association and Journeymen's Horse-Shoers Association continuously competing and cozying up to government officials to secure the contract. Rhinelander took the political favors out of the equine equation by installing traveling horseshoe wagons—akin to the traveling dog-grooming vans of today. Instead of sending horses to the shop and getting replacement horses for the day, the wagons—drawn by two horses and equipped with a forge, anvil, portable vise, shoes, tools, and nails—called directly at the engine houses. The wagon team would occupy the stalls of the regular fire horses, who would get shod on the street. Should a call come in during the shoeing, the wagon team was trained to take out the engine, hose cart, or ladder truck.

Each shoeing wagon employed a farrier who received a salary of $116.66 a month and a helper who earned $83.33 a month. These men had to pass a civil service examination and be experienced and professional in handling horses. Each of the twenty wagons in service had a district route that the men followed every month, allowing every horse to receive new shoes monthly. Some of the farriers also worked night shifts in the event a shoe became loose and required a quick resetting. Under the new system, the cost to shoe a horse was less than $4 a month, compared to about $7 a month with the contract system. Captain Charles Field, who supervised the Brooklyn wagon teams, told a reporter, "The men who are taking care of the horses are all experienced and clever. We have found the system to be more satisfactory, aside from the monetary end, than previously existed."

Engine 205: Eamybeg, Bucknell, Penrod, Waterboy, and Balgriffin

The thunder of steel shod hoofs, beating out an accompaniment to the shrill screams of a fire engine siren, resounded in the streets of New York today for the last time.

—"Gotham Fire Horses Answer Gong's Clang for Last Time,"
Buffalo Courier, December 21, 1922

There were still eighty-four horses in service in outlying parts of Brooklyn and Queens in June 1922 when the FDNY, under Commissioner Thomas J. Drennan, purchased twenty more gasoline-powered engines to complete the historic conversion from horse-driven to motorized apparatus. On December 21, 1922, Engine 205 of Brooklyn Heights would be the last company in the department to become motorized. Part of the delay was war related, but nostalgia also factored in: Engine 205 was one of Brooklyn's oldest, most famous, and most influential fire companies. It was also the closest to Borough Hall, which fit in perfectly with Commissioner Drennan's plans to turn the last run into an official publicity event. Even more appropriate, Engine 205 was reportedly the first company in Brooklyn to have horse-drawn apparatus.

The Brooklyn Heights engine company was organized September 19, 1846, by upstanding young men from wealthy families of downtown Brooklyn. Back then it was a volunteer company called Pacific Hose 14—the "Dude" Company of the Heights. Pacific Hose was originally located on Love Lane near Henry Street, but on October 11, 1853, the men secured more spacious quarters at 160 Pierrepont Street, which the city had purchased from Edgar L. Bartow.

The company reorganized as Steam Engine 5 under the Brooklyn Fire Department in 1869 and then as Engine 105 one year after the Brooklyn Fire Department merged with the FDNY. During the 1890s, the engine company had four horses under the care of Driver Michael O'Neill: Tom, Dick, Jerry, and Speed. As the only engine company house in Brooklyn Heights and the closest to the government buildings, the company was always on stage, so to speak.

Driver George W. Murray with Eamybeg, Balgriffin, and Penrose on the final call for the last horse-drawn engine in FDNY history. (Library of Congress, Prints & Photographs Division [LC-USZ62-63811])

Visitors often stopped by to feed the horses or see how quickly the teams could respond to calls during speed drills. The members and horses of the company also protected valuable property in the city, including the Court House, Municipal Building, Grand Opera House, Brooklyn Library, and the Polytechnic and Packer Institutes.

On the morning of December 20, 1922, Commissioner Drennan, Brooklyn Borough President Edward Riegelmann, Jiggs the over-weight Dalmatian fire dog, and numerous firemen and city dignitaries gathered behind Borough Hall to pay their final tribute to the fire horse. The men polished the animals' fur until it was shining, all while giving them loving pats and sharing kind words with their four-legged companions. Observed one reporter, "These men of the company are a hard, two-fisted gang of firemen, afraid of nothing, as they have proved time and again, and they are not given to sentimentalities. But, under the cover of banting and joking, their attachment for their equine co-laborers could easily be seen."

At 10:15 a.m., Assistant Fire Chief "Smoky" Joe Martin tapped out the final call at the fire alarm box at Joralemon and Court Streets: 5, 93, 205 (translation: An engine is wanted, Station #93, let Company 205 answer). When the alarm sounded, Balgriffin took his place

Jiggs howled in sorrow with Engineer Thomas "Smoke" McEwan as the men bid farewell to the last horses of Engine 205 and the FDNY. (Photograph from the Collection of the Connecticut Firemen's Historical Society, Inc.)

in the middle spot of the hitch for the engine, with Eamybeg and Penrose on each side. George W. Murray drove the engine this day, with Captain Leon Howard on the ash pan, keeping his hand on the whistle rope, and Engineer Thomas "Smoke" McEwan pushing coal into the firebox. Veteran John J. Foster ("Old Hickory"), who had just completed his course in automotive engineering, took the reins of the hose wagon drawn by Waterboy and Bucknell. The horses dashed down Fulton Street and along Court Street to Joralemon Street, "striking sparks from the pavement with their flying hoofs." When they reached the rear of Borough Hall, Jiggs, the company's senior coach dog, ran circles around the engine, obviously anxious and confused as to why no one was hooking up to the hydrant or taking the nozzle.

The muster ceremony ended as Riegelmann placed wreaths on each horse while the news photographers captured the poignant moment in black and white. Then the last official fire horses of the FDNY were swapped for the shiny new motorized pumping engine and hose wagon driven by Fireman Raymond McGill. The old horse-drawn equipment would find a home in a small town or village. The horses, all about nine years old, would find homes at upstate farms, where they'd have everything a good fire horse could ask for, save for the thrill of racing to fires. As a reporter for the *New-York Tribune* wrote, "They have done their duty faithfully, and perhaps if they could speak, they would say that there are worse things than being taken to a place where lush green grass replaces asphalt and where sundown means the end of a day's work."

HISTORICAL HOOK

One of the most popular and well-known firemen in the history of the FDNY is Chief Joseph B. Martin, aka Smoky Joe. According to the men who worked with him, there was "no more loveable character or better fire fighter in the department." When asked how Martin received his famous nickname, Chief Croker related this story to the *New York Sun*:

> It was one of those cellar fires over in West Street, with smothering black smoke putting out many of the bays. Well, there was hell to pay in the cellar. If ten men came out unconscious, why thirty certainly did. I observed that water in one hose line was still being used below. I yelled out to ascertain who had left a buckling nozzle loose in the cellar. No one answered. We tallied the crew of each line and then discovered that a rattling fine chief was missing—Joe Martin. Next thing I was groping in the cellar. I never took such punishment in my life. After three attempts, crawling on all fours, I finally followed the line and came up against Martin. He had wedged the nozzle between two large crates of furniture and behind this defense was slashing the fire. Grasping him by the collar, I dragged him to the street. A score of reporters crowded around. "Gentlemen, this is Smoky Joe Martin, and he certainly does love it," I concluded. The name has stuck to him ever since.

The nickname stuck and, as legend has it, was the basis for naming the mascot of the National Forest Service, Smokey Bear, in 1945. Smokey Bear was the brainchild of the Forest Service and the National Advertising Council, which worked together to create a symbol to represent the fight against forest fires. They commissioned artists to create a mascot for the Forest

Service, with *Saturday Evening Post* contributor Albert Staehle's drawing of a bear winning out over a squirrel. Unfortunately, Martin didn't live to see this ursine representation of him. He died four years earlier, on October 24, 1941, at the age of seventy-eight.

2

Fire Dogs

Fire dogs have been famous in New York since the good old Tweed days, and long before that for that matter, for a fire company without a dog is certainly only half equipped.

— "Animal Mascots of Police and Firemen Aid to Stop Thieves and Save Lives," *New York Evening Telegram*, December 3, 1911

When Bess, the queen Dalmatian of the FDNY fire dogs, retired to Flushing, Queens, in 1914, the *New York Evening World* remarked that New York City was witnessing the end of an era: "Her fate points the end of a picturesque scene of city life in which plunging horses of the department and the bounding, barking Dalmatian dogs who ran ahead to clear the traffic for the firefighting apparatus were the features. Horses and dogs are doomed. In another five years, the whole department will be motorized."

For more than two centuries, Dalmatians have served as mascots for firefighters in the United States. In fact, the breed's evolution from carriage dog to fire dog began as early as the mid-eighteenth century. British aristocrats had employed the dogs to guard their stables and protect them from threats on the open road. With their speed, endurance, guarding instincts, and kinship with the horses, Dalmatians were the carriage dog of choice in England as far back as the seventeenth century. When New York's volunteer fire corps began trading manpower for horsepower, the Dalmatian was a logical choice to run alongside the new horse-drawn engines.

Although fire dogs didn't make the official department records, they were just as valuable as the men and the horses. The dogs were like modern-day sirens, racing and barking ahead of the apparatus to clear the way of pedestrians and pushcarts and warding off stray dogs that could have caused the horses to lose their gait and stumble. They also watched over the valuable horses and helped keep them calm while the men were busy fighting fires. Some fire dogs made lifesaving rescues or even helped extinguish fires, such as Jack of Engine 17 on Ludlow Street, an Irish setter who would seize the hose nozzle with his teeth and help Captain Peter Halon and his men drag it to a burning building. Those dogs who stayed behind earned their brass collars by guarding the firehouse until the men returned.

In the days of the city's famous three-horse hitch, Dalmatians reigned supreme as the chief canine mascots of the FDNY. Other purebreds and mutts also served as excellent fire dogs, as many of the following stories prove, but it was the Dalmatian that received the most glory. According to the old records on file with the New York City Fire Museum, Brooklyn's volunteer fire corps, which provided fire protection for what was then the City of Brooklyn, was among the first to employ Dalmatians. The Brooklyn fire dogs were first and foremost companions for the horses, often sleeping in the stalls and sharing mealtime with their equine friends. The horses in turn took care of the dogs when responding to fires—although there were accidents, some fatal, the horses almost instinctively avoided hitting the dogs racing alongside them.

When the FDNY began replacing horses with motorized vehicles in 1910, the city's fire dogs began spending more time in the firehouse with the cats than with the men on fire calls. As Captain John F. Kelly of the Fire Department School of Instruction told a reporter in 1936, Dalmatians found it hard to adjust to the new-fangled fire engine. Not only did they miss their horse pals, but

Fire dogs were like modern-day red lights and sirens, racing and barking ahead of the apparatus to clear the way in all kinds of weather. (Photograph provided courtesy of the New York City Fire Museum)

they were often maimed or killed by the motorized fire apparatus and other vehicles on the road. To be sure, Dalmatians remained popular and prolific in the outer boroughs of Queens, the Bronx, and Staten Island, which took longer to replace their horses. For example, Mandy, the Dalmatian mascot of Hook and Ladder 117 on Astoria Boulevard in Queens, gave birth to almost one hundred puppies during her eighteen years of service. (When she passed in 1931, the men buried her in the backyard of the firehouse.) But over time, as gasoline-powered engines and trucks took over the horse stalls throughout the five boroughs, the firemen lost interest in the Dalmatian as a working dog, convinced that its day, like that of the horse, had passed. The introduction of new working shifts during this era was also a factor in the fire dog's demise. With firemen now off duty and away from quarters two or three days at a time, it was difficult for one master to provide the proper training and care required for a full-time fire dog. Many dogs began living at their masters' homes instead of the firehouse.

Dalmatians continue to be popular fire company mascots. Lacy
was born in Staten Island in 1983 and joined Brooklyn's Engine
247 in 1985. She died in 1997, one year after posing for this
photo during the company's centennial celebrations. (Photograph provided courtesy of the New York City Fire Museum)

By 1936, however, there was a resurgence in Dalmatians, with
about twenty-five still serving the FDNY. Many of these dogs
of the Dalmatian brat pack were sired by Rex, the popular mascot
of Engine 39 in Manhattan, and Pal, a prize-winning Dalmatian of
Engine 271 in Brooklyn. These dogs were mostly stay-at-home mascots who stood guard while the men were out on calls (Brooklyn's
Ladder 105 even placed an announcement in the *New York Daily
News* seeking a Dalmatian or police dog who was "good at sniffing
fires and strangers" to protect their firehouse from looters while
they were away). However, some dogs, like Cappy of Engine 65 and

Chief of Engine 20, continued to ride along as a passenger on the motorized vehicles. According to Captain Kelly, even though the dogs no longer watched over horses, they did have a sixth sense for danger when it came to the firemen. Rex, for example, would howl whenever the men were in a dangerous situation. If someone got into trouble inside a building, Rex sensed it as soon as it happened—before the injured fireman even came back outside.

Captain Kelly surmised that at the rate Rex was fathering pups, there would soon be a Dalmatian for every company in the department. He wasn't far off: in 1949, there was just shy of 101 Dalmatians in the FDNY, many of them the progeny of Rex, Pal, and the mother-daughter duo of Bess and Peggy.

Hope Hose Company 9 and Ladder 18: Jack and Jack

In 1885, J. Frank Kernan, author of *Reminiscences of the Old Fire Laddies and Volunteer Fire Departments of New York and Brooklyn*, wrote the following about the fire dog:

> One of the most interesting subjects in connection with the history of the Old Volunteer Department is that of the dogs attached to the various companies. There is not today an old vamp who may chance to read my work who has not a vivid remembrance of the dog belonging to his own or some rival organization. The utmost care and attention were lavished upon the intelligent animals, which in turn knew, to a man, each particular individual belonging to the company by which they were claimed. No outsider would attempt to take any liberty with an engine dog; while itinerant canines, seeming to intuitively apprehend danger, studiously avoided approaching the vicinity of an engine-house.

According to Kernan, the most famous fire dog of Brooklyn's volunteer department was Jack, who belonged to Hope Hose Company 9 at Van Brunt and Carroll Streets. One cold night during the winter of 1859, the "poor trembling brute" stood outside the door of the house, hoping someone inside would save his life. Perhaps he sensed that the firehouse was home to kind men who would let him spend the night beside the warm stove. Although the men didn't plan on keeping the dog, his intelligent expression convinced them that he would make an excellent pet for the company.

After spending some time at the firehouse, Jack learned that the men wanted to wake up at the first tap of the alarm bell. Whenever the alarm sounded at night, he'd instantly dash to the bunk room and bark incessantly until everyone was awake. Only then would he rush for his position in front of the carriage. Jack performed his fire-dog duties faithfully for nine years, running to every fire with the company until he died just as the bell struck for a second alarm on August 5, 1868. According to the *Brooklyn Daily Eagle*, which ran a short obituary for the veteran fire dog, all the members of the company cherished Jack and wished to have him "stuffed and preserved."

Another well-known fire dog in the late nineteenth century was also named Jack, described as a "large, sober-looking brown-and-black shaggy full-bred shepherd dog." Jack was attached to Ladder 18 at 84 Attorney Street, but he was the official pet of Captain Thomas O'Hearn. In 1897, a photographer from the *New York Times* took a picture of Jack, which was featured in an article about famous fire dogs and cats of the FDNY.

Every morning, Jack would report to work by standing with his paws on the desk and waiting until the foreman released him. On the fire scene, Jack was the first member to dash recklessly into a burning building to search for victims. The shepherd enjoyed scrambling up the ladder behind the firefighters, albeit he didn't always make it to the last rung (he also needed assistance getting down). Once during a fire on Forty-Second Street, he made it to the roof and refused to leave his human partners. Jack's paws were severely burned because he insisted on staying with the men on the hot tin roof. Maybe he stayed on the roof because he couldn't get down the ladder, but perhaps he stood by his people because that was what the FDNY expected a good fire dog to do.

Ladder 10, Engine 29, and Engine 13: Nell

Like many FDNY fire dogs, Nell was a pro at clearing the streets for the horses, running ahead of the team, and creating a scene whenever something got in their way. She could also decipher the alarms and knew exactly which combination of gongs sent Ladder 10 out. But what made Nell stand out was her ability to deliver hot coffee to the men while they were inside burning buildings.

According to a battalion chief who told the story to a *Washington Post* reporter in 1912, Nell first appeared at Ladder 10 at 193 Fulton Street around 1894. The men thought the St. Bernard had been abandoned by a Spanish schooner that had been lying at the foot of Fulton Street. The dog couldn't understand English, but an Irish fireman named Tobin took great fancy to the Spanish dog and volunteered to teach her English commands. Tobin also taught her how to carry hot coffee in a pail through all the smoke and confusion of a fire scene.

A young canine mascot poses with the men and horses of Ladder 10. (Firefighters and engine of Hook and Ladder Company No. 10, New York City, 1891. Robert L. Bracklow Photograph Collection. PR 008, 66000-20. New-York Historical Society)

When Tobin transferred to Engine 29, where the future fire chief John Kenlon was lieutenant, Nell became an engine dog. She learned how to pick out the hose line belonging to her engine and follow it through any tangle of hoses belonging to other companies until she found her men at the nozzle end. Only the Engine 29 men could take the pail of coffee from her; if any other fireman tried to take the pail, she'd put it down and growl a warning. One of her greatest achievements was during a large fire in the twelve-story Morton Building at Nassau and Ann Streets in February 1902. The engine driver handed Nell a pail of coffee, although he didn't think she'd deliver the goods due to the dense smoke and the torrent of water washing down the stairs and freezing on each step. It took her nearly an hour of slipping and sliding to reach the eleventh floor, but she finally delivered the pail to the men of Engine 29 "without having spilled any appreciate quantity of the coffee."

Nell also learned how to deliver the daily newspaper to the captain. Every day at 5 a.m., when the fireman on watch fed the horses, Nell would take advantage of the open door and walk down Chambers Street to a newsstand on West Broadway. The man would hand her a paper, which she would return to the engine house and place on the captain's desk.

Engine 29 also had a feline mascot who was on very friendly terms with Nell. When the cat gave birth to six kittens in the cellar, Nell took great interest in them, frequently visiting and standing guard over them. About two weeks after their birth, the mother cat left the firehouse and never returned. The firemen taught the little ones to drink from a saucer, and Nell took each kitten outside for fresh air by placing them in her mouth and depositing them on the sidewalk. If one of the kittens ventured too far or got too close to a cellar grate, she'd go after it and bring it back. Gradually the kittens learned to climb the stairs on their own, at which point Nell lost interest in them.

Nell followed her friend Lieutenant Kenlon to Engine 13 at 99 Wooster Street when he received a promotion to captain. But after nine years of service, she could no longer perform her fire duties. Captain Kenlon sent her to his country home "to end her days in peace and quiet comfort."

Engine 56: Bang Go

Most fire dogs of the horse-drawn era ran ahead of the horses on the ground. Bang Go vaulted through the air—about eight feet high in the air, to be exact.

Bang Go was the son of Go Bang, a prize-winning wire-haired fox terrier worth $2,500 and owned by Governeur Morris Carnochan, chairman of the American Kennel Club Rules Committee. His siblings were Baby Fireaway and Baby Ding Dong. Carnochan presented the dog to Captain Michael J. McNamara of Engine 56 at 120 West Eighty-Third Street when Bang Go was a puppy in 1899. The captain was leery of accepting the tiny dog at first. "In fact, when we first saw him," the captain told the press, "we all gave him the 'Gee-hee.' I knew nothing of wire-haired terriers then and did not realize his value and intelligence. But in a few days, he had earned for himself the affection and interest of all the firemen in the engine house."

Although the tiny dog longed to go to fires with the men, the captain didn't want him to respond, and so he locked up Bang Go whenever the company banged out for a call. But one day he couldn't find the dog before the engine set out. When the engine had gone a few blocks, Bang Go showed up, barking and racing with the horses in his excitement. On their way home, the men saw him pacing in front of the firehouse, warding off all passersby on that side of the street. From then on, whenever he had a chance to run with the horses, he'd dash down the street and repeatedly vault in the air with flying leaps. If he didn't want to run far, he'd run and do vaults in circles.

The high-energy full-bred dog also ate different meals than other fire dogs. For breakfast, he had bread and coffee with milk and sugar. Lunch was a large bowl of soup, plenty of meat and vegetables, and bread and butter. Another cup of coffee topped off his night, which explains why Bang Go was a wired wire-haired fox terrier.

Ladder 15: Spot

Spot became a fire dog much the same way most dogs of Old New York joined the FDNY: he walked into the firehouse and endeared himself to the firemen. Spot also ran to fires much the same way the other fire dogs ran, except Spot ran on two legs—his two left legs. This trick, born of necessity, made Spot one of the most remarkable fire dogs in the city in the early twentieth century.

Spot made his home with Ladder 15 on Old Slip, between Water and Front Streets (now the site of Old Slip Park). An injury to his right hind leg slowed him down, which caused one of the horses to step on his front right foot. For some time, Spot couldn't move at all; he'd just lay on a mat and whine whenever the company went on a call. Little by little, he learned to hobble on three feet. In this way he could get around, but only at a snail's pace. That was not fast enough to run with the horses.

Gradually, Spot adjusted to standing on his two left legs. Then he mastered running on those two legs. It was quite an amazing sight to see him balancing himself while leaning well over to the left, sort of as a wagon would do as it went around a sharp corner on two wheels. He never regained his former speed, but he could keep up with the heavy truck and the horses. Then one day in January 1904, Spot disappeared. The mourning firemen thought someone must have stolen him, because he would never have run away from home. This was the era of dime museums and vaudeville in New York, so perhaps someone nabbed him for a curiosity show. Sadly, we'll never know.

Engine 26: Baltimore

At 10:50 a.m. on February 7, 1904, Fire Patrolman Archibald McAllister discovered smoke coming from the basement of the wholesale dry-goods firm of John E. Hurst and Company in downtown Baltimore, Maryland. Ten minutes after he turned in an alarm, the roof and floors of the Hurst building had collapsed. By the time firemen arrived, the building was engulfed in flames, and the harbor winds were fanning the fire toward the downtown district. For more than two days, the fire raged eastward, consuming an area of more than 140 acres, destroying fifteen hundred office and manufacturing buildings, and leaving twenty-four blocks of Baltimore's business district "a graveyard of smoking black embers."

As the fire spread, Baltimore Fire Chief George W. Horton sent telegrams to Washington and Philadelphia requesting the neighboring cities to rush all available apparatus to his city. The following day, David J. Smyth, Philadelphia's director of public safety, contacted FDNY Acting Fire Chief Charles Washington Kruger at his headquarters on Great Jones Street. He explained that Philadelphia's fire engines were incompatible with Baltimore's saltwater hydrants, and all help was needed. With orders from New York City Mayor George B. McClellan, who told the chief to round up as many engine companies as he thought he could spare, Chief Kruger alerted the Pennsylvania Railroad and Central Railroad of New Jersey that flat cars would be needed at a moment's notice. Then he assigned the following companies to the Baltimore detail: Engine 5 on East Fourteenth Street, Engine 7 on Charles Street, Engine 12 on William Street, Engine 13 on Wooster Street, Engine 16 on East Twenty-Fifth Street, Engine 26 on West Thirty-Seventh Street, Engine 27 on Franklin Street, Engine 31 on Elm (Lafayette) Street, Engine 33 on Great Jones Street, and Ladder 5 on Charles Street.

The first six companies were under the command of First Battalion Chief John P. Howe. The other four companies were under the command of Foreman William Behler of Engine 33. Both crews took ferryboats to Jersey City, where trains of the Central Railroad and Pennsylvania Railroad were waiting for them. The firemen boarded coaches, the horses boarded box cars, and giant steam cranes loaded the engines, tenders, and ladder truck onto flat cars. In total, 105 men responded with about nineteen pieces of apparatus, sixty horses, and twelve thousand feet of hose. It took three hours and thirty-four minutes for the express trains to reach Baltimore.

When the men arrived in Baltimore, they headed to the waterfront. There, they helped stop the fire from jumping across Jones Falls to the factories and lumber mills on the other side of the narrow neck of water. According to Chief Howe, they focused most

Baltimore District Chief August Emrich with FDNY Battalion Chief John Howe and New York firemen following the Baltimore fire in February 1904. (Photograph provided courtesy of the New York City Fire Museum)

of their efforts on a large cold-storage house and several icehouses belonging to the American Ice Company. "There was a bigger body of fire there than I ever saw before," Howe told the press. "It reminded me of the 'Fall of Rome.' Great buildings were falling, and we had to dodge walls and wires all the time. Conditions there were bad." With engines three times as powerful as those of the Baltimore Fire Department, the men were able to hold the fire where any other company would have been defeated. The icehouses also helped their cause, holding the flames for three hours and serving as a main stopping point for the conflagration.

It was during their time in Baltimore that a plain yellow dog began following the members of Engine 26 and doing all he could to get in their way. The men called him Baltimore and decided to make him their mascot. When the firemen arrived back in Jersey City the following evening, the dog was with them. As the members of Engine 26 boarded the ferryboat to return to New York, Baltimore ran ahead of the horses, who seemed pleased to share his company. The ferryman tried to corral the dog, but the firemen yelled, "Let Baltimore alone!" as they explained that the dog belonged to them.

During Baltimore's first few days at the firehouse at 220 West Thirty-Seventh Street, he refused to eat any meat except ham. The men thought he might be a seafaring dog who preferred oysters. But then a dog fancier suggested dog biscuits, which he devoured with delight. The firemen determined that he must have been the dog of an aristocrat. As one man noted, "A dog reveals the manners of his master."

On February 13, the reporters who had traveled to Baltimore presented the dog with a collar of heavy leather, decorated with brass studs. The collar had a plate bearing the inscription, "Baltimore, Feb. 9, 1904. A Waif from the Flames." One fireman said Baltimore was a foxhound, "or if he ain't that, he is of a breed not to be questioned, because if he is different from standard breeds he is a breed all to himself." Baltimore was afraid of the reporters at first, perhaps because they didn't look or smell as they did on the train, covered in soot and reeking of smoke. He hid behind his firemen friends until he saw them welcome the strangers into their firehouse. When a reporter placed the prized collar on Baltimore's neck, he strutted around to show it off in front of the horses. The stray mutt had won a forever home in New York.

HISTORICAL HOOK

Although the Baltimore fire was the first time New York had ever traveled outside the city limits to fight a fire, the FDNY was well prepared. According to Battalion Chief Howe, the boilers on the steam engines required some fresh water, but the engines were equipped to work with Baltimore's saltwater hydrants. He also noted that several years earlier, at a convention of fire chiefs, the men had voted to adopt a uniform size for hose couplings and hydrants in all large cities in the United States. New York and Baltimore were thus compatible. Unfortunately, not all cities had fully adopted the standard by 1904. The lack of uniform threads has been cited as a contributing factor in the extensive destruction caused during the Baltimore fire.

During the early years of the United States' fire service, hydrant threads and hose-connection threads used to couple the hoses differed among the many manufacturers. For many years, members of the International Association of Fire Engineers had discussed adopting a standard thread for fire hose and hydrant couplings. The movement to standardize hose couplings began in earnest following the great Boston fire of 1872. At the first convention of the National Association of Fire Engineers, which coincidentally held its first meeting in Baltimore in 1873, the members recommended that a universal coupling standard be adopted throughout the United States. They also suggested the use of reducers and expanders to cut down on the costs of a full conversion to this standard.

At the association's convention in 1876, the men adopted a resolution recommending that "every department commence at once and order all new hose with couplings having this standard thread" and that "an ample supply of reducing couplings, both male and female, be supplied in each department." It wasn't until the 1891 convention in Springfield, Massachusetts, that a special committee approved a standard coupling for two-and-a-half-inch hose (inside diameter) comprising an outside diameter of three and one-sixteenth inches with seven and a half threads to the inch. (The committee also submitted standard specifications for eight sizes of hose up to six inches inside diameter.) This standard was adopted by the National Fire Protection Association (NFPA) and the American Water Works Association in 1905. Uptake was slow, with only 287 of the 8,000 cities and towns in the United States equipped with standard hose couplings and hydrant outlets; only 700 cities were on board by 1924. Even today, many cities and towns do not have NFPA-standard hydrants or hose couplings and must rely on adapters during mutual-aid calls. New York City has partially complied with the national standard, having standard pumper connections but nonstandard hose connections.

Fireboat *George B. McClellan*: Ginger

In 1905, Captain John Barney Conlon received a puppy named Ginger. He brought the little fox terrier to work to see if the dog would make a good recruit for the fireboat *George B. McClellan*, then attached to Manhattan's Engine 78 and located at the foot of Gansevoort Street. The puppy took to his new role like a fish to water and was soon one of the most popular mascots in the Marine Division.

Ginger was always the first crew member on deck when an alarm came in, taking his post at the hawsehole in the bow, where he'd quiver with excitement until the boat reached the fire. If the men had to go ashore to fight the flames, Ginger would be the first to spring off the boat, making the longest leap of all the firemen. When he wasn't helping the men fight fires, Ginger kept busy making trips around the West Washington Market, where everyone knew and loved the dog. One of his civilian fans who lived on the waterfront even engraved a plate for Ginger's collar.

Two years after joining the FDNY, Ginger mysteriously disappeared after going ashore with one of the men. A small boy said he had seen a canal-boat captain carrying a fox terrier that looked like Ginger, but the firemen had no clues how to find him. A year later, while returning from a fire, the *McClellan* passed a line of canal boats moving in the opposite direction. Just as the fireboat was opposite the last boat in the tow, a fox terrier began barking excitedly. "It's Ginger! Stop the boat!" a man cried. At the sound of his name, the dog dove into the river and swam toward the fireboat. The men said they'd have to pay the canal-boat captain a visit the next time he came into port. They didn't mean that in a nice way.

HISTORICAL HOOK

Like Ginger, Captain Conlon was super popular. He was also a distinguished, if not underrated, firefighter in the city's history. In 1885, the year he joined the department, the Life Saving Benevolent Association of New York presented him with a medal for saving multiple victims from drowning. He also received the Congressional Gold Medal for another drowning rescue in 1912.

Conlon joined the FDNY on August 4, 1885, beginning his career at Engine 21 on East Fortieth Street. It was here he saved the life of Driver Edward J. Leavy when one of the horses stumbled and pulled Leavy from his seat. Conlon, who was standing behind the driver's seat, grasped the horse's reins in one hand and Leavy's ankle with the other. Somehow, he managed to drive the engine for three blocks and get everyone safely to the scene. For this heroic feat, he received an honorable mention and placement on the department's Roll of Merit.

In 1902, as captain of Ladder 24, Conlon had the pleasure of meeting Prince Zaizhen (aka Tsai-Chen), a Manchu prince of the Qing dynasty. Prince Zaizhen, the first royal prince of China to ever visit the United States, wanted to see fire apparatus in action during his visit, so he showed up at Ladder 24 at 115 West Thirty-Third Street accompanied by thirty attendants. The prince and his entourage watched the firemen conduct a response drill in which they slid down the pole while the three horses ran from their stalls and got into position with their harnesses. The men completed the drill in less than eight seconds, to which the prince responded, "It's the most wonderful thing I ever saw. We have nothing like this in my country." The men invited the prince to slide down the brass pole, but he gracefully declined.

Conlon received a promotion to battalion chief in charge of the fireboats in 1906. He retired on August 4, 1911, with twenty-six years of service and died in 1935 at the age of seventy-seven. As for Ginger, a few years after she joined the department, the FDNY added three new fireboats to its fleet. Engine 78 and the *McClellan* relocated to East Ninety-Ninth Street on the Harlem River. Ginger had it good on Gansevoort Street, so she felt no need to jump ship and move uptown. Rather than move to the Upper East Side with the *McClellan*, Ginger stayed with the men of the new *Thomas Willett*. The fox terrier was still on active duty as late as 1911.

Engine 39 and Engine 8: Oakie and Bess

Oakie and Bess, the king and queen of fire dogs, were two of the most famous fire dogs in the history of the FDNY. They were also two of the last great fire dogs to run with the horses before the department replaced the horse-drawn apparatus with motorized vehicles.

Oakie was born and raised on Oakland Farm in Newport, Rhode Island. This was no ordinary farm but rather the country estate of Alfred Gwynne Vanderbilt, the great-grandson of Commodore Cornelius Vanderbilt. The younger Vanderbilt gifted Oakie to Engine 39 after reading about the death of Pinkie, their pedigree coach dog, in March 1907. Pinkie was the mascot of the company for many years, but his special friend was Driver "Silver King" Jimmie Oates. Every night, Pinkie slept in a small bunk next to Oates's bed on the second floor. And on every fire call, Pinkie sat next to Oates on the engine. On the night of March 8, an alarm came in, and Pinkie slid down the pole, just as he'd learned to do (dogs typically left the pole sliding to the men and the cats). When Oates took his seat on the engine, he noticed that Pinkie wasn't there. After returning to the firehouse, the men found Pinkie lying on the rubber mat at the foot of the pole. His back was broken. A few minutes later, he took his last breath in the soothing comfort of Oates's arms. None of the firemen ever confessed to dropping onto Pinkie while sliding down the pole.

After reading about how Pinkie's devotion to duty had brought about his death and how every man in the engine house was now in mourning, Vanderbilt sent the following letter to Captain Edward J. Levy:

> Dear Sir: The account in last Saturday's papers of the sad event which so suddenly plunged the members of Engine Company No. 39 in mourning attracted my attention. To take the place of "Pinkie," who was so suddenly taken from this world, I would be pleased to present to the members of your company a Dalmatian puppy that first saw the light nearly six months ago. Its parents were both imported. I have given instructions that the strongest and best marked puppy be sent to you by express from my Oakland Farm at Newport, R.I., and I trust that you will accept him or her, as the case may be, with my compliments.

On the day Oakie arrived at the circa-1886 firehouse, colocated in the department's headquarters building at 157 East Sixty-Seventh Street, Captain Levy and his fourteen men drew up in two lines and laid down a rug to receive their new dog. "Attired only in black and white, as a gentleman should be on formal occasions, Oakie of Newport and New York" arrived at his new home with full honors. After Fireman Charley Fay ripped open the crate, the dog, "black where he wasn't white, stood forth in all the perfect beauty of a job typed front page of a special night extra edition." The men celebrated with free hot dogs provided by saloon keeper Henry Zimmer while Oakie sat on a couch and posed for his adoring paparazzi. Originally, the men were going to name the dog either

Van or Gwynne in honor of his donor. But they chose Oakie instead for Oakland Farm.

The celebration continued with a formal reception in the captain's office. In addition to the firemen, others in attendance included Police Captain Nat Shire of the East Sixty-Seventh Street police station, Roundsman Ben Ashley, FDNY Captain John Rush, Supervisor Joseph Shea, Battalion Chief Howe, and Sport, the pet dog of Commissioner Francis J. Lantry. Sport took considerable interest in Oakie, but the former Vanderbilt dog "did not so much as deign to notice Sport, and turned up his aristocratic nose at the commissioner's dog." The fire horses—Bull, Baby, Tom, Paddy, and Jerry B—also looked on in wonder at their new canine boss.

Following the reception, Police Captain Shire issued the following edict: "Immediately upon the first tap of the alarm in the fire house next door, the members of the force stationed in this house will repair to the fire house in a body and surround it until the members of No. 39 get back from the fire to watch their own mutt. No one is to be permitted to take the dog out of the house without a special order from Fire Captain Levy. This does not apply, however, to any cop who can swipe the dog for us and get away with it."

A month after the noble dog arrived, he decided to forsake Third Avenue for Fifth Avenue to visit society's upper crust on Millionaire's Row. According to a company fireman, the men had asked four boys to take Oakie for a walk "out on the avenue." As soon as they reached Third Avenue, Oakie put his tail between his legs and headed west. "You ought to know what Third Avenue would mean to a dog of Oakie's breeding," the fireman told a *New York Times* reporter. "He was too swell for us. He's gone to the effete west." The next day, however, having seen enough of the rich and famous, Oakie returned to the firehouse and settled in as an FDNY working dog.

Oakie got busy with the ladies only a few months after joining the firehouse. His first mate was a Dalmatian named Bessie, a former Bellevue ambulance dog who was presented to the fire department when an order was issued banning animal mascots for the ambulances. After giving birth to five puppies in July 1907, Bessie bit six boys and one young man who had begun taunting her and blocking her way while she was taking a walk. Although Dr. W. F. Braisted of the Board of Health said she tested negative for rabies, Commissioner Lantry believed that she was dangerous and called for the SPCA to take her away. Oakie showed no interest in his puppies, so the firemen took turns feeding them from a bottle and spoon. As one newspaper noted, "there are milk stains on every uniform in the company."

Oakie may not have been interested in his own puppies, but he did save a human baby girl who was only a few weeks old. According to the story, one night Oakie hurriedly left headquarters for no apparent reason. When he returned, he was carrying in his jaw a bundle, which he carefully placed in front of the engine. The baby was wrapped up, but she was nearly dead from exposure. The fireman warmed the baby and brought her to the police station. Then they set out with Oakie to find out whether he was a kidnapper or a lifesaver. Oakie led the men to the basement of a house and picked up a shawl on the floor. The men concluded that the dog had found the baby girl lying on the basement floor.

Oakie's next mate, another Bess, also came from a litter of aristocratic dogs, but her master was an anonymous member of a Fifth Avenue family. He reportedly admired the work of the firemen who had responded to a fire at his house, so he wanted to give them a Dalmatian. One day he drove up to Engine 8 quarters at 165 East Fifty-First Street in his touring car and gave them a puppy. He didn't say who he was but told them that the dog's name was Bess and that he wanted her to be a real working fire dog.

While Bess was still a young pup in 1908, the men took turns bundling her up and carrying her home for meals. Boisterous and beefy Fireman Michael Creegman and Fireman Alonzo Weiss (aka Wise) were two of Bess's favorite firemen, so she often went home with them on the Third Avenue streetcars. As Bess got bigger, though, the conductors began objecting to her riding along with the men. When the conductors told the firemen that they could no longer take Bess on the streetcars, she started running after them. And so in July 1908, Captain Joseph Donovan and Driver David M. Lynx took Bess to the office of the receiver for the Third Avenue Railway Company. Bess barked and wagged her tail while the men applied for a special permit for her. The pass read, "To conductors: A permit is hereby granted for the bearer or bearers to carry a dog on the Third Avenue Railway cars. This permit expires on September 1, 1908. Frederick W. Whitridge, Receiver." To celebrate her rail pass—which Whitridge said he'd renew in September—the firemen bought Bess a new collar with a brass helmet on it. With her fire department badge, collar, and permit, Bess was now free to come and go as she pleased. Sometimes she'd take the car by herself to visit Fireman Weiss in the Bronx on his days off.

Over the next few years, Bess and Oakie had five litters of puppies—including a litter of eight puppies in February 1909—all of whom found homes with the firemen. One of these puppies was Mike, owned by Driver Lynx. Mike eventually took over his mother's former role as mascot of Engine 8 and acquired her Third Avenue railcar pass in 1910. Bess and Fireman Weiss moved to Fire Headquarters when Weiss transferred to Engine 39.

When Bess wasn't having puppies, she was a working fire dog. In addition to mastering ordinary dog tricks such as begging and playing dead, Bass understood the alarm system and knew almost as well as the men the location of the various boxes. Over at Engine 39, she cleared the crossing at Third Avenue and Sixty-Seventh Street about forty times a month, barking a warning to surface-car motormen, truck drivers, and pedestrians. She also followed her master into burning buildings, always abiding by the rules to stay one floor below the nozzle men (the department had established this rule for fear that a dog might cause the fireman to stumble).

But then one day in February 1912, the three horses she loved—Tom, Malden, and Charion—exited the firehouse with Driver Oates for the last time, never to return. The hose-truck horses, Enright and Anterash, were led by Driver John Leamy to the training stables. Then the men, headed by Captain Seymour J. Guy and Lieutenants Weiss and Harry J. Gallagher, removed the horses' harnesses, blankets, and feed bags to make way for a gasoline-powered engine. While the evicted horses stood in front of their firehouse, the $10,000 gasoline-pumping engine (nicknamed "The Giant") and the automobile hose wagon backed in to take their place. Bess, who had followed the horses to the street, returned to quarters to

On February 25, 1912, Bess the Dalmatian said good-bye to Tom, Malden, and Charion, the last of the Engine 39 fire horses. (Photograph provided courtesy of the New York City Fire Museum)

inspect the new machines. Not liking what she saw, she checked on the horses of the neighboring Ladder 16 to make sure they were still there. She refused to return to her station for some time.

On February 25, 1912, the new apparatus made its first three runs. Bess, for the first time in years, failed to follow along. When the gong sounded, she pranced about, and it looked as if she might join the men. But when the motor started, she tucked her tail between her legs and sought refuge upstairs in the sleeping quarters. There, she "howled until she gave everyone in the neighborhood a headache." In October of that year, a woman drove up to Fire Headquarters and presented Captain George Fox of Ladder 16 with a young Dalmatian to thank the men for their work. The men named him Chief. By this time, Bess had totally given up on responding to calls, albeit she still tagged after the men when they went for dinner. Chief took her place.

In March 1914, Bess and Lieutenant Weiss transferred to Engine 274 at 150-18 Forty-First Avenue in Queens. This company, which had been organized under the FDNY only a few years earlier in 1908, still had horse-drawn apparatus. Lieutenant Weiss and Bess were pleased with the horses, but the lieutenant knew it was just a matter of time before the Queens company transitioned to motorized vehicles. "There is no telling when it will happen to us again," he said, explaining that the engine companies at Corona and Elmhurst had been motorized and the horses at Murray Hill were from a company in Manhattan now using gasoline power. As the lieutenant spoke to the reporter, Bess looked up at him as if sensing his worry. "Now there's a dog worth loving and worth being loved by," Weiss said. "She is a ribbon dog. Got her honors at Madison Square Garden in 1910. She was a natural born mascot."

At about the same time Bess retired to Queens, Captain Levy also retired from the FDNY. Oakie went with him and spent his final years watching his master play pinochle with his FDNY pals in the back of a little café on Fifth Avenue and Fifty-Sixth Street. Lieutenant Weiss retired in July 1919, stating that he had tired of the job after twenty-five years of service and that he no longer wanted to continue working as a smoke eater.

HISTORICAL HOOK

One of Oakie's many visitors at Engine 39 was King Jock, an English bulldog of high pedigree owned by John C. Wakely, the steward of the Hahnemann Hospital at Park Avenue and Sixty-Seventh Street. King Jock was a show dog valued at $2,500, so it was no surprise that he and Oakie were quite amicable and enjoyed each other's company. Wakely was not only a friend of Captain Levy's but also one of the fire buffs attached to Engine 39.

Like the runners of the volunteer era, who helped pull the apparatus and work the ropes and pump handles, the buffs of the nineteenth and early twentieth centuries were an exclusive group of men who hung around the firehouses and accompanied the apparatus on calls. According to the *New York Press*, being a fire buff was "an honor to be held highly." Buffs had been "a recognized institution" since the fire department's inception, and they were among the firemen's best friends. The reporter explained,

The buffs are not recruited from any one walk in life, but comprise in their informal circle the workman out of a job and the millionaire with more money than he is able to spend. Although the conditions of life of the two men are entirely opposite, their aim is the same, and that is to be present at every fire which is dignified by two or more alarms. There is a fascination in watching the firemen extinguish a blaze and seeing their deeds of heroism which appeals strongly to the mind of the true buff. If he is an ordinary citizen he hangs about the firehouses, running errands for the firemen and waiting intently for the welcome sound of the gong. If he is a man of wealth or political influence he has an alarm, connected with the nearest fire station, in his bedroom, and at the sound of a second alarm leaves his comfortable bed and hastens to the scene of action.

There are several legends surrounding the origins of the word "buff," but the one most likely—although not proven—is that the term is derived from the Buffalo Corps of the New York Fire Department, of which New York State Governor Alfred E. Smith was a member in the 1880s (he was a buff for Engine 32). The organization dates to around 1865, when the city replaced the volunteer system with a paid fire department. Many volunteers who didn't transition to a paid position continued going to fires and sleeping in the firehouses. The new department would not supply them with bedding, so the men reportedly brought heavy buffalo robes to sleep in. Their nickname, "buffaloes," was shortened to "buffs."

During the early 1900s, some of Manhattan's and Brooklyn's recognized buffs included Dr. Harry Mortimer Archer, Assemblyman John McKeown, Magistrate E. Gaston Higginbotham, Colonel N. B. Thurston, David Woodhouse, and Simon Brentano. The men wore rubber boots and coats, as well as metal fire department badges—with the word "Buff" in the center instead of the fireman's number—that allowed them to get inside the fire lines. Buffs with clout had alarms in their homes, which were wired to the nearest firehouse and paid for by the department. Some of the buffs, such as Dr. Archer, provided medical assistance for the firemen, while others brought the men coffee and rolls. Well-to-do buffs endowed hospital beds and purchased medical equipment for injured firemen, established loan funds for the men and their families, and raised money for recruiting campaigns.

In December 1905, Chief Edward Croker issued an order prohibiting buffs from entering the firehouses and fire lines. Some of the wealthy buffs who had helped the chief get reinstated after Fire Commissioner Thomas Sturgis suspended him in August 1902 threatened to use their influence to force him to withdraw his order. But the chief doubled down in July 1906, ordering that all metal fire badges issued to the buffs be returned to headquarters. Chief Croker said that his men were greatly hampered in fighting

Deputy Fire Commissioner Dr. Harry Mortimer Archer. (Photograph provided courtesy of the New York City Fire Museum)

fires with so many people within the fire lines who had no business being on the scene.

The issuance of badges may have ended, but fire buffs continued following the fires and crossing the fire lines for many more years. In 1920, Dr. Archer—or "the prize buff," as he was called—had already put in thirty-four years as a buff and was now an honorary deputy chief and medical officer for the fire department. A graduate of Columbia University and Bellevue Medical and chief surgeon for the Aetna Life Insurance Company, Dr. Archer made the time to attend eight thousand fires and other disasters and treat about twenty-two thousand firemen and civilians who had been injured or overcome by smoke. His fire telegraph signal, which he kept in the uplifted right hand of a stuffed bear in his home library, was always in service. He also had his own ambulance with a chauffeur always waiting (the ambulance, first placed in service in 1914, was for firemen only). "I have never missed a second or third alarm fire in the thirty-four years," Dr. Archer told a reporter in 1920. Asked why he was buff, Dr. Archer said, "I do not know. I don't like fires, but I go because frequently there is need of medical assistance, and I give this gladly." Dr. Archer, who was appointed deputy fire commissioner in charge of Brooklyn and Queens in 1940, gladly performed his services until his death at the age of eighty-six in May 1954.

Engine 6: Jess

When Jess, the three-year-old Dalmatian of Engine 6, broke her leg while responding to a fire in September 1910, she wasn't about to let a major injury stop her from doing her job. Even if it meant disobeying her master, breaking the rope keeping her back, and running with a heavy plaster cast on her leg.

Jess was the domestic pet of Fireman Sheehan, who lived near the firehouse, then at 113 Liberty Street. When she was a puppy, she became accustomed to running from Sheehan's home to the firehouse and "dashing out in a wild state of puppy excitement to every fire the engine attended." Once formed, this habit of fire chasing became impossible to break. The men of the company decided to welcome her into their home, providing a clean pile of hay next to the stalls for her bedding.

One day Jess got too close to the hoofs of Acting Chief Sweet's horses while running ahead of his buggy. A horse struck her left foreleg, breaking it in three places. The chief couldn't stop to help her, but a kind-hearted civilian carried her back to quarters. Captain Flynn telephoned Mrs. Harry Ulysses Kibbe, president of the Bideawee Home for Animals, who in turn sent Dr. Kohstann to the engine house. The veterinarian set Jess's broken leg in a cast and ordered her tied up in the cellar to keep her from following the engine. Dr. Kohstann obviously didn't know Jess very well.

Jess stayed cooped up in the cellar for a few days, but when an alarm came in for Pier 5, "recuperating went to the winds." She broke loose from the rope, "and with the broken, plaster-incased leg held awkwardly in the air, ran on three legs directly in front of the three galloping fire horses all the way across town to an East River fire." By the time the men noticed their dog, it was too late to stop responding. All they could do was anxiously watch the horses and pray they didn't hit Jess as they galloped to the fire. Jess made it to the fire safely and seemed none the worse for wear when the company returned to quarters.

Engine 67: Chief

Most fire dogs of Old New York made the newspaper headlines when they saved a life, went missing, or died while on duty. From time to time, however, a dog would get publicity for doing something bad or comical. As P. T. Barnum may or may not have said, "There's no such thing as bad publicity." The men of Engine 67 might not have agreed with Barnum when their dog, Chief, earned the following headline in the *New York Evening World*: "Firehouse Dog Sleeps in Flat after a Blaze: Women Fail to Dislodge Him and Fire Fighters Are Recalled." But this bad publicity has earned Chief a few paragraphs in this book, so that's a good thing.

The news-making story took place on September 19, 1911, in an apartment at 500 West 170th Street. Mrs. Emanuel Pearson had just left her kitchen when she saw smoke pouring from a bedroom door. In response to Mrs. Pearson's screams, Mrs. E. W. Cope, the next-door neighbor, came to the rescue. Soon, more women came to help, each grabbing a bucket to form their own bucket brigade until Engine 67, just a few doors away at 518 West 170th Street, arrived. When the firemen ran into the apartment, they found the women celebrating for having extinguished the flames on their own. Confirming there was no need for any further action, the men returned to quarters. They inadvertently left one member behind.

While the women were celebrating, Chief, described as "a long, lean, smoke-eating greyhound," decided to make himself at home. He lay down on a rug under the parlor table and fell asleep. When Mrs. Pearson and Mrs. Cope tried to tell him that they no longer required his services, "he merely opened his blood-shot eyes and growled." When the women tried to dislodge him with a broom, he showed his long teeth. That sent the women running into the hall, where they grabbed shoe brushes and galoshes to throw at the unwelcome canine guest. He didn't budge. Following some discussion, the women sent a young boy to the firehouse to let the men know that their dog had overstayed his welcome. A delegation of firemen responded to the new emergency. As soon as Chief saw the blue coats and silvered buttons, "he meekly dropped his tail and ears and followed them back to his proper home." The embarrassed firemen told the press that their dog loved the smell of smoke, which is why he didn't want to leave Mrs. Pearson's apartment.

Engine 261: Bess and Molly

Bess, unlike most fire dogs of her era, preferred to stay at home and guard her Queens firehouse rather than run with the horses and engine. When an alarm came in, she'd sit at the head of the stairs leading to the locker rooms, "and woe would be unto him who would pass her until the firemen came back!" Bess also had an aversion to most men in uniform, especially letter carriers, policemen, and strange firemen. She loved the men of Engine 261, but whenever someone new transferred to the company, Bess would express her displeasure for several days until she learned that he was now a permanent member of her family.

Bess joined the company in 1911, when it was still called Engine 161 and located at 231 Radde Street (now Twenty-Eighth Street). During her nine years of active service, she gave birth to three litters of puppies, all of which were distributed to the neighbors (one of her sons moved in with the family next to the firehouse, but he remained a domestic pet). With each litter and each year of service, Bess began to pack on the pounds. By the summer of 1920, the ten-year-old dog was ready to retire.

On July 30, 1920, Bess went into the rear yard and plopped onto the ground. When Fireman Fred Niki came outside to check on her, she licked his hand, "as if sensing her approaching end, and as though grateful to the boys of the company for what they had been to her." Fireman John Green did what he could to make her last minutes of life as comfortable as possible. Captain Matt O'Farrell and his men had tears in their eyes as they buried Bess in the yard where she died. Not long after Bess passed away, Engine 261 got a new mascot named Molly. This Dalmatian was the last of the company's fire dogs to share her home with the four horses who pulled the engine and tender.

In October 1921, Battalion Chief Albert Reid announced that the horse-drawn vehicles would be replaced by motorized apparatus. When the four horses—Tony, Enuf, Franklin, and Exmurr—were taken away for the last time, Captain O'Farrell, Lieutenant Charles Riley, and all the men on duty lined up along the curb to send them off. Driver George McGowan, who had driven the engine for sixteen years, and Driver Fred Larkin delivered the horses and old apparatus to Winfield (now part of Woodside, Queens) while Molly checked out the new La France six-cylinder engine and tender combined. The men told a reporter for the *Brooklyn Times Union* that Molly would have to stretch her legs to keep up with the new engine unless she preferred to ride on it. Upon returning to the firehouse after leaving the horses at Winfield, Driver McGowan said, "Instead of oats now I guess we'll feed it gasoline."

Hose 6: Jack

When someone on the top floor of 354 Fulton Street (now Jamaica Avenue) in Queens carelessly tossed a lit match out the window, setting fire to an awning, Jack put his nose in gear and went into action. The black-spotted dog of Hose Company 6 was trotting past the office of Piquet & Piquet in August 1912 when he got a whiff of the smoke. He immediately began barking, attracting the attention of the building occupants. As real estate brokers Albert and Eli Piquet tried to tear down the blazing awning, Jack ran to his firehouse less than one block away on Herriman Avenue (now 161st Street). He rushed up to Fireman Gilmore W. Overacre and tugged vigorously at the man's trousers. Sensing trouble, Overacre followed Jack into the street. He grabbed a chemical extinguisher and quickly put out the flames, which had begun spreading to the building. The Piquet brothers said they'd buy Jack a new collar with a real fireman's badge attached to it to thank him for saving their property.

HISTORICAL HOOK

When Jack saved the Piquet's office building in 1912, Hose 6 (now Engine 299) had been a part of New York's paid fire department for only five years. Prior to 1907, the company was an independent volunteer organization and then briefly part of Jamaica's volunteer fire department before the town's volunteer companies disbanded.

The Jamaica Fire Department was founded in 1797, when the village of Jamaica had fewer than fifty houses. Following a few meetings to discuss fire protection for the growing village, forty-one men and women, including James and Elizabeth Herriman and John D. Ditmars, pledged contributions to purchase a fire engine. At a meeting of the subscribers on January 30, 1797, at the home of John and Joanna Hinchman, the townsfolk resolved that John Battan be captain of the fire company. An act of the Legislature of the State of New York titled "An Act for the Extinguishing of Fires in the Village of Jamaica, in Queens County" passed on April 1, 1797.

The village's first engine and ladder companies—Protection Engine and Atlantic Hook and Ladder—were quartered in the southwest corner of the Presbyterian churchyard on Fulton Street (now Jamaica Avenue) between Johnson and Clinton Streets (163rd and 164th Streets). In 1855, the village trustees built a house on Union Avenue (162nd Street) for the two companies. Several other companies joined the department throughout the nineteenth century, including Neptune Engine, Continental Bucket Company, Continental Hook and Ladder Company, Excelsior Hose Company, and Woodhull Hose Company.

Horse-drawn apparatus was not a standard feature in the Jamaica Fire Department, and even in 1903, the department's board of officers was still on the fence about introducing horses: the exception was a horse named Ben V, purchased for the department in 1897. Sets of regulation harness were sent to all seven companies (Fosdick, Excelsior, Woodhull, Distler, Resolute, Atlantic, and Continental), but each firehouse would have to undergo alterations to accommodate horses. Foreman Joseph Kaiser of the Excelsior Hose Company offered to stable up to three horses in his barn if that would help facilitate matters. The next day, someone put a wooden carpenter's horse and a handful of hay next to the Excelsior's engine; a real horse materialized about a week later. By June 1903, Chief Engineer

Valentine Bangert had delivered one horse to each engine company and two horses to the ladder companies.

In May 1907, Jamaica's fire department welcomed the independent Jamaica Hose Company into its folds. Two months later, on July 5, 1907, FDNY Fire Commissioner Francis J. Lantry disbanded all the companies of Jamaica's volunteer department and replaced them with new companies under New York City's paid fire department. The *Brooklyn Daily Eagle* reported, "The rapid growth of Jamaica and the erection of large, costly buildings have made it imperative that more adequate fire protection be secured. The apparatus with which the volunteers have done so much effective work in the past has outlived its usefulness in a great measure and must be replaced by more modern appliances for the fighting of fires, and men must be always ready in the fire houses, both night and day, to go out at a moment's notice."

Five new hose companies and three ladder companies were installed in Jamaica, replacing all but Jamaica Hose Company 6, which took over the former quarters of Woodhull Hose Company at 17 Herriman Avenue, just north of present-day Jamaica Avenue. Approximately 420 volunteers were mustered out, with only a handful accepting salaried positions with the FDNY. One of the "volunteers" who accepted a position with the paid department was fire horse Ben V, who was handed over to FDNY Hose 6 when the volunteer department was disorganized. When Ben V died in May 1913, his canine pal Jack was reportedly just as sad as Lieutenant Charles Brown and the other firemen were.

The last two horses to run with Hose 6 were Al Carroll and Allen Boy, who were retired on August 12, 1919, to make way for a new motorized hose wagon. Lieutenant Thomas Forgea told the press, "We are all sorry to lose the horses we have had for years. They were always on the jump at the tap of the gong. This is a progressive period and like others, the horse must give way to the most modern devices."

Ladder 12: Sparks

Like Oakie of Engine 39, Sparks was also a pedigree Dalmatian with ties to the Vanderbilt family. According to Ladder 12 Captain Lawrence McGuire, Sparks's mother and father were both gifted to the FDNY by Mrs. Alfred Vanderbilt, which automatically made Sparks a remarkable mascot.

Sparks was presented to Ladder 12 at 243 West Twentieth Street in December 1914 when he was about a month old. Upon his arrival, the men set out in search of puppy food. When they returned, Sparks was gone. Following a cursory search of the firehouse, they were about to give up finding the dog when Fireman Jimmy Canning grabbed his coat. There was Sparks, with his nose deep inside the coat pocket, attempting to chew on a plug of chewing tobacco. Testing to see whether the puppy really wanted to eat the tobacco, one of the men broke off a piece and handed it to Sparks. "Greatly to our surprise Sparks snapped the tobacco up voraciously and chewed on it to his heart's content," Captain McGuire said. "He really appeared to enjoy it, but he was not so chipper five minutes later when his head began to spin and his eyes to grow dim." Although Sparks didn't have a good first experience with the tobacco, it didn't stop him from chewing on it whenever given the chance.

Although Sparks shared his home with the horse who still pulled Deputy Chief George Ross's buggy, he didn't like to run with this horse or the company's auto truck, preferring instead to stay behind and guard the firehouse. However, he did enjoy playing tag in and around the truck with Smoke and Blackie, the feline mascots of Ladder 12. The agile cats often proved too much for Sparks, so he'd seek a safe spot among the helmets or pike poles to get away from them and take a nap. On more than one occasion, Sparks would wake up to find himself in the truck responding to a fire. Fortunately, he had good sense to stay on the truck while it was in motion.

Although Sparks was only six months old in the spring of 1915, he was quite clever when it came to firefighting. He could extinguish a lighted cigar or cigarette butt using his paw without injuring himself. He also learned how to attract the attention of a policeman whenever he discovered a bonfire in the street by circling around the fire and barking like mad until a policeman responded and extinguished the fire with his nightstick. As the proud captain told a *New York Sun* reporter, "His vigilance has prevented many fires."

Engine 19: Ted

During World War I, in the Forest of Argonne, the men of the gas battalion of New York's Seventy-Seventh Division sent messages between the front and rear lines by calling on a small Dalmatian named Phosgene. The French dog was one of dozens of stray dogs that associated themselves with the American battalions heading for the front lines during the war. Every contingent that landed in the French ports came upon the street dogs, which, like all war refugees, were hungry and smart enough to know that the soldiers "were friends worth having." Phosgene attached himself to Sergeant Harry J. Bailey of Company G of the gas battalion shortly after the Battle of Saint-Mihiel in September 1918. It took only a handful of kibbles for the dog to know that Sergeant Bailey and his men were his people.

One night the gas battalion was on the front lines observing German artillery, which included a large mixture of gas shells. The men tried to send a message to the back lines using messenger pigeons, but an hour later, they realized that the birds had fallen from the sky, wounded by shrapnel. That's when the soldiers got an idea to train Phosgene to do the work of the carrier pigeons. In short time, by breaking into small groups and hiding in the dense woods, the men were able to train the dog to carry messages from one group to another. Time and again, Phosgene did his job, tramping back and forth from the rear to front lines with messages hidden under his specially made silver-plate collar. The dog had many narrow escapes from bursting shells, but he never hesitated to complete the mission. According to the *New York Herald*, he was "a marvel at leaping across shell holes and trenches. He seemed to know just what he was doing and how it should be done."

Following the Armistice of November 11, 1918, Phosgene returned to New York with the division. The men smuggled him aboard a transport and took him to Camp Merritt, New Jersey, which is where Fireman William Kennelly of Engine 19 found him. The timing was perfect. Kennelly was just about to leave the service and rejoin the FDNY, and Phosgene needed a good home in the United States. Kennelly promised the soldiers that he would provide a good home to the dog at the Chelsea firehouse at 355 West Twenty-Fifth Street, so they let him take their foreign friend. Kennelly changed his new dog's name to Ted.

In telling the press about Ted and the dog's new career with the FDNY, Captain Ferdinand Butenschoen said, "Why, all the village is crazy about the dog. When anyone looks at his collar and sees that he has been to war they make friends with Ted forthwith." According to the captain, Ted was highly intelligent, especially when it came to getting the hose tender ready for an alarm. When the gong sounded, he'd run circles around the chauffeur to make sure he was going to crank up the motor on the vehicle. As soon as the driver touched the crank, Ted would leap onto the rear of the wagon and ride to the fire. "I am very glad that he rides on the wagon, because it means he will not meet the fate of other fire house mascots who run ahead of the apparatus and get killed," Butenschoen said. "He is a wise little fellow and, like a lot of the boys from around here who went to war, he learned something in France."

Engine 33 and Engine 55: Smoky Josephine

At first, no one knew just how many lives Fireman Frank Maixner had saved during a fire at 52 East Fourth Street on December 11, 1922. But every fireman of Engine 33 at 42 Great Jones Street and Engine 55 at 363 Broome Street hoped he had saved enough lives for everyone to share.

The fire had started in a loft on the second floor of the five-story building shortly before midnight. By the time the two engine companies reached the scene, the loft was filled with dense smoke. As Maixner groped through the loft to open the windows for ventilation, he heard a dog crying in a far corner. He made his way through the smoke until he found the dog, who was now in great distress. Placing the injured animal under his arms, he made his way down the stairs. Once outside, Maixner saw that he had rescued a brown collie. The firemen immediately named the dog Smoky Joe after the FDNY's second in command, Chief "Smoky Joe" Martin. Oops. While firemen O'Brien and Snyder of Engine 55 were working to revive the dog, they noticed that Smoky Joe was a Smoky Josephine. They changed her name on the spot. They also noticed that the arrival of "junior 'Smoky Joes' and 'Smoky Josephines' was imminently expected." Battalion Chief John J. P. Waldron put the dog in his red fire vehicle and drove her to the Ellin Prince Speyer Animal Hospital, where Mrs. George Bethune Adams and Dr. Bruce Blair saw to her treatment. The firemen waited with bated breath for the delivery, hoping Smoky Josephine would have a large litter so everyone could adopt a puppy. The *New York Times* reported, "Brown collie pup mascots are expected to be the style in firehouses in the neighborhood soon."

HISTORICAL HOOK

On January 10, 1919, the day Wesley Augustus Williams reported as a driver for Engine 55, Captain Charles Nolan retired after taking roll call. In a time when discrimination and segregation were the norm, Captain Nolan didn't want to be associated with the first company to have an active African American fireman. The other men couldn't quit so easily, so they asked for transfers. Department officials imposed a one-year moratorium on transfers with hopes that the men would adjust to Wesley. They adjusted by making Wesley perform demeaning tasks and damaging his uniforms.

Prior to joining the FDNY, Wesley had been a Red Cap luggage carrier at Grand Central Terminal and a sandhog who helped build the subway tunnel connecting the South Ferry to Brooklyn. He scored one hundred on the FDNY's physical fitness exam (he was the only applicant to pass with a perfect score) and later competed in department boxing and wrestling tournaments. Wesley endured the constant discrimination and prevailed simply by being a great fireman.

On September 16, 1927, Wesley became the FDNY's first African American officer when he was promoted to lieutenant for Engine 55. At that time, there were only three Black firemen of six thousand men in the department. Promotions to captain and battalion chief followed in 1934 and 1938, respectively. In 1940, when there were forty Black men in the department, Wesley founded the Vulcan Society to fight racial discrimination in the FDNY. The society was reportedly the first to purchase a lifetime membership in the National Association for the Advancement of Colored People. Battalion

Chief Wesley retired in 1952, following an accident on the way to a fire. He died at the age of eighty-seven on July 3, 1984, at Physician's Hospital in Queens. During the funeral services in Harlem, Robert Lowery, the city's first Black fire commissioner, stated, "He was an inspiration to me as he was to a number of young, black firefighters."

Engine 205: Jiggs

When eight-year-old Jiggs died on August 14, 1925, the *Brooklyn Daily Eagle* called him "Brooklyn's fattest dog, if not the fattest in Greater New York." Jiggs had a bad habit of making the daily rounds at the Brooklyn Borough Hall restaurants, and when he died, he tipped the scales at 121 pounds. It wasn't his weight, though, that killed him. Unfortunately, the Brooklyn SPCA had to humanely dispatch him because Jiggs had become a grumpy old man in his final year of retirement.

Jiggs was born on March 17, 1917, and presented to Engine 205 in Brooklyn Heights on Decoration Day (Memorial Day), when the company was located at 160 Pierrepont Street. Right away, Jiggs bonded with Engineer Thomas J. "Smoke" McEwan, and over the years, he rarely left McEwan's side. The only other person he really liked was the woman who kept a newspaper stand near Borough Hall. Every morning, he'd follow her after she delivered the newspaper to the firehouse until she gave him candy. Jiggs also took a liking to Bum the fire cat and her kittens. Bum was a longtime mascot of Engine 205—her mother cat joined the FDNY after the men found her cold and starving on the street near the firehouse in 1909. Bum and all her siblings stayed in the neighborhood, but only Bum was lucky enough to get a permanent home at the firehouse.

Jiggs was hyperactive in his youth, barking and crazily jumping whenever the gong rang for a fire. Bath time was always a struggle for McEwan and Fireman Frank Wolf, but they managed to bathe Jiggs four times a week. Sometimes young Jiggs would get a little too friendly or too ambitious. Once he picked the wrong time to make friends with one of the horses—the horse responded by booting him through a rear window. Another time he broke his leg while trying to slide down the pole.

During Jiggs's first few years as a fire buff, he was a buff Dalmatian, never weighing more than seventy-one pounds. He was fast with the horses and present on every call, no matter what the size of the fire or incident. In his first five years of service, he responded to more than ten thousand fire calls. But then he struck up a friendship with John Martin, a chef in Joe's Restaurant at the corner of Fulton and Pierrepont Streets. John couldn't help but give the dog a few treats every day, and with a menu that listed more than four hundred food choices, there was plenty to go around for Jiggs. After befriending Martin, Jiggs discovered other friendly chefs at nearby restaurants. The chefs encouraged the dog to eat and often bragged that the famous fire dog preferred their cooking to another's.

Jiggs couldn't have become a canine epicurean at a worse time in the history of the department. One by one, each company had been replacing its horses with motorized apparatus. Brooklyn's Engine 205 was the last to relinquish its horses in 1922. With the horses gone, Jiggs could no longer get his daily exercise. Refusing to accept a pension and move to a retirement farm, Jiggs tried running with the motorized apparatus a few times, but it nearly killed him. An overweight Dalmatian was no match for a motorized engine that could go up to forty miles an hour.

By 1923, Jiggs weighed 118 pounds. Twice the firemen sent him to an exclusive farm for canine reduction treatments, but both times he made his way back to Pierrepont Street without reaching his weight goal. Then, on October 12, 1923, Jiggs received treatment for painful swelling in his right paw, which turned out to be gout. Jiggs was put on a strict diet and lost weight over the next two months. But before long, when McEwan wasn't watching him carefully, Jiggs got back into his bad ways and was soon heavier and lazier than ever. He spent his days lying outside the firehouse sunning himself and, as the firemen said, never partook in "any such feminine activity as dieting to reduce." Captain Leon Howard told the press that the men never fed Jiggs—he fed himself—and the fatter he got, the more he wanted to eat.

In July 1925, Engine 205 relocated to 274 Hicks Street. For Jiggs, Hicks Street was a long way from Borough Hall and all his favorite restaurants that he had visited "with the regularity and fervor of an old-time rounder at the cocktail hour." Unable to adjust to the change, the good-natured dog soon grew remorseful and bad tempered. That month, police at the Poplar Street station charged Jiggs with biting a passerby who had reportedly kicked him in front of the station while the engine was out. The men sent the dog to the Butler Street pound in a wagon donated by the *Brooklyn Standard Union*, and he remained there in confinement for ten days until authorities confirmed that he didn't have rabies. Upon his release from the pound, Jiggs was issued a silver-plated muzzle and a dog license. Fire Commissioner Thomas J. Drennan told Captain Howard, "Put him back on active duty. He will neither be fined nor his pay deducted. Jiggs is one of the best dogs in the history of the Fire Department."

Apparently, Jiggs didn't wear the muzzle, because a month later, he was still snapping at people, including children, and was a danger to the public. The men of Engine 205 had no other choice but to ask the SPCA to euthanize their beloved fire dog. Sadly, McEwan was on vacation at the time, and the men were not able to locate him before Jiggs took his final breath.

HISTORICAL HOOK

In 1903, New York Alderman James Cowdin Myers introduced an ordinance requiring the muzzling of all dogs on the city streets during summer months. If caught without a muzzle, the dog went to the pound, and the owner had to pay a three-dollar release fee. The primary purpose of the law was to prevent "mad dogs" from biting people and spreading rabies during the dog days of summer. This wasn't the first time such an ordinance had been issued in the city—legislation requiring summertime muzzles and licenses went into effect as early as July 1877—but Myers's proposal garnered much more publicity and colorful comments. During a hearing on the ordinance, Mrs. M. Jennings said that it wasn't right to muzzle dogs just because bad boys were making them go mad. "I don't think the city is a place for dogs, but for that matter it's no place for children," she told the board. Two doctors who spoke during the hearing argued whether rabies even existed or not.

The proposed ordinance created much discontent among New Yorkers, especially in families where some members agreed that muzzling was a great idea and others—referred to as the anti-muzzlers—thought that it was criminal to muzzle the family pet. When asked whether city dogs should wear muzzles or not, one man told the *New-York Tribune*, "There is no use talking. This dog question is the question after all. They may talk as much as they please about our relations with foreign countries, tariffs, bond issues and little things like those, but, after all, the dog question is the one that gets closest home. Why, that question would break up families."

Some people questioned the legality of the muzzle mandate, while others claimed that existing laws requiring leashes rendered the legality question a moot point. One woman, when asked why she so vehemently opposed the proposed mandate, said, "Well, try it on yourself and see how you like it." A man who had overheard her replied, "Wonder how she'd like being led around by a rope." The ordinance passed in June 1903.

In July 1908, the Board of Health took the ordinance ten steps further by ordering the killing of any dog running at large without a muzzle or a leash no longer than four feet long. Whether the dog had a license or not was of no importance, and the sixty sanitary police assigned to the detail did not have to report how many dogs they shot. All they had to do was be careful not to endanger human life. Health Commissioner Thomas Darlington explained, "It makes no difference whether the dog is worth five cents or $5,000. If it is found loose or unmuzzled, off to be killed it goes, and there will be no redeeming these animals at the pound, as before."

Needless to say, the men of the FDNY were outraged by this law, because it meant that their dogs who ran with the horses could be shot and killed just for doing their job. Most companies chose to keep their dogs locked up in the firehouse in summer months, when the ordinance was in effect. Oakie of Engine 39 was one such dog who stayed behind. A few companies tried muzzling their dogs, but that didn't go over well with the canines. As one fireman from Engine 76 explained, the fire dogs ran with their mouths wide open; when the company's dog Nellie tried running with her jaws clamped tight with the muzzle, she found it impossible. She also scared their other dog, Mongrel, who spent ten days hiding in the cellar after seeing Nellie "under the muzzle torture."

There were a few companies that were not about to let the law deter them from allowing their mascots to be true fire dogs. Some of those companies, such as Ladder 6 at 77 Canal Street, paid a heavy price for disobeying the law—its dog was shot and killed by a Health Department worker for not wearing a muzzle while roaming about on Allen Street. Engine 8's

Firefighter Michael Creegman, also known as Mickey the Breeze, was particularly outraged and told the press that he'd fight any man who tried to kill his fire company's beloved dog, Bess. "She's a smoke eater," Creegman told the *New York Times*. He explained how Bess would hang close to the men inside burning buildings and dip her nose on the wet hose or in puddles when the smoke got too dense. "We couldn't keep her away from a fire. It would break her heart. That dog is a fire dog and you might just as well tell a fireman he musn't help rescue people from a burning house because it's his day off and expect him to obey the order as to tell Bess to stay home at the clang of the gong." Another fireman chimed in, "God knows what'd happen if anybody shot Bess when Mickey was around."

In 1914, the Board of Health took another big step and made the muzzle ordinance effective year-round. The intention was to eradicate rabies—which doctors had now proved was a legitimate lethal disease—by preventing dogs from biting humans and other animals. The unpopular law was effective: in 1915, there was only one death from a bite (down from eight in 1914), and 992 fewer citizens received bites. That year, the press reported that rabies would probably disappear from New York City altogether. As the fire dogs began disappearing from the streets, so did the firemen's objections to muzzling their dogs.

One fire dog who didn't seem to mind wearing a muzzle, even when he was just hanging around the firehouse, was Brownie, the "chunky little Irish terrier" of Engine 53 at 175 East 104th Street. Brownie's muzzle was special, because it was capped by a small fireman's hat. The little terrier spent much of his time in the firehouse, but the instant an alarm came in, he'd bark excitedly and push aside any curiosity seekers before jumping up to take his high place beside the driver. The muzzle didn't stop him from going into burning buildings—and it may have even assisted him in his job. In November 1928, one reporter for the *New York Times* opined, "The little terrier seems immune to smoke fumes which would seriously inconvenience a human."

In December 1934, New York's Board of Health modified the strict dog-muzzling law to make muzzling optional if the dog was confined on a leash not exceeding six feet in length. The amendment to the Sanitary Code was no doubt a relief to every fire dog and every company with a canine mascot.

Ladder 16: Pooch

When Ladder 16 Fireman Patrick J. Murphy crushed his leg after falling beneath the truck, Pooch went on a hunger strike. For two weeks, as Murphy recuperated in Bellevue Hospital, the Dalmatian mascot refused to eat anything.

Pooch joined Ladder 16 at 159 East Sixty-Seventh Street in 1928, when she was just a pup. During her three years of service, she refused to eat any meals but those served by her master, Fireman Murphy. On June 2, 1931, Murphy slipped on the wet floor in the firehouse while trying to jump onto the moving ladder truck in response to an alarm. Pooch was heartbroken and had to be held back as the ambulance took Murphy away. She immediately stopped eating and slowly began to starve to death.

Other firemen as well as policemen from the station next door tried to tempt Pooch with tidbits. Civilians also stopped by to offer her candy and other treats. "But not even orange lollypops, her favorite, could bring her out of her lethargy." She spent most of her time mourning by Murphy's cot. By the middle of the month, the malnourished dog could barely manage to stagger about the firehouse. The men tried to let her visit Murphy, but hospital officials told them that dogs were unsanitary and that there was thus an unbreakable rule against them. Department officials reached out to a "big shot politician" who was able to make a deal with Deputy Commissioner of Hospitals James H. Fay to admit Pooch as a visitor.

On the morning that Murphy was set to be released, Pooch was given a cool shower and placed in her Sunday finery—a harness studded with a miniature helmet. Ladder 16 Captain Louis Moran drove her to Bellevue in his car and carried her in a basket to the accident ward. As soon as she saw her master and heard him call her name, she leaped to his side, snuggled against him, and barked with glee. Then she showed off the medal she had received in the mail that morning from the Animal Protective Union, which had enrolled her as an honorary member. After posing for photographers and newsreel men, she returned home to devour a bowl of shrimp salad.

Pooch must have continued eating a lot, because five months later, when she won a silver medal from the New York Anti-Vivisection Society for being faithful to her master, the *New York Daily News* described her as "a fat, waddling Dalmatian." Murphy, who was still using a cane, told the press that "the spotted black and white barrel" was the result of overfeeding by a sympathetic friend who had read about his dog's vigil.

Engine 65: Cappy

One of the most photographed Dalmatians of the FDNY was Cappy, who joined the department in 1936. Cappy found his way to the circa-1898 engine house of Engine 65 at 33 West Forty-Third Street when a New Jersey fire buff and advertising man named Cal Jones presented the men with a young puppy he had raised. The men named him Cappy and made him a mascot of Engine 65.

Unlike many fire dogs of this era, Cappy always jumped onto the engine and rode to the scene with the firemen. He loved the speed, and as he balanced on his perch, he'd lift his muzzle into the wind and treasure every moment of the adventure. Sometimes, when the engine was taking a sharp curve, passersby would gasp because Cappy seemed to be hanging on by only his toenails.

During Cappy's early years, the men allowed him to follow them into burning buildings. One time he not only carried a cat from a burning building but also went to the Ellin Prince Speyer Animal Hospital to visit the cat while it was recovering. Eventually, as Cappy got older, the men had to secure his leash to the seat so he wouldn't follow them or roll off the engine as it took sharp curves. (They may have gotten their idea from Engine 20, which built a special cab with a safety chain on the running board to keep their Dalmatian, Chief, from falling off the engine on the way to fires.)

When Cappy wasn't responding to fire calls, he spent his downtime patiently waiting in front of a Spanish restaurant for his daily handout. He had to watch his figure, though, because Cappy was an advertising star. Engine 65 was near the city's advertising district.

Because Cappy was so handsome and photogenic, the firemen offered his services as a model for national magazines. "He could sell anything, he was so glamourous and friendly, automobiles, gasoline, soap, sports clothes, whisky, air travel, or raise money for the March of Dimes," Captain James Brennan told a reporter shortly after Cappy died in 1950. "We used to let him out to illustrators for $5 a day, and we kept a special bank account just for him. We spent the money for his food and occasional veterinary bills."

In the fall of 1938, Cappy spent a few days at the Ellin Prince Speyer Animal Hospital for treatment of laryngitis. While Cappy was in the hospital, a fire broke out in some storage lofts near the hospital. As Mrs. George Bethune Adams, the ninety-year-old resident director of the hospital, ran outside to make sure none of her charges were in danger, Cappy began leaping at the door of his cage. Hearing the clanging of the fire bell and smelling the smoke, he wanted to go to work, but he couldn't bark to express his desires.

Five months later, in March 1939, Cappy went missing after leaving the firehouse for his daily trip around the neighborhood. According to the *New York Times*, one of the sandhogs working on subway construction at Sixth Avenue and Forty-Eighth Street found him and took him home to Queens, thinking the handsome spotted dog would make an excellent pet. Cappy was properly muzzled, but he wasn't wearing his FDNY collar that day; so the worker had no idea he was a fire dog. When Mrs. Bethune Adams heard about Cappy's disappearance, she posted a generous reward for his safe return. A few days later, the sandhog read a news story about the fire dog going missing. He immediately delivered the dog back to the firehouse, "well fed and quite his old self."

In between photo shoots, fire calls, and vet visits, Cappy kept busy with the ladies, fathering several FDNY Dalmatians. He even joined two of his sons, Raffles and Beau, in the 1941 exhibition of twenty-five FDNY Dalmatians at the Westminster Kennel Club's annual dog show at Madison Square Garden. Although the press surmised that Cappy would do well because of his modeling experience, it was King, belonging to Fireman George F. Donnelly of Ladder 311 in Queens, who was crowned the top pooch of the FDNY.

Cappy eagerly watches as Henry the cat slides down the
pole at Engine 65 in 1941. (Getty Images)

During this time, Engine 65 had a mascot tuxedo cat named
Henry. Henry would slide down the pole with the firefighters
whenever an alarm came in for the station. In 1941, a news photographer captured Henry sliding down the pole as Cappy watched
from below. Henry disappeared in 1942, which was the same year
Cappy took his last rides on the fire engine. By then, the modern
equipment was too fast, making it difficult for him to keep his bal-
ance when the vehicle made turns, especially with his aging paws.
Cappy remained back home, where he brooded over his retirement
in his bed near the warm chimney and whimpered when the trucks

rolled out until he finally dozed off into a fitful sleep. Observed a reporter for the *New York Times* in 1949, "To look at his rheumy eyes, bloated flanks, gray whiskers and sagging forepaws, you would not think that Cappy was formerly the glamour dog of the advertising business."

In April 1950, Cappy began to shake and drink excessive amounts of water. The firemen took him to the Ellin Prince Speyer Animal Hospital, where the vet diagnosed him with uremic poisoning. He died two weeks later on May 7. The following Thursday, a funeral took place at the Bideawee Pet Memorial Park in Wantagh, Long Island. Only Captain Brennan, Firemen Francis Hickey and Eugene Uhl, and a few other off-duty men were able to attend the ceremony, "but they brought with them the grief of all 31 desolate men in New York who couldn't attend." Brennan told a reporter, "We'll be out every so often to say 'Hello' to Cappy. He never forgot us, and we're not forgetting him."

Following the funeral, the men hung a photo of Cappy framed in a black ribbon and topped with a mourning palm outside the firehouse. The legend under the photo read, "CAPPY—1936–1950." On the front door, they chalked up a code signal: "5-5-5-5. Our Mascot. 8:30 AM" (5-5-5-5 is the department's signal code for a line-of-duty death). "Yes, Cappy died Sunday morning," Captain Brennan told all the office workers, residents, and shoppers who stopped by when they saw the sign. Asked if the company would ever get another dog, the captain shook his head and replied, "Sure will miss that dog. But please don't tell anybody we'd like to have another. A modern firehouse in the midst of a big city is no place for a fire dog. No dog could ever replace Cappy, anyway."

Engine 257, Ladder 123, and Engine 271: Bess, Peggy, and Pal

For almost four months in 1936, Bess was the most famous mother of all the Brooklyn fire dogs in the FDNY. But then her own daughter took over the Top Mom title.

Bess was the blue-ribbon holder of Engine 257 at 1361 Rockaway Parkway. In February 1936, she presented her firemen friends
with eight Dalmatian puppies. Not to be outdone by her mother,
Peggy—one of Bess's daughters from an earlier litter—duplicated
her mother's maternal feat. In June 1936, the blue-ribbon-winning
Dalmatian of Ladder 123 at 423 Ralph Avenue also gave birth to
eight puppies. As was the tradition, the firemen shared the sixteen
puppies with other companies in need of a fire dog.

The father of Bess's pooches was Pal, another prize-winning Dalmatian attached to Engine 271 at 394 Himrod Street. Following his
death in 1939, the *Brooklyn Daily Eagle* wrote a short tribute to Pal.
Lieutenant Joseph Oesau of Ladder 170 also praised Pal in an article
published in the *New York Daily News* in 1949.

Pal arrived at Engine 271 sometime around 1931. He took to the
job quickly and early on showed evidence of becoming a great fire
dog. Although he sustained a broken leg while still a pup, when the
leg had completely mended, he returned to chasing the fire engines
on every call. In addition to being a strong runner, Pal knew all
the sounds of the fire engine and alarm bells. He could also distinguish between the alarms for his company and for the neighboring
company, Ladder 124. According to Lieutenant Oesau, he'd never
go out if only the truck rolled. When he wasn't responding to fire
calls, Pal kept busy earning his title as "the daddy of most of the fire
dogs." He knew every brewery in the neighborhood, and he had a
favorite sweetheart across the street in a peddler's cart yard. When
the carts moved to a new location about two miles away, Pal would
frequently visit his girlfriend at her new home.

During Pal's final year of life, he started staying behind when the
engine rolled. In September 1939, the men took him to the Ellin
Prince Speyer Animal Hospital, where he died of uremic poisoning
on October 3. According to the press, a heavy gloom hung over
the firehouse following Pal's passing. Not willing to settle for a
backyard burial, Pal's pals made arrangements with the New York
banker James Speyer (the second husband of Ellin Prince Speyer),
who had a small private pet cemetery at Waldheim, his country
estate in Scarborough, New York. Unfortunately, none of the men

with whom Pal worked most closely were able to attend the funeral, but their thoughts were with him as he was "laid away among the tall pines."

Engine 20: Susie

Susie, the mascot of Engine 20 at 253 Lafayette Street, was another of the many dogs who were part of the FDNY's Dalmatian brat pack. Not only did she earn a big, bold headline in the *New York Times* in August 1936, but she also got her photo in the paper, sitting at the wheel of the motorized engine. No, Susie didn't save a child or a fireman from a burning building. And although she had recently given birth to eleven puppies, that momentous occasion wasn't what caught the newsmen's attention. What this new mom did was help save her own engine house from burning down.

It was a beautiful Sunday morning on August 9, and Susie was taking advantage of the warm sun for a nap outdoors. All her puppies had recently found homes with other fire companies, so her maternal responsibilities were over for now. Her duties as a fire dog, however, were ongoing. Smelling smoke coming from the building next door, she barked excitedly until Lieutenant William Neilan looked out the front door to see what all the fuss was about. He couldn't miss the dense smoke and orange flames rolling from the top floor of the New York and Brooklyn Paper Company, a paper and twine storage warehouse at 245–247 Lafayette Street.

As a brisk north wind drove the dense smoke and flames toward the firehouse, the lieutenant realized that the fire was already too far gone for his company to extinguish on its own. Deputy Chief Peter George called in a second alarm, which brought Chief George L. McKenna and numerous pieces of apparatus. Susie seemed overjoyed by all the action as she barked and frisked about in the street while the firemen laid out their hose. While the other companies focused on putting out the fire, the men of Engine 20 focused on saving their own house from the terrific heat of the blazing paper warehouse. The fire gutted the fourth floor of the warehouse, causing considerable damage. The smoke made its way down through the gratings of the subway, creating much discomfort for passengers at the Spring Street station. The men were able to save their firehouse and a Board of Education warehouse to the north of the burning building. Susie received credit for sounding the first alarm and celebrated with a special dinner that night.

Engine 224: Butts

When Butts arrived at his new home in September 1941, the name inscribed on his pedigree papers was Bronzeville. But then a neighborhood boy called him Butts, and that stuck for the rest of his life as the mascot of Brooklyn's Engine 224. "He just got that name all of a sudden," one of the firemen told a reporter. "Everybody likes it. It's easier to shout."

Butts was one of a litter of three Dalmatians born to Hollow Hill Buttons and Hollow Hill Rooster—the latter a champion male—on the Hollow Hill estate of Mrs. Paul Moore in Convent, New Jersey. Two puppies went to Manhattan fire companies, and Butts went to Brooklyn. At only six months old, Butts was already eighteen inches high and two feet long when he joined the firehouse at 274 Hicks Street. "Boy, what a dog he's going to be when he stops growing," an officer said. Although Butts was shy at first and inclined to nip the hands of those who tried to pet him, he quickly became a favorite with the firemen and neighborhood children, perking up his ears when the alarms rang, climbing a few rungs of the ladder, and doing all the right things that gave promise of him becoming a real working member of the company. Unlike the old-time fire dogs, though, Butts wasn't taught or encouraged to leap onto the apparatus or ride to fires—no ifs, ands, or buts about it. "We want to keep him in the house as much as possible," the officer said.

During Butts's probationary period, one man on each of the three shifts was responsible for seeing that he got plenty of exercise and ate healthy foods. A couple of solid bones, dry cereal with milk, raw carrots, and raw meat constituted his daily chow. Within a weeks' time, the frightened young pup who cringed in a corner when the alarm bells went off now looked at the bell in anticipation. The men thought that in no time at all, he'd recognize the "fours" and "fives" leading off the alarms that the company answered. His ladder scaling wasn't great—he had to be carried down after climbing two or three rungs—but he showed promise for going higher and coming down on his own. The men were also sure he'd be a blue-ribbon dog like his pop: only one week after Butts arrived at the firehouse, the men began planning on carrying on a thirty-year FDNY tradition by entering their dog in the department's next Dalmatian show.

3

Fire Cats

Born on the fourth of July in 1895, Tootsy was an all-American feline firefighter with Engine 27 at 173 Franklin Street. Unlike most cats, Tootsy loved the smell of smoke as much as she treasured a fresh-caught mouse. She was a genuine fire cat who loved riding on the engine, conversing with the firemen, and sleeping in her favorite horse's harness. She was also quite beautiful and drew much praise from the public and the press when she appeared in the National Cat Show at Madison Square Garden. According to the *New York Press*, the firemen adored Tootsy so much that they would have rather parted with their shields than lose their "white-fleeced feline fire fighter."

Although fire dogs were and still are an institution in the FDNY, Old New York had its share of feline mascots. Some companies and organizations even preferred cats. For example, Fire Patrol 3 on West Thirtieth Street wasn't anxious to have a dog mascot because a dog would follow the apparatus to fires. As a salvage corps, Fire Patrol 3 covered a much larger territory than the engine and ladder companies did. The long runs would have been too much for a dog. A cat like Tootsy or their own cat, Nellie, could ride along on the apparatus, curled up next to the driver or nestled inside a helmet.

Mickey the cat of Engine 47 was one of only a few felines who posed for photographers in the early twentieth century. She's pictured with her pal Jack, who's donning a tiny silver helmet on his collar. (Photograph from the Collection of the Connecticut Firemen's Historical Society, Inc.)

Sometimes fire cats, dogs, and horses would fraternize as one happy family, but usually the firehouse dog and cat were sworn enemies, with the dog taking reign over the apparatus floor and the cat ruling over the living quarters. The *New York Press* summed up the fire department cat as follows:

It is a curious feature of the fire department cats, and yet thoroughly characteristic of the animal, that they take no interest whatsoever in the active work of their company. The noise and activity that always follows the ringing of an alarm, the wild dash of the men for the sliding poles and the thundering rattle of the engine and tender as they leave the house have practically no effect on these cats. They learn to scuttle out of the way of the firemen, but beyond that they pay no attention to the commotion. And while the fire-engine dog is barking like mad and tearing around the opened doors of the house, his serene highness the cat has rolled himself up for another nap on one of the fireman's cots.

To be sure, the firehouse dogs and horses were generally more popular with the neighborhood children. But when it came to publicity, the fire cat was on equal footing with its four-legged friends. Fire cats often made the newspaper headlines, especially when they got into unimaginable trouble or broke the mold by responding to fires. Some stories were only filler copy of about two or three column inches—such as the short-but-sweet tale of Buck, the Brooklyn fire cat of Engine 208 who refused to eat anything Fireman George "Babe" Hartigan offered, preferring instead to make a daily trip to Eddie McDonald's lunch room, "where he'd put away at least three pork chops or a good porter house steak a day." But the press also loved publishing larger stories of favorite mascots such as Hattie, the blind and deaf cat of Engine 303 in Queens, and Dan, the enormous cat who lost forty pounds on an accidental diet at Engine 40 in Manhattan. Due to the private and skittish nature of most felines, however, very few cats got their pictures published in the newspapers; unlike the fire horses and dogs, they had to settle for unflattering cartoon-like illustrations. Photos or not, the old news articles provide evidence that firehouse felines were respected and adored by firemen, who loved nothing more than a chance to brag about the antics of their cat to any press agent who'd listen to their story.

Ladder 10: Patsey

On August 1, 1891, Ladder 10 was designated as ready for active service with what was then the Brooklyn Fire Department. The new company, headquartered at 264 State Street, protected one square mile in the Second District, which, according to Brooklyn Fire Department records, represented "more value than that of any other equal portion of the city." It included all the expensive residential buildings in Brooklyn Heights, a considerable portion of the Hill (Cobble Hill), and the large shopping district lying between those two neighborhoods. Ladder 10 responded to calls from 117 boxes on a second alarm, with the most remote box located at the end of Red Hook Point.

Ladder 10 was one of the earliest to have a truck equipped with a three-horse-hitch. Its three horses, Larry, Billy, and Dick—who were black, dark brown, and dapple bay, respectively—could set up in their harnesses and depart the firehouse in just twelve seconds. Billy, who was nearly seventeen hands high and more than fourteen hundred pounds, was the veteran, having served for five years with a prior truck company. He was so well versed in the telegraph alarm system that no amount of persuasion could encourage him to leave his stall on a test run.

Two days after the company went into service, a new member joined the roster. Patsey, a small cat "who wore a fur coat which in color resembled a tortoise shell," entered the bay door on August 3, 1891, settled into a chair, and, through her general demeanor, indicated her intentions to stay. The men welcomed her with warm milk and christened her Patsey. Although Patsey's name didn't appear on the payrolls at Brooklyn's fire headquarters, the men considered Patsey to be an official fire cat. They even presented her with a silver collar.

Life was good for the former street cat, largely due to all the wonderful features of the new two-story firehouse. One of the highlights was a large gymnasium in the cellar, where the men could work out with rowing machines, dumbbells, heavy and light hammers, Indian clubs, and something called quoits, which was a traditional game that involved throwing rings over a set distance. Patsey loved spending time in the gymnasium—her favorite activity was taking lessons in high vaulting and running jumps. Another favorite activity for Patsey was napping. She loved to sleep on top of the men's coats on the tip of the extension ladder.

One day as Patsey was taking an afternoon nap, an alarm sounded from a box at Hoyt and Warren Streets. Normally, she was on the alert as soon as the gong sounded, but on this occasion, she didn't wake up until the truck was heading to the fire. At Dean and Pacific Streets, Fireman Collins discovered Patsey with her claws buried deep into one of the coats. When the truck arrived at the scene, the men transferred Patsey to the driver's seat and covered her with a coat. She remained on the seat while she watched all the action with amazement. Like Tootsy, she appeared to enjoy the experience and made it a habit to remain sleeping on the truck as the alarm sounded.

HISTORICAL HOOK

Prior to about 1885, every horse-drawn apparatus in New York's Metropolitan Fire Department used only one horse or a team of two horses. As the engines and trucks began getting larger and heavier with longer ladders and new lifesaving equipment, the department began gradually adding three-horse teams to accommodate these heavier loads. Although the Brooklyn Fire Department reportedly had the first ladder truck with a three-horse team, the first team in Manhattan to receive a third horse was Ladder 10 on Fulton Street. The switch to a triple hitch (or three-abreast hitch) proved so successful that the department continued adding a third horse to all the truck teams in the city. The transition was slow, and by 1888, only twelve pieces of apparatus had three-horse hitches. That year, the one- and two-horse teams were put to the test.

On March 12, 1888, a blizzard of epic proportions pummeled the Atlantic coast, from the Chesapeake Bay to Maine. Snowfall amounts reached forty to fifty inches, with snow drifts as high as forty feet tall. More than four hundred people died in the storm, including two hundred in New York. During the first night of the storm, multiple alarms came in. The first was a fire at 9–11 Laight Street, which quickly spread through the building. The second was a fire in a five-story building at 559 West Forty-Second Street, which spread to a neighboring building. Of the five companies assigned to the first fire, only one engine and one ladder could make it, arriving in twenty minutes. At the second fire, only three pieces of apparatus were able to get to the scene. Some men tried to push their way to the fire, while others left their rigs behind and carried tools to the scene. With conditions worsening, the FDNY accepted offers from local breweries and streetcar lines to place their horses and sleighs in service for the fire department. Spike hitches, which placed the experienced horses out in front, allowed the men to temporarily attach four or five horses to the engines and trucks, while sleds were used to carry the heavy hose.

Lessons learned during the blizzard put the transition to three horses on a fast track. By 1894, every one of the twenty-two ladder trucks and almost half of the engines (especially the heavier engines and those assigned to

It took more strength and skill to drive a three-horse team than a two-horse team, but the FDNY had no difficulty finding trained equestrians who could take on the challenge. (Photograph provided courtesy of the New York City Fire Museum)

companies in the hilly districts of the city) were drawn by a team of three horses. The remaining companies had equipment that would allow for a three-horse team in the event of an emergency. The only one-horse tenders at this time were at double companies—those with two complete sets of apparatus—primarily located in crowded parts of the city where there was inadequate room for a four-wheeled, two-horse tender.

In 1894, Chief Hugh Bonner told the press that the three-horse team was advantageous in every way. As he explained, it took about two or three more seconds to hitch up a three-horse team, but those few seconds lost were more than gained back on the road. (For a three-horse team, it took about twenty seconds to hitch up and get the apparatus out of quarters, with the horses trained to come to their places under their harness on a gallop.) The chief also admitted that it took more strength and skill to drive a three-horse team, but the department had no difficulty finding men who could handle the task. Not only could three horses get the company to a fire quicker, but they also fared better in winter. As the *New York Sun* noted, "One now rarely or never hears of a fire apparatus stuck going to a fire; the three-horse team goes right ahead through the very worst going." The one drawback of the three-abreast team was that the middle horse—the most experienced—was typically the first horse to break down and go lame. Once this happened, the entire team often had to retire, because many firemen believed that replacing one horse in an established team would be a bad omen for the company. Incidentally, the business world took notice of the FDNY's actions. According to the *Sun*, the visible increase in three-horse delivery wagons was probably due to its success in the fire department.

Engine 40: Dan

This is a tale of a cat. Of a cat with a tail fourteen inches long. It is a true tale. It is vouched for by a fireman, a policeman and the appearance of the cat. A woman, a basket, a hole in a ceiling, a doctor and some medicine also figure into the tale.

—"Dan's Tribulations," *New York World*, January 5, 1894

Dan was a beautiful cat, with glossy-black fur and bright yellow eyes. From the tip of his nose to the tip of his tail, he measured thirty-three inches and, if one can believe, weighed forty-eight pounds. Within a four-week period between Thanksgiving and Christmas Day in 1893, the three-year-old tubby tabby had shrunk down to eight pounds.

According to the remarkable tale, Dan was raised by a kind woman who doted on him. Sadly, just before Thanksgiving, the woman learned she had to move from her comfortable home. There was no room for Dan in her tiny new apartment, so poor Dan was destined to be homeless. The woman knew that police stations sometimes took in human vagrants, so she went to the Twenty-Fourth Police Precinct on West Sixty-Eighth Street to report Dan's dilemma. As Sergeant Townsend listened to her woeful tale, he looked out the window and scratched his head. Across the street, he saw Assistant Foreman Francis Casey looking out a window in the newly constructed firehouse for Engine 40. The sergeant invited Foreman Casey to visit him. He then presented Dan to the foreman as a housewarming gift in honor of the new firehouse.

Foreman Casey was a sixty-one-year-old veteran of the fire services. He joined the volunteer department when he was twenty-five in 1858 and moved up to foreman of the new Engine 40 in December 1874. Having spent so many years in the department, Casey no doubt had much experience with firehouse cats. Dan immediately began purring in the fireman's ear when Casey bent down to pet him. The woman, trusting that her cat was in safe hands, wiped a few tears from her eyes and walked away. What happened next was one for the books.

The trouble began when Foreman Casey hoisted Dan onto his shoulders. The cat dug his claws into Casey's hair, sending the fireman into a full-blown panic. As he ran across the street and into the firehouse, the enormous cat clung on tight. Inside the firehouse, a carpenter was making a hole for a new steam pipe in the wood ceiling. He had just taken a three-foot board down when Casey ran into the firehouse, waving his arms frantically over his head. Suddenly, a second alarm for fire sounded. "The gong ranged and clanged. The horses pawed and jumped. Men rushed to and fro shouting and yelling." Casey sprang to take charge of the engine. Dan sprang for the hole in the ceiling. The engine pulled out, and the doors closed. Four hours later, when the men returned to the firehouse, Casey searched for Dan. The huge cat was nowhere to be found. The next day, the carpenter and a machinist finished installing the steam pipe. Then they closed the hole in the ceiling. Dan was apparently taking a long catnap and had no idea his fate was also being sealed.

Four weeks and five days passed with no sight of Dan. These were long and hard days for the once pampered pet. As the *New York World* reporter noted, he suffered one day for every inch of his length. During this time, the men began hearing strange noises between the first and second floors. Some of the more superstitious firemen thought the eerie cries they heard were coming from a ghost. Luckily for Dan, though, the steam pipe didn't work properly. After removing the faulty pipe, the carpenter and machinist left the hole in the ceiling open. The next day, Christmas Eve, as Casey and Fireman Reynolds were standing directly under the hole, they heard a strange noise, as if a human baby were crying out in distress. They looked up and saw two bright balls of fire glowing back at them.

"It's a ghost!" Reynolds shouted. "I knew the house was haunted."

"Meow," cried Dan in response.

"Worse than ghosts!" Casey said. "It's Dan the cat!"

While the men spoke, Dan began squeezing and wriggling himself from the ceiling hole. The men were shocked when the tiny cat fell to the floor. "Yes, it was Dan. But, oh! how he changed!" the reporter wrote. "The glossy coat was ragged rough; the bright eyes were dim and glassy. Forty of the forty-eight pounds had gone. The ribs stood out like stripes on a zebra."

Casey carried Dan up to his cot and called for Dr. Milligan. The doctor felt for the cat's pulse, which was very weak, and put his ear up to his heart. Then he fed Dan six drops of milk and brandy. The milk and brandy treatment continued for five more days in increasing doses. Little by little, the tiny cat got better. By New Year's Eve, he was able to drink tea from a cup. While Dan convalesced on the cot, the other pets of Engine 40—two all-white cats named Nell and Pete—stood guard. They gently licked Dan's coat and helped nurse him back to health. Somehow, they knew Dan was in bad shape.

A few weeks later, the reporter returned to the firehouse to check on Dan. The men told him that Dan had a relapse and had taken a turn for the worse. Casey said he had found the cat lying unconscious in the cellar on the previous morning. He immediately called for Dr. Milligan, who said that Dan had suffered from a fainting fit. He put ammonia on a sponge and held it up to the cat's nose. Dan shivered, wiggled his tail, and opened his eyes. "Saved again!" Casey exclaimed. The doctor advised the foreman to keep the cat in his bed for a while and away from any drafts. The next day, Dan was sleeping peacefully on the cot with his right paw resting on the tip of his nose. The press reported that Dan was expected to recover fully.

Engine 30 and Engine 1: Kitty and Hero

While fighting a fire on the fourth floor of a large, seven-story umbrella factory and apartment building at 522–524 West Broadway in March 1903, Captain O'Connell, Fireman Lindshaw, and several other firemen of Engine 30 heard a cry coming from the floor above. They stopped and listened. Then the captain yelled, "There's a baby up there! Lindshaw, go up and bring it down!" Plunging through the smoke to the stairway, the smoke so dense he could hardly see, Lindshaw groped his way to the floor above. Guided by the cries, he made his way across the room, where he found a tiny Maltese kitten wailing piteously near a window. As soon as the kitten saw the large fireman, she began to purr. Lindshaw tucked the cat under his coat and dashed back down the stairs. Engine 30 brought the kitten back to quarters at 253 Spring Street and adopted Kitty as its mascot.

The lucky kitten of Engine 30 was one of numerous animal mascots that joined the FDNY via a heroic rescue. One of the most amazing feline victims-turned-mascots was Hero of Engine 1, then stationed at 165 West Twenty-Ninth Street. Hero and about a dozen other stray cats were living with more than five hundred horses in the car stables of the Forty-Second Street and Grand Street Ferry Railroad on Twelfth Avenue and Forty-Second Street. On the evening of June 12, 1886, the night watchman, John Horner, noticed smoke coming from the third-floor paint shop at the northeast corner of the car stables. He ran out and sounded the alarm, but by the time the fire engines arrived a few minutes later, the entire stable, covering eight lots on Forty-Second Street, eight lots on Forty-Third Street, and the entire riverfront, was engulfed in flames. At the time of the fire, almost all the horses were in the building, including five who were upstairs in a special veterinary hospital. One sick horse was in a sling awaiting treatment. Under the direction of Superintendent John M. Calhoun, all the employees on site led every horse but the unfortunate horse in the sling safely outside.

While everyone on site was saving the horses, the cats were fighting for their lives as the building continued to burn around them. Many of the firemen from Engine 1 took it upon themselves to rescue the cats. Of all the cats they saved, there was one feline that evidently had at least ten lives. This kitty, whom the men of Engine 1 later named Hero, was rescued by Assistant Chief John "Bucky" McCabe. According to the *New York Times*, the tabby had been lurking behind a chimney on top of the wall on Forty-Second Street just after the roof had collapsed. As the firemen approached her, she ran quickly along the wall toward the Hudson River, trying to limit the amount of time her paws had to land on the hot bricks. At one point, she tried to jump from the wall to a telegraph pole, but instead she scurried along to a portion of the wall nearest the river, where the bricks were cooler. When the firemen found her again, they directed a stream of water against the wall below her to cool off the bricks. This only frightened her more, causing her to hide in a space in the wall.

The cat continued to hide for about an hour, until the firemen had to direct their hoses toward her once again to extinguish flames in the area. Everyone assumed that the poor cat had roasted to death, but when the water hit the wall, she jumped out of her hiding spot and tried to escape again. About five minutes later, "a forlorn-looking cat, with her hair well singed off" jumped from a window on Forty-Third Street. Assistant Chief McCabe caught her and, wrapping her up tenderly, turned her over to the care of one of the firemen from Engine 1. The men brought Hero to the firehouse and treated her burned and blistered paws with liniment and tender care. According to news accounts, by the next day, Hero was recovering at her new forever home.

Engine 59, Engine 252, Engine 239, Ladder 25, Ladder 107: Barney, Jerry, Peter, Dick, and Thomas

One of the most famous FDNY fire cats was Barney of Engine 59 at 180 West 137th Street. Barney's claim to fame in the early twentieth century was sliding down the brass fire pole, which he did "as gracefully as any member of the company." He didn't swoop down in a flash like the men did, but by wrapping his four paws around the brass rod, he was able to slide down rather quickly. Sometimes the firemen played a mean trick on Barney by placing their Dalmatian at the foot of the pole. Barney would notice the dog about halfway down and immediately stop to plan his exit strategy. As soon as he saw an opening, he'd drop onto the dog, scratch him a few times, and then rush to the cellar to avoid repercussions.

Another fire cat possessing fire-pole skills during this era was Jerry of Ladder 25 at 205 West Seventy-Seventh Street. Even though he was old and had lost most of his teeth by 1910, the black cat was "still as ardent in answering an alarm when he [was] upstairs in the dormitory as the newest recruit." Whenever an alarm came in, Jerry would spring from his bed and go down the pole. Sometimes he'd slide down by clasping it with only his front paws, but as he got older, he preferred hitching a ride on the shoulders of one of the firemen. Once on the lower floor, he'd leap aboard the truck and curl up on an old coat that the men had placed there for him. Although Jerry never missed a fire call in seven years, by 1910 he was spending at least twelve hours a day sleeping on the truck. If an alarm came in while he was on the truck, he'd open one yellow eye and cock his ear, as if counting the gongs. If Ladder 25 wasn't needed, his ears would fall back, and his eyelids would close. The firemen often discussed Jerry's health and did everything possible to make him comfortable. A young man who wrote a letter about Jerry published in the *New-York Tribune* said he wouldn't be surprised if the men draped crepe bunting at the firehouse when the cat passed away.

In 1913, the *Brooklyn Daily Eagle* told the story of two Brooklyn fire cats who had mastered the pole. The first was an orange tabby cat of Engine 252 at 617 Central Avenue, who not only was a pro at sliding down the pole but also climbed ladders "with the agility of a veteran." According to the men, Peter could make the descent from the third-floor sitting room to the ground floor in three seconds. At the first sound of an alarm, he'd dash to the pole and, with a flying leap, throw his paws about it and slide down. Then, with one more leap, he'd land on the driver's seat of the hose wagon. The firemen said he always seemed proud to be the first member ready for action. Peter joined the men on every call and would follow them up the ladder as far as possible, until the smoke and flames drove him back.

Peter's feline rival was Dick, a large tortoise-shell cat attached to Ladder 107 at 79 New Jersey Avenue. Dick never used the stairs to go down, always choosing the pole as his preferred method of descent. This cat also had an excellent attendance record at fires and was reportedly the happiest when perched on the driver's seat responding to a call. At the end of each call, Dick would rest on the horses' warm backs or purr contentedly at their feet.

In 1931, a newborn kitten—so small that his eyes had not yet opened—made his way to Brooklyn's Engine 239. By the time Thomas was a year old, he was one of the boys at 395 Fourth Avenue. Like the other cats, Thomas was a pro when it came to sliding down the brass pole. In fact, he liked to make a game of it. Whenever he saw one of his friends in uniform making for the pole hole, he'd beat him to it and slide down first. Then he'd jump aboard the apparatus and give a haughty wave of the tail while the men were still donning their boots and gear. In addition to being a smart-aleck cat, Thomas was also a proud feline. He'd never answer to any fireman who called him Tom or Tommy. He also refused to approach any stranger who didn't properly address him: only when addressed as Mr. Thomas in a respectful tone would he take that as a sign of reverence and a cue to put on his friendly cat act.

HISTORICAL HOOK

Many nineteenth-century city firehouses were constructed of two or three stories. In New York City, the fire department established the red-brick, three-story design in 1865, when it organized an assortment of volunteer fire companies into one paid, fully horse-powered Metropolitan Fire Department. The multiple-storied firehouse wasn't built to conserve land space but to separate the horses from the men. Until 1922, under an act authorized in 1857 by Chief Engineer Harry Howard of the city's volunteer department, firefighters were required to live at the firehouse, serving around the clock, save for one-hour dinner breaks. Horses and the apparatus occupied the first floor, with the second floor reserved for the firefighters' living quarters and kitchen. The third floor served as a storage area for the horses' hay and recreational space for the men.

According to one legend, fire horses would sometimes ascend the stairs in search of the food they could smell cooking on the second floor. Horses have difficulty descending stairs, so they'd get stuck on the second floor. Spiral staircases prevented wayward horses from accessing the upper floors, but it wasn't easy for firemen to quickly descend a spiral staircase. Sliding poles were a solution that came to the rescue, so to speak.

While this legend has not been completely debunked in other cities, according to officials at the New York City Fire Museum, it doesn't apply to the FDNY. The reality is that only a few firehouses in the city had or have spiral stairs; fire poles were installed because the men kept tripping and falling while trying to scramble down the straight narrow stairs whenever an alarm rang. Furthermore, FDNY horses remained secured in their stalls, so unless they figured out how to escape, they weren't free to roam about the firehouse and attempt to climb the stairs. That being said, at least one fire horse did learn how to escape and climb the stairs: Jerry of the Atlantic Engine Company—later Engine 166—in Rockaway, Queens. In October 1902, Fireman George Vreeland returned to the firehouse following a brief errand to find Jerry poking his head out a second-floor window. It took more than a dozen men three hours to lead the horse safely down the stairs.

In 1873, Captain Daniel Lawler installed a polished wood pole at Engine 13 at 99 Wooster Street. According to an article in *Fire Engineering* about the captain's accidental death in 1927, Lawler, a carpenter by trade, cut a hole in the dormitory floor and installed the wood pole without getting approval. Fire officials soon noticed that Engine 13 was arriving on the scene a minute or two before other companies. Although Lawler was reprimanded, no action was reported. In fact, the officials agreed with Lawler's suggestion that a brass pole would work even better. Soon, the FDNY began erecting poles in all the city's fire stations. Before the end of the century, the brass pole had become a standard fixture in every firehouse, helping firemen—and fire cats—save valuable seconds by whizzing down to the waiting horses and apparatus.

With no railings or guards in place, poles created a hazard for the men, especially during the sleeping hours. In December 1889, for example, Fireman Charles H. Morris of Engine 17 on Ludlow Street fractured his skull and died after plunging down the pole hole in his sleep. According to the *New York Evening World*, Morris's bed was just two feet from the hole, and although he knew he was prone to sleepwalking—in fact, on one other occasion, he slid down the pole while still asleep—he didn't take any precautions to prevent another accident. A few years later, the press reported several similar accidents, including one in which Fireman George T. F. Harris of Engine 8 fractured his skull after falling through the hole while

Fire poles were installed to prevent the men from tripping down steep, narrow stairs whenever an alarm rang. (The Miriam and Ira D. Wallach Division of Art, Prints and Photographs: Picture Collection. "An alarm." *The New York Public Library Digital Collections*. 1877-10)

sleepwalking; one in which Fireman Gustave Nagel of Engine 25 broke his back when he missed his footing after waking up for an alarm; and another involving Fireman James Potter of Engine 32, who was not seriously injured when he tumbled down the pole hole after falling asleep in a chair. In 1903 alone, four firemen were killed and many others were wounded after falling down the pole. Following the death of the third fireman that year, the department issued an order to place guard rails around the holes. Full compliance with this order took decades.

In 1928, doctors and surgeons associated with the Police and Fire Surgeons and Medical Directors of Civil Service Commissions warned that hernias, sprains, and fractures were "the direct result from use of brass sliding poles in fire stations." FDNY Medical Director Dr. John J. White agreed that the poles "were a menace to firemen" and suggested a plan to replace them with chutes. Dr. Harry Archer suggested using grass pads instead of rubber mats, which was the practice in Europe.

In 1974, the FDNY announced plans to build the department's first one-story firehouse in Rockaway, Queens. A one-story station would allow the department to circumvent the need for stairs or dangerous poles. "We've had a lot of pole-hole injuries over the years," Chief John R. Travell, head of the department's safety division, told the *New York Times*. In addition to numerous leg and ankle fractures, Chief Travell also cited two deaths, in 1960 and 1962, when tired firemen accidentally fell fifteen to twenty feet through the holes. It would take another thirty years before the quarters of Engine 265 and Ladder 121 opened on Rockaway Beach Boulevard in Queens. By then, the department had abandoned plans to build more similar firehouses due to the lack of space. There was simply no way a sprawling, one-story firehouse could replace the narrow, multistoried firehouses throughout the congested city.

By 2005, the humble brass conveyance system was well on its way out, as the department began building new stations in Queens and Staten Island and remodeling the old firehouses in Manhattan, the Bronx, and Brooklyn to conform with modern building codes. While some firehouses still have poles (for example, Engine 33/Ladder 9 on Great Jones Street boasts the longest of any fire pole in the city at twenty-eight feet from the third to second floor), many of the older firehouses in Manhattan and Brooklyn lost their poles to ventilation systems during renovations. At the FDNY Fire Academy on Randall's Island, instructors also stopped teaching new recruits how to slide down poles. Veteran firefighters who supported the department's intense loyalty to tradition did not support the decision to remove or enclose the sliding poles.

Today, some fire stations across the country are turning to chutes and slides, either of the plastic looping kind or a more traditional steel playground slide. Although the National Fire Protection Association takes no official stance on whether firehouses should remove their poles, it leans toward removal as a matter of safety. For those stations choosing to keep the old pole, it must have a landing mat and a door or gated enclosure—not that a gate would ever stop a fire cat.

Ladder 68: Tabbie

Until Tabbie the cat showed up in the winter of 1910, Mac the Dalmatian held a monopoly on mascots at Brooklyn Fire Headquarters at 365 Jay Street, where Ladder 68 and Water Tower 6 were quartered. It was Mac whom Deputy Commissioner Arthur J. O'Keefe presented to Ladder 68 in 1909, and it was Mac who was on duty 24/7 guarding the stable. It was also Mac who received all the attention from the firemen and the press. After all, the smart dog knew all the signals (the men said he could even smell an incoming alarm), could easily climb a ladder, and even once saved a fireman overcome by smoke in a hallway.

But then Peter Carroll, the engineer detailed at Fire Headquarters, had to ruin it all by rescuing a kitten he found crouching behind a corridor door, hungry and shivering with cold. Carroll took the poor little thing to the warm and comfortable engine room, where he shared his lunch with the kitten. Tabbie quickly made friends with many of the firemen and, unlike Mac, proved to be a first-grade mouser. However, during her first few months at Fire Headquarters, Mac wouldn't allow Tabbie to enter his domain. Time and again, she tried to get into the stables to control the rat population, but Mac wasn't about to give up his territory, even though he was a lousy mouser.

Opportunity finally knocked one fall day in 1911. Mac, responding to a command from one of the firemen, went off duty for a moment. This was enough time for Tabbie to enter the forbidden premises, which she instinctively recognized as fertile hunting ground. When Mac returned to the stables, he didn't detect anything amiss. Then suddenly he heard a strange and unwelcome noise as Tabbie appeared in the doorway with a rat of monstrous proportions in her mouth. According to the *Brooklyn Daily Eagle*, "Mac let out a howl of jealous anger and denied his rival the privilege of passing him." Hearing the commotion, several firemen appeared in the stable. Although Mac had always been their favorite, most of the men sympathized with Tabbie, even going as far as calling Mac away from the situation. When he refused to budge, two men held him off, allowing Tabbie to make her getaway in a flash to the engine room. Following that incident, the men agreed that overseeing the stable would now be Tabbie's assignment, even if it meant escorting her through the prohibited passage daily to let her do her job.

Unfortunately for Mac, the firemen didn't have to escort Tabbie for too long. In 1912, Deputy Chief John F. O'Hara ran over Mac with his vehicle while responding to an alarm. Although he didn't die, Mac sustained enough injuries to place him on the sick roster. Fireman Warren Schneider, who was Mac's best pal, had a friend with a hotel on Shelter Island off the coast of Long Island. He pleaded to take the dog there to live out the rest of his life. The men took a vote, and with many regrets, allowed Mac to retire. A report that Mac had been banished for poor behavior, general laziness, and a bad habit of waking up the three horses at headquarters was "vigorously denied and resented by the men of 68." Mac thrived in his new retirement home under the care of proprietor Henry Walther; he even became a fire buff for the Shelter Island Fire Department.

Fire Patrol 3: Bouncer and Nellie

There was a deep gloom pervading the quarters of Fire Patrol 3 on West Thirtieth Street in August 1915. The *New York Sun* reported, "If it were not for the absence of crape on the door, a visitor would be led to believe that the company had just lost its most popular member. The firemen move about without animation; their fighting spirit, developed through constant battle with fire and smoke, has disappeared." The reason for the despair was that Fire Patrol 3 was soon to lose its two beloved feline mascots.

The New York Fire Patrol, which originated as the Fire Police in 1835, was a paid fire salvage service chartered and funded by the New York Board of Fire Underwriters in 1867 to protect and preserve property and life during and after fires. Although not officially affiliated with the FDNY, the men worked alongside the city's firemen and took orders from the FDNY commanding officers. Patrolmen were private civilians, but they were also firefighters trained in the art of salvage, forced entry, and overhaul. Many FDNY firefighters began their careers with the Fire Patrol.

On September 10, 1895, Fire Patrol 3 moved into new headquarters at 240 West Thirtieth Street. The four-story patrol house featured stalls for five horses on the ground floor, a dormitory on the second floor, a large billiard room and sitting room on the third floor, and workshops and supply space on the top floor. An elevator for passengers and freight was in the rear of the building. Behind the station was a two-story brick stable with feed rooms and a hayloft. This building had two box stalls with a thick flooring of Irish peat, where the horses could recover from their long, hard runs.

Five years after moving in, the patrolmen were still without a mascot. They wanted one, but they didn't want a dog. As a salvage corps, Fire Patrol 3 had an immense territory to cover—from Fourteenth to Fifty-Seventh Streets between the two rivers—which made it impractical for them to have a dog trained to follow the apparatus to fires. So, when the opportunity to acquire a proper mascot presented itself at a fire in October 1900, the men acted immediately.

According to the report, the men were working on an upper floor when they came upon two kittens on a rear fire escape. The tenants had abandoned the kittens in their flight to escape the burning building. Trained to ensure nothing with a rightful owner was removed from a fire scene, the men tried to find the owners of the kittens. When no one came forward to claim the cats, they adopted both. They named the gray tiger-striped kitten Bouncer and the black kitten Nellie.

Bouncer was the more intelligent cat, although Nellie was also a smarter cat than most. Four months after moving into the patrol house, Bouncer had mastered the fire pole, wrapping all four paws around it before making his descent. Bouncer was a polite cat who never slid down until all the men were done—he'd wait patiently with his ears erect and his tail puffed up in excitement until it was his turn to catch the pole with "a well-aimed spring." When it came to the landing, he outdid every member, striking the rubber mat "as gently as an autumn leaf landing on the turf." Bouncer also answered to his name during roll call in the morning: After the captain called out each member's name, he'd shout, "Bouncer!" and the cat would arch his back, answer with a "meow," and head upstairs to the sitting room with the men. While Bouncer never ran past the front door when an alarm came in, Nellie's specialty was riding to fire calls, curled up in one of the helmets.

Three years after Bouncer and Nellie moved in, the men took in a pet goat named Willie, who lived with the horses in the stable. Willie got into trouble in February 1903 when he took advantage of an open stable door and went on a half-hour romp along Fifth Avenue. First, he charged at some young boys who threw snowballs at him, knocking one boy down. Next, he knocked down a few pedestrians and ran under several horses, which were not accustomed to seeing goats running loose on Fifth Avenue. As a crowd of cab drivers and small boys with sticks and snowballs chased him, he ran north to the Waldorf-Astoria, knocking down one of the hotel porters. Eventually he made his way back to the stable. As the *New-York Tribune* concluded, it was no big deal. "No one had been seriously injured."

By 1915, Willie was no doubt gone, and the fifteen-year-old cats were blind and could no longer care for themselves. The thirty-two members of the salvage corps, including Lieutenant John Sanders and Sergeant John Butler, decided it best to euthanize the cats. And so they assigned Captain Jimmy Rice the job of sending for the SPCA wagon to take them away to a painless death. Every man hoped he would not be on duty when the wagon called. Captain Rice told the press that when he signed the death warrant for Bouncer and Nellie, he wouldn't sign his own name. He would only sign, "Patrol 3. Commanding Officer."

Engine 31: Smoke

Once upon a time, a fire cat named Smoke lived in a fairy-tale castle of a firehouse that was home to Engine Company 31, Water Tower 1, and Battalion 2. Designed by Napoleon LeBrun & Sons and completed in 1895, the French Renaissance firehouse at 87 Lafayette Street was what the department called "The Finest Firehouse in the World." The large three-bay structure was constructed of brick and Indiana limestone topped by a dormered slate roof lavished with intricate copper cresting, gargoyles, and spires. Designed with horses in mind, it featured three doors large enough for seventeen horses to all charge out at once. In the stable at the rear of the apparatus floor were stalls with doors that opened automatically as the fire bell rang. There was also a large tower that masked a shaft in which Captain Smoky Joe Martin and his men could hang their hoses to dry.

By 1924, the horses had been gone a dozen years, and the apparatus floor had been converted to accommodate the new motorized vehicles. The main attraction of the firehouse was now a fire cat with a penchant for sliding down poles and catching rubber balls. Visitors by the hundreds couldn't get enough of the feline's antics.

Now, Smoke was reportedly a modest cat who didn't actively seek publicity. She enjoyed being pampered by the firemen, sleeping beside the warm boiler, and living in the lap of luxury. But one day a reporter from the *New York World* learned of her tricks, and her easy life as a beloved mascot came to an end. For weeks, fans stopped by to watch her repeatedly slide down the pole and catch the balls. In addition to tourists and news reporters, noted scientists reportedly came to give her intelligence tests. Catnip manufacturers begged for permission to use her picture in their ads. Moving-picture companies offered her jobs. Smoke fended off the paparazzi for a while until she could take it no more. One night she walked out of the firehouse and disappeared.

A few days after Smoke ran away, Lieutenant Charles Kohlenberger and Fireman Charley Farley found the cat in poor condition near the Edison Company's plant on Lafayette Street. Workmen in the plant had been trying to tempt her with liver and fish, but she refused to eat. According to a tongue-in-cheek story originally published in the *New York World*, the firemen had told Smoke to stay away from the plant on previous occasions because "she had returned from there so often in a lit condition."

Apparently, some tough cats hung around the backyard of the plant, and according to the men, many of these cats were envious of Smoke and expressed their intention of making her pay for her lifestyle. The firemen thought perhaps One-Eyed Horace, a cat with a bad reputation, had roughed her up, which then caused her to get sick and lose her appetite. The men took Smoke home, where she continued her hunger strike. At a loss for words for why their cat wouldn't eat, the firemen came up with a few other theories. Perhaps she was a sympathizer with the Irish Republicans who had gone on a hunger strike in Belfast, or maybe she just wanted to get away from publicity. A few other engine companies offered her better liver and more mice if she would leave Lafayette Street and become their mascot, but in the end, nothing worked. The men brought Smoke to the Ellin Prince Speyer Animal Hospital, where, despite attempts at forced feeding, she slipped into a coma and died on August 26, 1924.

Engine 303: Hattie

When the firemen of Engine 303 in Queens moved into their new firehouse in February 1931, they did so with mixed feelings. Sure, they were pleased with their new quarters at 104-12 Princeton Street, which they would be sharing with Ladder 126. But they were sad about having to retire their fire cat, Hattie (aka Patty), before settling into their new home.

For more than twenty years, Hattie, a deaf and partly blind cat, had been the Engine 303 mascot. Firemen Robert Hieronn and Fred Kranz attested to her length of service, telling a reporter that they had both been with the company for more than eighteen years and knew that Hattie had joined long before their assignment for duty there. Over the years, the neighborhood children grew up with Hattie, whom they said was "the most human cat in the world." Hattie loved to sleep under the potbelly stove in the old firehouse at 61 Bandman Avenue (105th Avenue), but she was a smoke eater at heart. In her younger days, she enjoyed going to fires. She was also a great friend of Jiggs, the famous fire dog of Brooklyn's Engine 205. The two apparently met up at large mutual-aid fires; their friendship ended when Jiggs refused to ride on the motorized vehicles after the horse-drawn engines were scrapped from the department. Hattie didn't let the motorized vehicles faze her. Until her health began to deteriorate, she was always on the engine before the gong stopped.

When the firemen learned that the Princeton Street firehouse would soon open, they attempted to acclimate Hattie to the new building and teach her to stay there. But the stubborn old cat always came back to her familiar potbelly stove. And so, following a conference, the men decided to retire their veteran cat. Rather than have her live in a vacant building, they thought it best to take her to the SPCA shelter in Jamaica, where they advised the custodian to take special care of her. Soon after Engine 303 and Ladder 126 moved into their new home, the men agreed to search for a new firehouse mascot.

Engine 203: Blackie

Blackie knew she couldn't go to fires with the men of Engine 203 in Brooklyn. In fact, she normally had no desire to ride the apparatus, preferring instead to retreat to the back of the station at 533 Hicks Street or go to sleep on the captain's desk when a call came in. But one day, the proud mother cat couldn't resist. She had to show off her four black kittens as soon as the newborns opened their eyes. One by one, she hoisted them onto the red hose wagon and took them on their first call. When the wagon arrived at the scene, the firemen were amazed to find their feline mascot with her offspring on the vehicle.

Blackie, a black-and-white former alley cat, joined the FDNY around December 1943. According to the *Brooklyn Daily Eagle*, a fireman found her half frozen on the running board of an automobile. She soon became a favorite with the other firemen, especially Captain William Neilan, who called her a "rascal" and "an old terror." Blackie loved all the men, but she didn't like women. Whenever the widows of deceased firemen arrived to make the beds upstairs, she'd stand aside and watch suspiciously as they worked. If a woman dared to come too close to the cat, Blackie would warn her off with a hiss.

Every morning and evening at roll call, Blackie would line up with the fourteen firemen reporting for duty, answering with a plaintive "meow" when she heard her name read off the roster. Although she didn't report to fires, she did a great job keeping the mice away. And like many other fire cats, she was a master of the brass pole. One morning—January 27, 1944, to be specific—Blackie decided to show off her skills by "saucily sailing down the brass firehouse pole." On that day, a truck had dumped ten tons of nut coal at the firehouse as part of a citywide plan to address coal shortages during World War II. Under this initiative, the city established emergency coal stations at fire and police stations, where attendants would supply people with fifty- and one-hundred-pound lots on a cash-and-carry basis. One of the stations selected to serve as an emergency coal station was Engine 203. A newsman from the *Brooklyn Daily Eagle* who was photographing the firemen shoveling the coal was distracted by Blackie and had to set up the photo again. For this exploit, Blackie received publicity in the newspapers, and two motion-picture companies reportedly made newsreels of her.

In addition to the firemen, Blackie loved the neighborhood male cats—or at least they loved her. The firemen often spoke of her love life and her boyfriend, Tom, whom they referred to as "a big bruiser who hangs out on the wall in back." Tom, a dirty black-and-white cat with no apparent owner, spent hours on top of the brick handball-court wall in any kind of weather, just waiting for his lady cat to appear. During her time at the firehouse, Blackie gave birth to two litters of kittens. Fortunately for the kittens, they were all much in demand due to their mother's fame as a fire cat. Each one went home with a fireman's family, who raised them to be Brooklyn firehouse cats just like their mom.

Fireboat *John J. Harvey*: Corporal Gussie

Corporal Gussie may have been born an ordinary brown-gray tabby cat, but by the time she was only a few weeks old, she not only was an FDNY mascot cat but was also on her way to becoming the first and only FDNY cat to serve her country during World War II.

Like many of the famous cats of the Ernest Hemingway Home and Museum in Florida, Gussie was a polydactyl (six-toed) cat. In 1944, the men of the FDNY fireboat *John J. Harvey* found Gussie and her littermates on the wharf at the Battery in Lower Manhattan. They chose Gussie as their newest feline mascot and brought her to their station behind the New York Aquarium, then located in the old Castle Clinton. Gussie followed a long line of FDNY cats on the *Harvey*, starting in 1932, when the men of the new fireboat had to fire one of their first cats for failing to do her job. According to the press, this cat lived at the home station, but she only killed pigeons and sparrows. This forced the men to bring on a second feline mascot to exterminate the rats invading the wharfs.

With war efforts still in full force in the summer of 1944, Corporal Gussie didn't have an opportunity to rise through the ranks of the FDNY. Instead, the patriotic firemen turned her over to the

Army Service Forces, one of the three autonomous components of the United States Army during World War II. The Army Service Forces had a headquarters unit stationed at the North River Terminal of the New York Port of Embarkation (at Pier 86, where the Intrepid Museum is now). Gussie was one of several army cats who helped fight the war on mice and rats at the terminal. Only five days after her induction, Gussie rose to the position of corporal, and according to the *New York Sun*, she advanced steadily. Her commanding officer, Lieutenant Colonel J. W. Rafferty, even cited her "for meritorious service in the extermination of mice." The New York Women's League for Animals also made her an honorary member of its cat brigade, with the rank of brigadier.

In December 1944, Gussie received a brief military leave to serve as the official feline hostess for the Championship Show of the Empire Cat Club at the Hotel Capitol on Eighth Avenue. Guarded by Corporal John Adair and Sergeant Peter Rozembajgier, Gussie calmly viewed the proceedings from atop a grand piano in the Walnut Room, posed for photographers, and allowed the reporters to pet her. Corporal Adair introduced Corporal Gussie to the cats on display, which she didn't appreciate as much—photographers captured her hissing at one prize feline, giving the evil eye to two Siamese cats, and shunning the attention of Leo II, a handsome Chinchilla Persian. Apparently, the GI cat didn't approve of the aristocrats.

Under President Harry S. Truman, the Army Service Forces was abolished in June 1946. Hopefully, Corporal Gussie returned to the *John J. Harvey* and lived the rest of her life as a fire cat of distinction.

HISTORICAL HOOK

The United States Army Garrison at Fort Hamilton in Brooklyn was once an important staging area for the New York Port of Embarkation. At the start of the United States' involvement in World War II, more than one hundred new structures sprang up within the fort limits, including temporary barracks, warehouses, a theater, a service club, hospital buildings, and a new fire station for the Fort Hamilton Fire Department.

Chief Gustav R. Moje with Butch the toothless mascot.
(Chief Moje, Ft. Hamilton, [1947], Gelatin silver print,
NEIG_1012; Brooklyn Daily Eagle photographs, Brooklyn
Public Library, Center for Brooklyn History)

The Fort Hamilton Fire Department, installed in December 1941, was
one of many military installations within New York City that had a paid
civilian fire department during and after World War II, including Fort Jay
on Governor's Island, Fort Wadsworth on Staten Island, and Camp Rockaway in Queens. These federal fire departments cooperated with the FDNY
and operated at fires with FDNY units. Chief Gustav R. Moje, a former
FDNY captain who had retired in 1936 after thirty-two years of service,
took charge of organizing and overseeing the Fort Hamilton department.
The department started off with ten city firemen who were on the FDNY
appointment list but for whom city funds had not yet been allotted. These
men received a six-month leave of absence to help organize the army

post department, after which they returned to the FDNY. Following this six-month period, Chief Moje was responsible for training enlisted men as firefighters.

By 1947, the Fort Hamilton Fire Department had a force of twenty-seven enlisted men, four civilian assistant and senior firefighters, and one mascot dog named Butch. Next to Chief Moje, Butch had the longest record of service with the department. He had shown up shivering and without a license outside the chief's quarters on a frosty night shortly after the department was organized. Described as a "waddling fox terrier" with short legs and a stumpy tail, Butch was a fighting fireman—albeit he didn't fight fires but rather other dogs on the post. "That's why he hasn't hardly any teeth left," Assistant Chief Adolph Salvano told the *Brooklyn Daily Eagle*. "He'll tackle any dog regardless of size."

With the post back on a peacetime regime, Butch's main job was accompanying the men on their daily fire-prevention details: smoking in bed was a problem, and with 160 acres of old frame buildings, constant inspection kept the men and their mascot busy. During the six years that Chief Moje and Butch worked at the fort, there were no fires of any consequences.

4

Monkey Mascots

In twenty-first-century New York, it is illegal to import, possess, or sell wild animals—including gorillas, chimpanzees, orangutans, and gibbons—for domestic pet ownership. Under the state's Environmental Protection Law, these animals can only be imported, possessed, transported, and sold by certain listed entities, such as wildlife sanctuaries, educational institutions, and federally licensed exhibitors, provided they have the necessary permits and licenses.

This was not the case one hundred years ago, when traders regularly took thousands of monkeys from their homes in South America and South Africa and imported them to the United States. Once mostly associated with the immigrant organ grinders who trained them to tip their fancy hats for pennies, by the early 1900s, monkeys were in high demand. The major buyers of primates were the traveling menagerie shows, which renewed their stock every year. Zoological gardens, such as the New York Zoological Gardens (Bronx Zoo), also purchased numerous monkeys for their popular primate houses. During this era—particularly during wartime—monkeys were also popular mascots on steamships and among various military squads stationed around the world.

By 1907, the supply could not meet the demand, as small marmosets that could be "conveniently carried about in a muff, a wrist

At the start of the twentieth century, many small ape and monkey breeds, like these chimpanzees at the Bronx Zoological Park, were popular with high-society ladies and firemen. (Library of Congress, Prints & Photographs Division [LC-USZ62-47701])

bag or a coat pocket" began replacing the lap dog as the preferred companion for high-society ladies across the country. In New York City firehouses, popular monkeys such as Jennie of Engine 20 were also replacing the dog or cat as a preferred mascot. Some of these monkeys may have starred on the vaudeville stage before taking on the mascot role, while others were gifted to department members by captains of the freight ships that had transported the monkeys from their jungle homes to the concrete jungle. Sadly, most monkeys didn't survive long in the city climate, but the firemen did their best to keep their primate pals comfortable and happy while they were affiliated with the FDNY.

Engine 31 and Engine 165: Mrs. Herman

Mrs. Herman, aka Jocko, was a primate belle (possibly a long-tailed macaque) from Java, one of the Greater Sunda Islands in Indonesia. The pet of Captain Timothy J. McAuliffe, she joined the FDNY in 1904 and was reportedly the only "volunteer firewoman" at this time in the United States. Mrs. Herman's first home was with Engine 31 and Water Tower 1 at 87 Lafayette Street.

Mrs. Herman may have been of the fairer sex, but she didn't like women and didn't like wearing dresses (or any clothes at all). While she wasn't permitted to respond to fires, she enjoyed mimicking the men by chewing tobacco and smoking cigars—habits she acquired during her long days at sea before arriving in New York. Her favorite foods were ice cream and cake, which she ate with a spoon "with a propriety and a solemnity" that made girls envy her table manners whenever a fireman took her to the confectioner's shop. She also loved spending time with Pinky, the four-year-old female Dalmatian owned by Lieutenant Sullivan of Water Tower 1, and with the firehouse's seventeen horses. Pluto, the big gray horse of Water Tower 1, was her favorite. Mrs. Herman loved nothing more than riding around the block on Pinky's back every afternoon and taking naps on Pluto's back.

One of the many firehouse pets that Mrs. Herman truly adored was Minnie the cat. Although the two were the best of friends, they sometimes fought, as friends often do. Shortly after the cat gave birth to five kittens, the two female mascots got into an altercation. During the brawl, Mrs. Herman accidentally broke Minnie's back leg. Mrs. Herman took full responsibility for the injury and was extra careful with the mother cat, nursing her back to health in a tender manner. As for Boxer, the other firehouse cat, he didn't stand a chance with Mrs. Herman. In fact, she made his life miserable. When Mrs. Herman was around, Boxer was not a happy cat.

In November 1904, the men loaned Mrs. Herman to the Educational Alliance at 197 East Broadway. Founded in 1889 and originally established as a settlement house for eastern European Jews, the Educational Alliance provided immigrants a respite from their tenement lives. The center offered basic classes in English and US citizenship skills, as well as theatrical and recreational programs for children. From November 1904 through June 1905, Mrs. Herman brought much joy to the children by entertaining them while their parents attended evening programs. She even got a taste of stardom, appearing in the role of Ram Dass's pet monkey from Frances Hodgson Burnett's *A Little Princess*. Mrs. Herman had to give up the chewing tobacco to perform in the children's play, and although everyone treated her kindly, she was rather sulky at the daily rehearsals. During her first scene with a young girl who was playing the role of Sara Crewe, Mrs. Herman chewed gum and winked at a fireman who was at the facility inspecting the exits.

When Mrs. Herman returned to her fire duties in June, the first thing she did was explore her newfound freedom. During her stay at the Educational Alliance, Mrs. Herman had been kept on a leash to keep her from escaping and returning to the firehouse. She had never experienced a leash before, so it took her some time to realize that she was once again free to come and go as she pleased. Next, she practiced her pole-sliding skills and took a ride on Pinky. Mrs. Herman also showed off her three new outfits: everyone at the Educational Alliance had assumed that she was a male, so they made her a sailor suit, a fireman's outfit, and a policeman's uniform. She also ran around and pulled on the men's whiskers, which was a habit she picked up while she was away. To celebrate her homecoming, the men held a party in the street. Dozens of children gathered around as she turned somersaults, chewed tobacco, and extinguished lit matches handed to her. Poor Boxer did not receive an invitation to the party. He was relegated to a neighboring fence, from which he viewed the merry reception while sulking.

When Captain McAuliffe transferred to Engine 165 in September 1905, he took Mrs. Herman with him. Engine 165 was one of five companies established that year in Far Rockaway, Arverne, and Rockaway Beach as part of the first extension of the paid system that replaced the volunteer fire companies in Queens. Engine 165 was organized in the former quarters of the Arverne Engine Company at 63-21 Rockaway Beach Boulevard. The other new companies included Engine 164 (which replaced Oceanic Hose Company and Protective Hook and Ladder), Engine 166 (formerly Atlantic Engine), Engine 167 (which replaced Seaside Hose and Engine Company), and Ladder 71 (formerly Oceanus Hook and Ladder). The total firefighting force of the new Battalion 37 was fifty-five firemen, twelve officers, and one firefighter monkey.

Life was quite different for Mrs. Herman in the Rockaways. Unlike at the Manhattan firehouse, the men here allowed her to be a real firefighter and respond to every alarm. Mrs. Herman could count the signals and never missed a fire, day or night. As soon as the gong rang in the engine house, she'd be the first member of the company to slide down the pole and jump onto the driver's seat. She also learned how to get the mail from the post office a few times a day and carefully distribute the letters to the firemen as Captain McAuliffe called out their names. At night, she'd accompany the captain to his home, where she'd eat her dinner with the McAuliffe family "like a little lady."

While Mrs. Herman was still at Engine 31, she had learned how to clean out the neighborhood peanut stands by chatting up the proprietors while leisurely robbing them of their wares. Soon after arriving at the Rockaways, Mrs. Herman practiced her sleight-of-hand trick on Driver Andrew Munn—only this time she stole cash instead of peanuts. According to a report in the *Brooklyn Daily Eagle* (which called her Jocko), Munn was about to take a nap in the dormitory when he saw the monkey steal a roll of bills containing $62 from his vest pocket. Naturally, he thought the friendly monkey would hand the money back to him, but instead he watched as Mrs. Herman bounded out the window and climbed onto the roof. Captain McAuliffe finally coaxed Mrs. Herman down, but not before she had already chewed and eaten the money—or at least that's what the men thought had happened, since the cash never reappeared.

The new engine house on Rockaway Beach Boulevard didn't have as many horses and pets as her former firehouse had, but Mrs. Herman took steps to change that status by adopting a small kitten about a year after she arrived. The female monkey who once chewed tobacco and shunned girlie dresses became a devoted mother to the tiny kitten, feeding him milk with a spoon, rocking him to sleep in a tiny cradle, and giving him frequent rides in a baby carriage that the men had created for the small mother monkey and her baby kitten.

Battalion 9: Betsy and Bob

Betsy and Bob were probably the most troublesome mascots of the FDNY. Although the two monkeys appeared docile and obedient, that was merely a façade they put on in the presence of the firemen. Once out of sight, they were more like Bonnie and Clyde. The problem was, Betsy and Bob didn't have to abide by the rules of the firehouse or report their comings and goings. Perhaps if the men had set down house rules and treated the monkeys more like the horses, they would not have gotten into so much trouble.

Soon after Betsy and Bob arrived at the Battalion 9 headquarters at 248 West Forty-Eighth Street, numerous silver items began appearing throughout the firehouse. Why, the men wondered, were there silver napkin rings, silver-backed combs, and silver mirrors on the men's beds, in the recreation room, in the lockers, and in the chief's quarters? Where did they come from? How did they get there? And to whom did all these silver things belong? The situation created tension, especially after someone found a lady's silver comb in the chief's wagon. They knew there was no thief among them, and yet the men all eyed each other suspiciously. Some men began to lose sleep over the situation. The mystery of the silver objects lingered on for several days, and the number of silver and other shiny objects continued to increase. It was only by accident that the men solved the whodunnit.

According to the story, one of the firemen happened to be taking a nap with his feet up on the windowsill in the top-floor recreation room, which overlooked neighboring backyards. Suddenly a light flashed directly in his eyes, which made him blink and sit up. His back was to the sun, so he knew the sun couldn't be the source of the flash. He looked down into one of the yards, and there was Betsy, the larger of the two monkeys, cautiously making her way down a rain downspout. In her paws was a silver-backed hand mirror, which was what had caught the sunlight that flashed into the fireman's eyes.

It took only a brief investigation to discover that Betsy and Bob were regular "second-story thieves" who had been pillaging the neighborhood houses and stealing every shiny article they could grab. The firemen notified the nearby police station of the thefts, which allowed the police to close out numerous complaints of missing toiletry items. The chief of the battalion couldn't take any more chances with the monkey thieves, so poor Betsy and Bob were put behind bars in the cages at the Central Park Menagerie. Sadly, Betsy did not fare well in the cage; she died shortly after her banishment. Some folks said she died of a broken heart because she missed her best friend, Flo, a St. Bernard who shared the firehouse with Betsy and Bob. Every morning, Betsy would jump on the dog's back, grab his collar, and go for a ride. Betsy spent her last days on Earth pining for Flo and the life she had with Battalion 9. According to FDNY Secretary Alfred Downes, "the firemen always attributed the monkey's death to the fact that she was bereft not only of her reputation, but of her old companions as well."

HISTORICAL HOOK

Although the men of Battalion 9 eventually solved the mystery of the stolen silver items, perhaps the case could have been solved sooner had the men enlisted the help of a fire marshal. Betsy and Bob were not arsonists, but they certainly left enough clues about the firehouse for a trained eye to detect the cause and origin of the thefts.

The history of New York City's fire marshals dates to 1854, when Alfred E. Baker, a reporter for the *New York Herald*, started to question the large number of "peculiar fires of doubtful origin." Chief Engineer Alfred Carson asked the reporter to investigate the fires and apprehend the arsonists. After Baker successfully caught a few firebugs in the act, the department awarded him the title of fire marshal and issued him a fireman's red shirt, cap, and coat.

As the city's sole fire marshal, it was Baker's duty to attend to all fires, both night and day, and thoroughly investigate their origin. One newspaper noted that his "long practical experience in the police regulations of the city, combined with untiring perseverance, eminently capacitate him for the arduous task he has undertaken to perform." Baker didn't receive a salary from the FDNY at first; the insurance companies established a fund to reimburse him for his work.

One of Baker's first arrests came in July 1854, following an investigation at a frame dwelling at 96 Amos Street (now West Tenth Street). According to the report, James Turner, who had lived in a basement apartment with his wife, set fire to straw in a closet after his wife had left him and removed the furniture from the premises. Although the fire caused little damage, the *New-York Tribune* reported that had the fire gotten under way, the building and the adjoining frame building would have been destroyed and lives may have been lost.

Baker published a semiannual report titled "Fires and Their Causes— Incendiarism and Negligence" to document his progress. His February 1856 report for the period of May 31 through December 31, 1855, documented fifty-two fires related to acts of incendiarism—a decrease of sixteen fires compared with the corresponding months of 1854—and fourteen arrests for arson. Baker also made suggestions for reducing the number of fires, both accidental and incendiary. For example, his 1856 report contained "some interesting suggestions in reference to the construction of buildings" while also denouncing "the new and peculiar dwellings, called 'tenements.'" In an 1858 report, he suggested passage of a law authorizing the police to arrest young male members of "gangs of idlers," who accounted for the most incendiarism during that time.

Baker remained in his position until 1868. He worked as a portrait painter in his small studio at 1267 Broadway until his death in February 1889, at the age of about sixty-five. The position of fire marshal eventually morphed into the Bureau of Fire Marshals and then the Bureau of Fire Investigation. Today, FDNY fire marshals must have much more experience than Baker had when he created the job. Not only must they first serve as firefighters in the department, but they must also complete the New York Police Department's criminal investigation course and receive hundreds of hours of additional training. In 1992, Joann Jacobs and Margaret Moffatt were the first women appointed to the prestigious position.

Engine 40: The Anonymous Monkey

After returning from a fire call on February 16, 1910, the men of Engine 40 at 153 West Sixty-Eighth Street found a monkey sitting quite contentedly on the desk near the large alarm gong. He immediately mixed with his new firemen friends and established himself as "a desirable acquaintance." Thinking the monkey may have belonged to someone nearby, the men went to the West Sixty-Eighth Street police station to see if anyone had reported a lost monkey. They also checked the newspaper advertisements for lost and found items. A few days after the monkey appeared in their firehouse, the men told a *New York Times* reporter that they would adopt the monkey if no one claimed him. By that time, they were already beginning to feel that the yet-to-be-named monkey was their mascot—and the monkey agreed. Feeling quite at home at Engine 40, he learned how to respond to alarms, slide down the pole from the sleeping quarters, jump on the backs of the horses as they were preparing to go on a call, and sleep in bed. He also figured out how to climb out the window and walk across the window ledges of adjoining tenement buildings to steal food from open windows. The press never followed up on the outcome of the unknown monkey; hopefully the primate fire buff found a permanent home with Engine 40 and didn't end up behind bars at the Central Park Menagerie.

Engine 126: Fitz

New York State Congressman John Joseph Fitzgerald of Brooklyn didn't know much about ring-tailed monkeys when he received one as a gift while visiting Panama in December 1913. By December 1915, his experiences with the raccoon-looking monkey with a black-and-white-striped tail was more than he had bargained for—about $1,000 more.

Shortly after toting the small simian from Panama to Brooklyn as "excess baggage," Congressman Fitzgerald presented him to the firemen of Engine 126 at 409 State Street. Not knowing what to do with their new monkey mascot—which they first named Fido—the men kept him in captivity by tying him to an unused hose cart near a window using a thick leather strap. This contraption worked for about a month, but every day at dinnertime, Fido would chew at the strap. On January 31, 1914, the strap finally broke, and out the window Fido went. As he climbed up the fire escape of the adjoining tenement, someone sounded an alarm at the firehouse to alert the men of the escape. Within minutes, fifteen firemen were swarming over the roof of the apartment house, climbing up and down the fire escapes, and hanging out the windows trying to snatch the tiny monkey. To the delight of the small boys on the street and the young women boarders in the Harriet Judson YWCA on Nevins Street, Fido continued scrambling up and down the fire escapes without a care in the world.

According to the *Brooklyn Daily Eagle*, "the recapture of Congressman Fitzgerald's gift was as neat a bit of strategy as has been seen in a long while." First, the tenement janitor climbed onto the roof armed with just his hands and "a sinister black cloth in which to infold Mr. Monk with loving tenderness." The janitor got within two feet of Fido when the monkey "began a correspondence course of Simian cussing" and shrieking that sent the man backward through a window. Next, the firemen strategically placed themselves on the fire escape—one at the top, one at the bottom, and two in the middle—to cut off all avenues of retreat. Using gentle coaxing, Fireman Riley finally convinced Fido that his shoulder made a much more respectable perch than a fire escape. Alas, in attempting to pass the monkey through the window, he lost his grip, and Fido got away again. After waiting a few moments for the monkey to settle down, one man grabbed for his head, and another grabbed the tail. While the people on the street below cheered on the firemen, they placed Fido back inside, where a solid chain of steel awaited him. That evening, the men voted to rename the monkey Fitz in honor of the congressman.

About two years later, in December 1915, Mrs. Clara F. Burch filed a complaint against Congressman Fitzgerald and Battalion Chief John J. Dooley. Mrs. Burch, who lived in a ground-floor apartment at 417 State Street—three doors down from the firehouse—alleged that the monkey was of a "malicious, vicious, ferocious, mischievous, dangerous and unmanageable disposition, and possessed other vicious propensities." According to Mrs. Burch, Fitz would climb out on an extension overlooking the neighboring backyards. From there, he could climb along a fence into her yard and then jump into her window (as the *Brooklyn Daily Eagle* noted, "even a window screen was but a temporary inconvenience in the way of his entrance into her home"). One day, she said, not only did Fitz enter her apartment, but he also scratched and beat her until her husband heard her cries and chased the monkey away. Mrs. Burch said she sought $1,000 in damages for her medical fees, stating that she still suffered from the nervous shock and other effects of the monkey's unwelcome visit.

Chief Dooley told the press that after receiving Mrs. Burch's complaint, he remanded the monkey to the Prospect Park Zoo in the care of Head Keeper John O'Brien. Congressman Fitzgerald refused to speak to the press about the suit or go into any detail about the history of Fitz. As one reporter noted, based on the tone of his voice, it did not appear that the representative wanted to receive another ring-tail monkey as a gift.

HISTORICAL HOOK

Prior to the 1860s, when fire escapes on New York City tenements were first required by law, there were few forms of safe escape from a multistory building fire. Narrow interior stairs often burned away in a hot fire, making dangerous ladder rescues from windows and roofs a necessary option. Wooden extension ladders were not viable when they weren't long enough to reach the upper floors (the FDNY didn't purchase its first crank-operated aerial ladders until 1886). Inventors designed all kinds of creative escape mechanisms—including rope and basket devices, cloth chutes, parachute helmets, and extension ladders on wheels—but most were flimsy and would never instill confidence in people faced with a life-or-death situation.

On February 2, 1860, a fire broke out in a double six-story tenement at 142 Elm Street, which was occupied by a grocery and bakery on the ground floor and twenty-four families above. The fire, fed by dry hay and wood shavings in the bakery's storeroom, quickly spread, burning the interior stairway and cutting off any chance of escape for the people on the top

Inventors designed all kinds of creative escape mechanisms, including ladder chutes based on a device called a retreat (or escape) patented by M. Joaquim Smith of London in 1773. (Wellcome Collection)

floors. With even the longest of the ladders unable to reach above the fourth floor, all the volunteer firemen could do was watch as men, women, and children jumped to their deaths. The *New York Times* reported, "The shouts of the firemen, the groans and shrieks of the doomed creatures in this building, and the crackling flames, constituted a scene tragic enough to make the stoutest heart shrink with horror." Approximately thirty civilian lives were lost that day.

During a coroner's inquest and a hearing of evidence, a recommendation was made for the enactment of a statute prescribing a means of escape for the occupants of similar structures. The story received extensive coverage, and many opinionated New Yorkers put steel pen to paper to share their views on fire escapes. In one letter to the *New York Times*, an anonymous writer pointed out a serious flaw in a proposal for connecting outside iron ladders to chamber windows: "Such ladders would render every chamber accessible from the street and from the chambers above and below and would thus leave every family exposed to robbery. In a tenement building, where persons of every grade of character would be collected, the exposure of families to clandestine visits from their own neighbors, above or below them, would be a serious evil; to say nothing of the risk of burglaries from the street. Such ladders could only be attached to the hall windows, and would be of little use when the stairways and the halls were obstructed by flames or heat."

Another *Times* editorialist, B. B. Lewis, submitted several ways to remedy potential fire-escape flaws and suggested that "iron ladders could be constructed in such a matter that they could be folded up and form a kind of projecting sill to the windows, on which the inmates could place their house plants." He was onto something.

Inventors also jumped on the bandwagon, bringing their contraptions to the city for public demonstrations. The Pompier Corps, a German volunteer firefighting corps, exhibited their fire-escape system at Richard French's seven-story hotel across from City Hall Park. Their "pompier ladder" was a scaling ladder system in which a fireman would climb the first ladder resting on the sidewalk and use additional ladders with iron hooks to attach to upper-story windowsills as he climbed higher. C. D. Brown and W. J. Bunce demonstrated their fire-escape bag at City Hall and Thorp's Hotel at Union Square. Their device was based on a circa-1843 system used in London by the Royal Society for the Protection of Life from Fire. The society maintained an organized body of men, called conductors, who oversaw a series of interconnected ladders on two wheels that were stationed in different parts of the city. These ladders were special because they featured full-length canvas troughs made of sail cloth and covered with wire gauze. After running to the fire with the wheeled ladder, the conductor would throw it against the building and use ropes and pulleys to extend it sixty to eighty feet. The conductor would then enter a window and place victims in the canvas trough, allowing them to slide safely to the street. The *New York Times* reported that the London system "seemed most capable of being the readiest adapted to immediate use, when the cries of life in danger summon."

It wasn't until twenty years later, in 1884, that the FDNY would choose the pompier ladder system—also known as the Hoell Life Saving Appliance—which Lieutenant Christ Hoell had implemented in the St. Louis Fire Department in 1877. The first rescue using these ladders took place in April 1884, when Ladder 3 Firemen John Binns, Thomas F. Barrett, and Michael E. C. Graham rescued the elevator boy Louis Caistang from a seventh-story window during a fire at the St. George's Flats at 225 East Seventh Street.

While inventor wannabes were trying to sell their contraptions to the city, New York State legislators were busy writing a new law to address the public-safety issue. On April 17, 1860, the state passed a law titled "An Act to Provide Against Unsafe Buildings in the City of New York." Under Section 25 of this law, all dwelling houses built for more than eight families required exterior fireproof stairs or balconies connected by fireproof stairs on the outside of every floor. This law was updated in 1862 to add more requirements and was applied retroactively to all existing dwelling houses.

Unfortunately, most of the straight-ladder fire escapes of this era were shoddily built, and enforcement and maintenance were lacking; so collapse

FDNY firemen drill with scaling ladders in the early twentieth century. (Library of Congress, Prints & Photographs Division, [LC-DIG-ggbain-02989])

was imminent. In 1868, for example, there were close to twenty thousand tenements in the city, of which more than one thousand did not yet have some type of fire escape in place. The tenement laws also didn't carry over to other buildings, such as hotels, office buildings, and theaters. For example, when the iconic Potter Building (old New York World Building) was destroyed by fire on January 31, 1882, three men were resigned to sliding down a telegraph pole wire from the fifth floor because the ladders of Ladder 10 couldn't reach them and there was no other means of escape. An 1897 law requiring rope fire escapes in every New York hotel room was seen by some people as a better alternative to leaping to the sidewalk, but the ropes were mostly ineffective. During the horrific Windsor Hotel fire on March 17, 1899, in fact, numerous people fell or slid hard and fast to their deaths while using the ropes. Several bills were proposed to address fire safety following the Windsor Hotel fire, but as one editorialist in the *New York Times* pointed out, "To hang a hotel all around with iron ladders would make a disfigurement that might agreeably testify to the activity of legislators and swell the profits of ironmongers. But it would amount to little or nothing as a precaution. A burning tinder box is no safer for being inclosed [*sic*] in a cage of red-hot ladders called fire escapes." The writer suggested that the only solution was the construction of fireproof staircases, unconnected to the elevator shafts and independent of the building.

With the passage of the Tenement House Act of 1901, regulations for residential fire escapes were more strictly enforced. Under Section 12 of this act, fire escapes were defined as outside open iron balconies and stairs located on both the front and rear of the building at each story above the ground floor. The law also established strict rules about specifics such as balcony and landing size, drop ladders, and the angle of the stairs. Despite a $10 fine for any encumbrance, fire escapes became an extension of the living space, as tenants turned them into mini patios, gardens, storage spaces, summer sleeping quarters, and jungle gyms for children. A 1968 change in the city's building codes banned the construction of external fire escapes on almost all new buildings, placing the focus on fire prevention and the use of sprinklers and fireproof interior stairways. In recent years, developers have removed fire escapes from older buildings as part of their efforts to restore them to their original glory. As the FDNY spokesman Jim Long told the press in 2005, "Fire escapes are going the way of the dinosaur."

Ladder 24: Jack Johnson

In December 1908, Captain William Kehoe of Ladder 24 received a Brazilian monkey. He brought the monkey to the firehouse at 115 West Thirty-Third Street and made a bed for him on the second floor. The firemen named him Jack Johnson.

Two months later, on February 13, 1909, Jack made the headlines when he took advantage of an open front window and made his way onto Thirty-Third Street. Captain Kehoe saw the monkey escape and took off after him, shouting for his men to follow. As the firemen, five policemen, and hundreds of citizens ran after Jack, the monkey made his way through the refuse and building materials on the Pennsylvania Railroad and Hudson Terminal site (the site was being cleared to make way for a concourse for the old McAdoo tunnel system—today's PATH—at Thirty-Third Street and Sixth Avenue). Just as the monkey mascot began heading for Broadway, an Italian organ grinder headed him off and almost caught him before Jack turned south on Sixth Avenue. By this time, the neighborhood was in an uproar. As more people pressed in on him, Jack dove into the cellar of a new building between Sixth Avenue and Broadway. A young boy named Jimmy Cosgrove captured the monkey and presented him to Captain Kehoe, who rewarded the youth for catching the ladder company's mischievous mascot.

Ladder 20: Jennie and Chipper

One of the most famous monkey mascots of the FDNY was Jennie of Ladder 20, then headquartered in the circa-1854 Firemen's Hall at 155 Mercer Street in Manhattan. Jennie was a ring-tailed monkey born in Pará, Brazil, where she had suffered abuse while under the care of a young boy. The skipper of a tramp freighter reportedly rescued the tiny monkey and presented her to Lieutenant Edward F. Croker in 1895. The future fire chief welcomed the baby monkey and made a comfortable home for her in the corner of the firehouse recreation room. Jennie briefly shared mascot duties with Chipper, a Java monkey who joined the ladder company in 1900. Chipper had more years of service, but he didn't have the same hardworking press agent as Jennie had.

Jennie was affectionate with the firemen at first—and most of them adored her, too, albeit from a distance—but she especially loved Fireman Frank Murphy, who took charge of her and became her faithful attendant. Her favorite place was the sitting room, especially when the men returned from a big fire. Jennie would chatter away softly while swinging from one bed to another as the exhausted men undressed to prepare for a bath or a nap. According to the *New York Press*, she was so sympathetic that the firemen soon began to understand every word she said.

Like all monkeys, Jennie was a mischief maker and had a wild side. She often got into brawls with the firemen—one time she bit Fireman Frank Riley's hand so badly that he had to go on sick leave for a few months. She also spent a lot of time climbing on the barred windows at the rear of the firehouse and screeching at the women working in the factory building across the yard. At lunchtime, the women would respond by tossing bits of food at Jennie, which was exactly the response she wanted. Jenny was also mischievous with the horses, especially during grooming time. She'd often sit on the radiator and hold the horse's halter during the process; if the horse refused to stand quietly, Jennie would climb up the halter and slap the horse on the nose until it behaved.

As a monkey, Jennie was quicker and more agile than the dogs and cats in the neighborhood, and she made their life miserable whenever she got loose, which was quite often. One night she was crossing the fence into the adjoining yard when she came face to face with a large tomcat. The cat tried to escape by running up a tree, but Jennie chased up the tree close behind him. The cat eventually escaped, but Jennie spent the night in the tree.

Although the monkey didn't have good experiences with the neighborhood cats, she did adore the firehouse cat. Every time the cat had a litter of kittens, Jennie would take over as nurse and care for them, so all the mother had to do was feed them. One day, Jennie decided to take two of the kittens exploring outdoors. From the top-floor window, she carried the kittens down the outside of the firehouse. She then climbed up a tree and sat on a limb cuddling the kittens in her lap.

After years of escaping from the firehouse and causing trouble in the neighborhood, Jennie was eventually remanded to the bare gymnasium floor chained to a post. But every mischievous thing she ever did was all forgiven the day she saved the firehouse from burning down. According to a news report, the men had just returned from a fire on a frosty winter night. One of the firemen put some frozen-stiff clothes over a radiator on the top floor to thaw them out. He forgot about the matches still in the pocket. In short time, the heat set fire to the matches, which then set the clothes and woodwork on fire. One floor below, all the men were soundly sleeping in the dormitory. The only souls awake in the firehouse were the watchman, who was on the ground floor, and Jennie, who was confined to her sleeping area on the top floor. Unable to run down the stairs to alert the men, she did the next best thing a smart monkey could do. Grabbing a few pool balls from the pool table, Jennie hurled them down the iron stairway into the dormitory and screeched out a warning. The men instantly awoke in response to the loud clattering and primate alarm, and they doused the flames with fire extinguishers. In the official report of the incident, the men noted that it was Jennie the Monk who had rendered the fire-suppressive services.

Perhaps as a reward for Jennie's good deed, the firemen began allowing her to go to a few fires with them during the summer of 1907. One August day, she slipped from her blanket on the truck to investigate some hats thrown from the burning building. Just as she started to scramble over a hose, it burst and shot the shocked and drenched monkey about twenty feet in the air. Shortly after that incident, Jennie began acting up more than usual. One day, while out with Fireman Murphy on a Broadway streetcar, she snatched a woman's hat and tore it to pieces before Murphy could stop her. A few days later, she escaped from the firehouse, ran into a restaurant, and sat down on the counter. The proprietor was so frightened that he ran to the firehouse to get help. When the men entered the restaurant, Jennie was throwing cups, saucers, and bottles in all directions. During her "time out" punishment for these events, she got into some mischief in the chief's office while the men were on a call. She drank a bottle of paste, swallowed the ink eradicator, spread the chief's valuable papers on the floor, and poured ink all over them. She then tore open a pillow, rolled herself around in the stuffing, ink, and paste, and hurried back to her quarters. When the men returned, Jennie welcomed them with a big smile on her face. Back to her chain she went. Less than a week later, she died in the firehouse, possibly from the paste or from the injuries she had sustained at the fire. Following her death, Murphy was inconsolable. The men told the press that they would have her skin stuffed and mounted and placed in her favorite place in the firehouse.

HISTORICAL HOOK

In 1920, Joseph Charles Pohler was living with his wife and newborn baby on College Avenue in the Bronx and working as a second-grade fireman at Ladder 20 when he got an offer he couldn't refuse. Ironically, the offer came to him while he was shimmying up the brass pole in the firehouse gymnasium—sort of how a monkey like Jennie would do.

Engine 20 Fireman Joseph Pohler changed his name to Gene Pollar to play the role of Tarzan in *The Revenge of Tarzan*. (United Archives GmbH / Alamy Stock Photo)

According to the story, first published in the *New York Evening World*, Numa Pictures was in the market for an actor to play the role of Tarzan in a new movie based on the *Tarzan of the Apes* stories. Elmo Lincoln, the original actor in the role, had already made two Tarzan movies and wasn't interested in a third (though he would later return to the role). Director Harry Revere and corporate stockholder George Merrick came to the city to see if they could find a "physically satisfactory Tarzan" among the men of the New York Police Department. Although they came up empty during this search, someone informed them of a six-foot-four-inch firefighter weighing 225 pounds at Ladder 20. When Revere and Merrick arrived at the firehouse, the twenty-six-year-old Pohler was at the top of the pole. The men decided at once that he was the perfect man to play Tarzan in their new movie, *The Revenge of Tarzan*.

"Who sent you over here to kid me?" Pohler asked the men. After Revere and Merrick assured him that the offer was legitimate, Pohler resigned from the FDNY and went home to tell his wife. He got a new stage name, Gene Pollar, and a contract to make $100 a week plus expenses. (Pohler said he didn't want his landlord to find out he was making way more than the $1,400 annual salary for a fireman.) According to the *Evening World*, Pohler had always been interested in racing automobiles because he loved the thrill of the fast cars. He joined the fire department in search of even more thrilling adventures. After rehearsing on the set in California with nine lions—one weighing 925 pounds—Pohler told the reporter, "Being a 'Smoky Joe' is about as thrilling as a Quaker meeting."

The Revenge of Tarzan was surprisingly successful and more thrilling than *Tarzan of the Apes*, which was the original movie based on the Tarzan stories. Universal Pictures offered Pohler a two-year contract at $350 a week, but Numa Pictures refused to release him. With only the one film to his credit, Pohler ended his short-lived acting career and returned to his job as a fireman. He died at the age of seventy-nine in 1971 in Fort Lauderdale, Florida.

5

Happy Families and Best Friends

On the streets of Victorian London, one could oftentimes observe a crowd gathered around a large cage containing a variety of animals that in nature were natural enemies. The men who exhibited these collections of cats, rabbits, birds, monkeys, and other small mammals advertised them as "Happy Families." The animals in these families were trained to live in "perfectly good temper and joyous happiness" by the prospect of small rewards or punishments.

Happy families were not limited to London. Many traveling menageries and dime museums in Europe and the United States featured cages filled with creatures who were no doubt unhappy, relegated to a life of boredom and punishments for bad behavior. One of the most popular happy family exhibits in New York City was at P. T. Barnum's American Museum on the corner of Broadway and Ann Street. Located on the third floor and comprising a long wire cage filled with dogs, cats, monkeys, anteaters, squirrels, mice and rats, parrots, chickens, ducks, turkeys, quails and pheasants, guinea pigs, rabbits, turtles, snakes, frogs, robins, pigeons, and more, Barnum's happy family was one of the more interesting

On July 13, 1865, a horrific fire took the lives of dozens of mammals, birds, and fish at P. T. Barnum's American Museum, including all the animals in the happy family exhibit. (The Miriam and Ira D. Wallach Division of Art, Prints and Photographs: Picture Collection. "Burning of Barnum's American Museum." *The New York Public Library Digital Collections*. 1897)

of the many curiosities exhibited at the museum. Sadly, all these animals and many others in the museum died in a horrific fire on July 13, 1865.

In the late nineteenth and early twentieth centuries, the press often referred to a mixed group of working animals and mascots as happy families. Typically, a happy family comprised a few horses, dogs, and cats that had befriended each other, whether for comfort, safety, or amusement. One of the most famous happy families was the menagerie of Manhattan's Engine 8, which in addition to three turtles, included a popular horse, an aristocratic Dalmatian, and a playful cat who fraternized together. In Brooklyn, Engine 13 was also a strong contender for having the most four-legged friends with a "happy family of six animals that lived in harmony." Firehouses with two popular mascots, although not considered a happy family, also caught the attention of the press, especially if the duo had a unique symbiotic relationship.

Engine 13: Ben, Billy, and Nell

Billy the goat was one of the six animals who composed the large happy family of Brooklyn's Engine 13 at 137 Powers Street. Billy was the pet of Fireman Henry Reese, who had received the goat in 1891 when Billy was a young kid. Reese fed him from a bottle until Billy was old enough to indulge in paper, tomato cans, and other goat edibles. In 1895, the goat was sharing the firehouse with the company's three horses, a pretty kitten named Nell, and a Dalmatian named Ben (aka Spot).

Ben joined the fire department around 1893. Originally attached to the new Engine 34 on Bergen Street, where he was born, Ben received a transfer to Engine 13 as soon as he could leave his mother. Ben quickly became a favorite among the firemen, neighborhood children, and horses, but it was the engine house cat (possibly Nell's mother) who loved him most, especially when he let her sleep for hours between his paws. Ben also watched out for the horses; if one ever got loose, he'd bark until one of the men replaced the hitch.

As for humans, the friendly dog knew the habits and mealtimes of everyone on the block, which allowed him to visit specific families whenever they were serving his favorite foods. One of his favorite civilians was Isaac Smith Remson, a prominent businessman who owned a manufacturing business at 740–760 Grand Street. If ever Remson was away when Ben paid a visit, the dog would run around the corner to the barber shop that the businessman patronized.

Ben was a born firefighter who loved responding to fires. If he were visiting a family at mealtime and the alarm went off, he'd jump through any open window, carrying the window sash with him. Like the men he worked with at the second alarm company, he was often impatient for a run. When the horses stood on the floor waiting for a second alarm, Ben would pace back and forth in anticipation of the potential action to come.

One time Ben was locked in the cellar when the company received a call. A little girl who lived opposite the engine house heard him barking and let him out, but by then it was too late for him to respond. When the men returned, one of the firemen told Ben, "You will go down town on charges for this." According to a reporter for the *Brooklyn Daily Eagle*, "the dog appeared to realize that he was in disgrace."

On April 1, 1895, Ben was running ahead of the horses responding to a fire at Humboldt and Stagg Streets when a ferocious bulldog ran from Thomas Shanley's blacksmith shop on Powers Street and pinned him to the ground. The horses trampled the fighting dogs, breaking their backs. A policeman dispatched both dogs and laid them in the gutter. The men said they wanted to have Ben's skin stuffed and properly mounted so they could place him in his favorite corner of the firehouse, but his skin was irreparably damaged by the horses' hoofs.

Two weeks after this tragic incident, a stenographer at the Ewen Street police court dropped his notebook in front of the firehouse. Billy, who was in the habit of leaving the house every morning to forage, picked up the notebook and began eating it. The *Brooklyn Daily Eagle* reported the following:

> Billy had a remarkable digestive system, even for a goat, but a notebook, containing opinions, decisions, rulings, quotations from the classics, meditations uttered in Latin, lectures to delinquent husbands, advice to wayward girls, fatherly advice to boys who build bonfires in the streets, [and] choice bits of poetry with which Judge Watson burdened the public record in a single day is enough to give a dozen Williamsburg goats dyspepsia. Billy ate the notebook at one meal. He became extremely ill and hid himself in the darkest corner in the cellar. In vain he tried to rid himself of the deep distress in his stomach. . . . He had even digested a picture of Trilby and a petition from the citizens of the Fifteenth Ward praying the mayor and the health commissioner to abate the Newtown Creek nuisances. He had devoured a set of resolutions adopted by the anti-Worth faction of the Nineteenth Ward which denounced the charities reorganization bill. But Judge Watson's eloquence, wit and poetry did not agree with Billy.

Thinking a change of air would be good for the goat, Reese took him to his home, which was just around the corner from Engine 12 on Wythe Avenue. Fireman Edward Casey of Engine 12 told Reese he had a fluid that, if injected in the goat, would make Billy good as new. Reese gave Casey permission to administer the panacea that night. The next morning, Billy was dead. Casey said that had he known what was in the goat's stomach, he would not have given him the injection.

With Ben and Billy gone, the little kitten and three horses were all that remained of the happy family. The horses went on with their lives, even winning a first-place blue ribbon with Driver Eugene Pownall at the Riding and Driving Club annual horse show one month after Ben's and Billy's deaths, a first prize for hitching up the fastest in just over four seconds with Driver Charles W. Norris in 1896, and first prize in the show's fire department exhibition in 1897.

Two years later, in October 1899, the company was renumbered 113, but that did not eliminate the bad luck. On June 24, 1902, while responding to an alarm of fire at 120 Seigel Street, the tender collided with the Engine 116 engine, throwing all the men on the tender to the pavement "with great force." All three of the Engine 113 horses were also thrown to ground, and two were severely injured. Although all the firemen save for Captain Marks of Engine 116 refused medical treatment, the *New York Times* reported that one of the tender's horses would have to be killed. And the bad luck didn't end there.

On August 26, 1902, just two months after the accident, the engines of both companies collided on the way to a fire at 198 Johnson Avenue. The men of both engines jumped for their lives, but one of the horses was killed. Engine 116 managed to make it to the fire—where the company helped rescue Joseph Havens, his wife, and their three children—but the Engine 113 apparatus was too badly wrecked to continue. The cause of the fire is more than ironic: According to the *New York Times*, the fire started when a cat overturned a kerosene lamp on a mantel in the rear of Simon Flynn's grocery store. The newspaper described the feline arsonist as "a big black cat."

HISTORICAL HOOK

In January 1914, the *New York Sun* reported on a man who had walked into the elevator in the Atlantic Building at 49 Wall Street and asked the operator for the thirteenth floor. When told there was no such floor in the building, the man questioned how he was previously able to walk up one flight of stairs from the twelfth floor to the floor above. "That was the fourteenth floor," the attendant replied. "There isn't a thirteenth floor in this building." The *Sun* reporter then explained: "That thirteen is feared by not a few is evident from the number of tall office buildings in the downtown sections of the city that have no thirteenth floor. The floor above the twelfth, which ordinarily should be the thirteenth, in many buildings is the fourteenth floor or the "M" floor or some other kind of a floor. It is anything but the thirteenth floor."

In Western culture, the number thirteen is rooted in negative meaning and is often associated with bad luck and superstition. There is even a word for fear of the number thirteen: triskaidekaphobia. Researchers estimate that as many as 10 percent of Americans have triskaidekaphobia. This superstition has had a significant influence on real estate: even today, some hotel and high-rise developers rename the thirteenth floor or eliminate thirteen from room numbers. According to CityRealty, a New York City–based housing data and listings firm, of 629 condo buildings with thirteen or more floors, only 55 label the floor above the twelfth as the thirteenth floor.

During the early twentieth century, New York City high-rise designers often omitted listing a thirteenth floor for fear of turning off superstitious would-be tenants. Although some real estate developers believed it would be difficult to rent offices on the thirteenth floor, the fears remained largely unfounded, especially as skyscrapers became more common. In 1920, the *New-York Tribune* reporter Wilbur Forrest called the superstition an irrational "hoodoo" and pointed out some absurdities:

> If our Continental forefathers had suffered the fear of the supposed thirteen jinx as much as the builders of great office buildings on Lower Broadway, they would have eliminated the thirteenth state and the thirteenth star in the flag which they fought behind for independence. Lower Broadway builders of office structures have more often than not asked the sign painter to forget that there is a thirteenth floor and call it fourteenth, whereupon offices have rented as readily on the thirteenth floor as any other floor, though the said floor exists and goes through its material life under an alias, like the criminal who changes his name.

The superstition might be hoodoo, but there were in fact a rash of suicides and deaths caused by jumps or falls from the thirteenth floor in the first two decades of the twentieth century. In January 1908, for example, Caroline Bartlett Sears, wife of the Boston millionaire Herbert Mason Sears, jumped from her room on the thirteenth floor of the St. Regis Hotel on Fifth Avenue and landed on the roof of a neighboring building. A year later, the businessman Ervin G. Long leaped from his office on the thirteenth floor of a Hudson Terminal building at 50 Church Street and landed on an airshaft skylight on the second floor. The attorney Philip Keyes Walcott leaped or fell to his death from the thirteenth floor of his office at 63 Beaver Street in October 1914, and the salesman Richard D. Hudson plunged from the thirteenth floor of the Woolworth Building on Broadway in February 1919.

With all this superstition and bad luck, one can only wonder if the number thirteen had anything to do with the misfortune surrounding the Engine 13 mascots in the spring of 1895 and the Engine 113 horses in the summer of 1902.

Ladder 12: Billy and Mr. Jack

One popular horse and dog duo of the early twentieth century was Billy and Mr. Jack of Ladder 12 at 243 West Twentieth Street. According to FDNY Secretary Downes, Billy, an all-white horse, was a faithful worker and one of the gentlest in the neighborhood; not only was he the friend of every child on the block, but "his hand-shaking was the pride of the neighborhood." Mr. Jack, a Dalmatian, "was as fond of him as one animal could be of another."

Almost every morning following roll call, Mr. Jack would climb on Billy's back and go for a ride down the cobblestone block. Billy, ever loyal in his duty, would always stay alert for the signal bell as he trotted up and down West Twentieth Street with Mr. Jack clinging to his back. Should an alarm come in while the pals were out for a joy ride, Billy would gallop to the harness and take his place as the center horse of the triple hitch. Jack would then jump off the horse's back and take his place in front of the nigh horse, quickly switching into work mode to warn everyone to get out of the way.

Mr. Jack was a cautious dog when it came to leading the horses, especially in rainy weather or during snowstorms. But once on the scene, he was aggressive, following his two-legged friends into the buildings and staying by their side until they had completed their job. If he got injured on the job, Billy was always there to nurse him back to health. According to department records, one time Billy nursed Mr. Jack so carefully "that a wound upon the lower part of the foreleg was wholly cured by the gentle tongue of the dog-doctor."

Engine 131 and Ladder 70: Peter, Rocks, Nellie, and Abie

The FDNY permitted firemen to keep singing birds in the firehouse, but some men pushed the envelope by including parrots, pigeons, and even seagulls in the "singing bird" category. Engine 131 and Ladder 70 at 107–109 Watkins Street in Brooklyn had a large green parrot named Peter, who, over the years, shared the firehouse with the horses, three cats, a brindle bull terrier (or possibly bulldog) named Rocks, a fox terrier named Nellie, and a mutt named Abie. (The men told a reporter from the *Brooklyn Standard Union* that they had considered getting a goat at one point, but Brownsville already had too many goats.)

Peter was the star of the dual company and received the most press coverage. He came to the firehouse with Battalion Chief John J. Donohue around 1905, when the two companies first joined forces on Watkins Street. The men had originally intended to keep Peter indoors with the cats, but he soon grew restless remaining behind when his human and animal friends answered alarms. The parrot learned to fly down the stairs when the alarm bell rang and take his position on a rung of the ladder; if the men needed to raise the ladder on a call, he'd fly to another perch from which he could supervise the men in action. Not only did he attend fires, but he also took on the role of captain, barking out commands in both English and Yiddish "with an occasional mixture of profanity that at least would cause commotion if they came from the officer really in charge." "Wake up, you loafers! Get on the job! Beat it!" Captain

Peter would shriek when the alarm rang. One time, when the chief ordered a fireman to climb the ladder, Peter called out, "And be damn quick about it!"

Peter was also known to reprimand those civilians responsible for calling in a false alarm. "Now, even the birds are persecuting me," one upholstery store owner explained when Peter chastised him "so vehemently, with his features ruffled and his eyes glaring vindictively." The parrot didn't calm down until the man explained that a mattress had been on fire but some neighbors rushed in and put out the blaze before the firemen arrived.

When Peter wasn't responding to alarms, he enjoyed perching on the backs of the horses and taking naps on the men's cots. According to Chief Donohue, he also chewed tobacco and drank beer with the men and loved to brag about the burns and scars he received while performing his supervisory duties.

Like many mascots, Rocks the bull terrier did his job every day with little fanfare or press unless tragedy occurred. Rocks arrived at the double company in August 1907, a gift from a Brownsville resident who had "a soft spot in his heart for the fire laddies." He accompanied the truck to every fire and was a favorite in the neighborhood—everyone treated him with great respect as he dashed through the crowded streets at the heels of powerful horses. A few days before Christmas 1907, Rocks was leading the truck to a chimney fire, running at full speed and barking to encourage the horses to go faster. Forced to jump onto the sidewalk to escape the flying hoofs as the truck turned sharply onto Blake Avenue, he slipped on the pavement. Before he could recover, the front wheel passed over him. As the firemen continued to the fire, a citizen placed a blanket over Rocks's body. Captain James J. Mooney later carried the dog to the firehouse, where Rocks died in his arms. The men made a special box for Rocks and buried their canine friend in a neighboring yard.

Two months after Rocks died, the men were presented with a tiny fox terrier. They were still overcome with grief, but they tried to welcome this gifted dog, whom they named Nellie, into their home. The little puppy could do no more than bark at the horses, and the men were usually too preoccupied to pay attention to her, so she made her own fun. She tore apart their sheets and pillow-cases and hats and anything soft she could get her paws on. The men tried reprimanding and punishing her, but when they finally reached wits' end, they decided to give Nellie to the first farmer they met bound for some distant town on Long Island.

The first farmer to drive past the engine house was heading to Valley Stream with a cart filled with carrots. The men asked the farmer to take Nellie with him and drop her off at any corner. Seven days later, the little fox terrier appeared at the firehouse, looking tired and hungry. A *Brooklyn Times Union* reporter noted, "There was nothing to do but take the dog in, especially as her brown eyes pleaded so hard." No sooner did she settle in than the furniture "went through a siege of disaster."

The next farmer to pass by was heading to Mineola. Three weeks after Nellie's carriage ride to Mineola, she returned. The following day, the men sent her on her way with a coal-wagon driver headed to the Gowanus Canal. Nellie jumped off the wagon at Union Street and First Avenue and headed back to Engine 131. Frustrated and overwhelmed by the little dog's determination, the firemen were not kind to Nellie, but her pleading brown eyes appealed to the lieutenant. "Let her alone, boys," he said. "She can't help it because it's her nature to play with cloth caps and growl at furniture. If you fellows don't want the animal say so and I'll bring her home with me." The officer's words hit home with the men, who agreed to accept Nellie as their mascot.

Karma struck two hours later, when the fire bell rang. As a large crowd of children gathered around the engine house in anticipation, Nellie realized that something was expected of her. She quickly dispersed the crowd, allowing the men and the horses to respond without worrying about hitting a child. At that very moment, Nellie knew that her hard work had paid off. She had won the once-hardened hearts of the men of Engine 131.

Abie was just a career hobo dog living in the streets when he decided to get an honest job as a fire dog in 1908. He chose Engine 131, where he spent the next two years running with the horses. The little terrier was a natural fire dog who had no fear entering burning buildings with the men. One time he accompanied the men into a building on New Jersey Avenue, where he found a newborn puppy. The men allowed Abie to adopt the puppy, who also became a part of the growing happy family.

Like Rocks, Abie died in the line of duty, cutting his noble career short. On March 20, 1910, the company received a report of a three-year-old girl whose dress had caught fire at 423 Osborn Street. The girl's mother, Sarah Brown, was able to save her child and her home by tearing off the burning dress and forming a bucket brigade with some women to extinguish burning curtains. Mrs. Brown and her daughter were treated for their burns, but poor Abie was killed when the engine struck her while racing to the Browns' home. Driver Bill Dunn had thrown the horses onto their haunches to try to save the dog, but it all happened too fast. One of the men jumped off the engine to pick up Abie, who died in his arms a few minutes later. The press did not report on the reactions or comments of Peter and the other Engine 31 animals on the passing of Abie.

Engine 72: Jim and Rags

Rags was an orphaned, dirty-white terrier, but providence led her to the FDNY, where she became a popular fire dog attached to Engine 72 at 22 East Twelfth Street. Her best friend and stall mate was Jim, one of the company's three engine horses.

Like an unwanted newborn baby who has been dropped off at a firehouse under safe-haven laws, Rags arrived at the firehouse on January 4, 1905, when someone left her in the drawer of the watch deck. It had been a stormy night, and the men were out on a call during a heavy snowstorm. When they arrived back at quarters, one of the men heard the pup crying. After finding the tiny shaggy dog under a ragged coat, they promptly named her Rags and took her in as their mascot. Only three weeks old, Rags was too young to walk on her own or drink milk from a saucer. They purchased a baby's bottle at the drug store and, after a good deal of coaxing, bottle-fed the tiny puppy. Just as she finished the first bottle, another alarm came in. They put Rags back in the drawer, where she spent the next few weeks under the men's care.

Once Rags was able to get around on her own, she discovered the horse stalls. From then on, she slept in Jim's stall. Horse and dog became fast friends. Whenever Rags didn't wake up and leave the stall when an alarm came in, Jim would take her up by the back of the neck and run to the pole with her. When visitors came to the house to give the horses sugar, Rags would seize hold of them by their clothing and drag them toward Jim, so her favorite horse would get the first and largest lumps. If Jim dropped the sugar, Rags would retrieve the lump and place it where Jim could reach it. The other two horses got stuck with the smaller pieces.

Unlike Jim, who had to attend every fire call, Rags never went on calls. When she wasn't out visiting the families who fed her on Twelfth Street, her job was to stay behind on the watch desk until the company returned. No one could enter while the men were away unless they were wearing a uniform. Some of the telegraph boys in the neighborhood found out the little dog loved men in uniform, so they began visiting her when the company rolled. Rags must have thought they were good guys since they wore a uniform.

Rags and Jim's friendship was unfortunately short-lived. By 1910, Engine 72 would be the first company in the FDNY to replace its horses with a motorized, high-pressure hose wagon for use in those parts of the city equipped with new high-pressure fire hydrants. Six months after the new hose wagon arrived, Rags was run over by the vehicle and killed. Dora took her place, and the female Dalmatian learned to adapt to the motorized apparatus by running with it as far as she could before it got too far from her. If the men saw her getting too close when the hose wagon started out, someone would grab her and drag her onto the apparatus so she could ride along. But if no one grabbed her, she'd wait on the corner for another horse-drawn engine to come by. If a horse-drawn engine failed to appear, she'd head back home and wait for her family to return.

HISTORICAL HOOK

The decisive feature governing fire-fighting in all countries and under all conditions may in every case be summed up in the two words "water supply."

—FDNY Chief John Kenlon, *Fires and Fire-Fighters*, 1913

Although the five boroughs of New York City are surrounded by various bodies of water, getting adequate water to a fire was often a challenge for both the volunteer and paid firemen, whether they were relying on buckets, pumps, and cisterns or using steam-powered engines to draft water from small water mains that were of little use for great fires.

Prior to the introduction of the Croton Aqueduct distribution system in 1842 and before Manhattan had water mains and fire hydrants, the lower portion of the island had a network of wooden water pipes and fire plugs. The wooden pipes, which were essentially hollowed-out logs, were joined together and connected to about forty cisterns around Lower Manhattan and to reservoirs on Chambers Street and the Bowery at Thirteenth Street. This primitive water system, which was prone to rotting and leakage, was operated by the Manhattan Company, the corporate predecessor to JP Morgan Chase. The company maintained the mains from 1799, when its waterworks committee was empowered "to contract for as many pine logs as they think necessary for pipe and also for boring the same," until 1842. To access these mains, the volunteer firemen dug up cobblestones covering the logs and cut holes in them. Then they used fire plugs, which were like giant corks, to plug up the holes after the fire was out. The next time there was a fire in that vicinity, the men could remove the plug rather than cut another hole in the log.

The city's first primitive street hydrant (or fire plug, as the early hydrants were called), was placed in front of Mrs. Close's candy store on the northwest corner of Liberty and William Streets in 1808. The following year, an experimental wooden hydrant replaced the plug on the same corner. In 1817, the department's first modern hydrant went into service on Frankfort Street, in front of the home of George B. Smith, a volunteer fireman with Engine 12 who erected the hydrant at his own expense. Despite being in an elevated neighborhood, which would have provided some force for the water stream, the failure of the Manhattan Company to fulfill its obligations made the hydrant "practically useless," albeit it did earn Smith the title of "Father of the hydrant." Cast-iron pipes and hydrants began replacing the wooden mains in 1827, and hydrant companies—originally consisting of a foreman, an assistant, a clerk, and twenty men—were organized in 1831 to

Several of the Manhattan Company's wooden mains have been recovered, including a few sections of pipe that were found near the surface on Coenties Slip and on Beekman Street between Water and Pearl Streets. A small section is on display at the New York City Fire Museum. (Photograph by the author)

manage the hydrants and protect the existing plugs from damage. The city's four hydrant companies went out of service in about 1855.

In the early 1900s, as new skyscrapers began rapidly replacing the old two- and three-story buildings and disastrous fires of great magnitude were making the headlines, city planners realized that New York needed a high-pressure water system to supplement the Croton Aqueduct, which had supplied water to the city's hydrants since 1842. Between 1903 and 1908, four new high-pressure pumping stations—two in Manhattan, one in downtown Brooklyn, and one in Coney Island—were constructed to serve the city's new high-pressure zones. In Manhattan, both pumping stations were in one-story, fireproof buildings located close to tidal water, in a position where they could never be in the center of a conflagration. Connections were available to ensure access to adequate water in case problems arose with the Croton supply. About fifty-five miles of extra-heavy cast-iron main served Manhattan's high-pressure zone, which extended north from City

In 1910, Engine 72 was the recipient of the department's first motorized vehicle, a high-pressure double hose wagon. (Library of Congress, Prints & Photographs Division [LC-USZ62-119559])

Hall to Twenty-Eighth Street and from the North River (Hudson River) to Second Avenue. In 1909, the two pumping stations had a combined capacity of more than thirty thousand gallons per minute, which exceeded that of all the fire engines in the boroughs of Manhattan, the Bronx, and Brooklyn, working under normal conditions. By 1913, Manhattan had 2,066 hydrants (about one per acre), Brooklyn had 1,112 hydrants, and Coney Island's high-pressure district had 345 hydrants.

At the start of 1910, under Commissioner Rhinelander Waldo, the FDNY conducted its first practical test of a motor-driven apparatus in the city. The vehicle was a high-pressure double-hose wagon for use in the high-pressure zone. Engine 72 was the recipient of this first motorized vehicle. The wagon carried forty lengths of fifty-foot hose and could respond to an alarm at a rate of thirty miles an hour (twenty-five miles per hour in heavy snowfall). Responding to a first alarm from the box at the Twenty-Third Street Ferry took only five minutes, whereas it took Jim and the other horses more than fifteen minutes to cover the same distance. Ten men could ride on the wagon, and it had power enough to pull a load that would have required sixty-six horses.

By August 1910, the motorized wagon at Engine 72 had proved so successful that the FDNY contracted for more hose wagons of the same model. Engine 58 on West 115th Street received one, and Engine 20 on Lafayette

Street received two. Commissioner Waldo told the press that he was quite impressed with the high-pressure hose wagon, noting that it cost only $50 a year for its maintenance, as opposed to $900 a year to care for three horses.

Engine 21: Mike, Mack, and Mabel

In February 1909, a *New York Sun* reporter interviewed Lucy Fox, the young daughter of Captain George J. Fox of Engine 21. The company's beloved fire dog, Mike, had been killed a few days earlier while responding to an alarm from Ladder 2 on East Fiftieth Street. According to the report, Mike was visiting the ladder company when the call came in. As soon as the gong sounded, he instinctively got out in front of the horses. When they reached Second Avenue, he paused to see which way the horses were going to turn. As he turned to stay in front, he slipped on the pavement and went under the wheels. The driver picked up Mike's lifeless body and delivered him to Engine 21, then located at 216 East Fortieth Street. To honor the brave Dalmatian, the newspaper published happier memories of Mike and the engine company's happy family as told by eleven-year-old Lucy.

During the interview, Mack, the Panama monkey mascot of Engine 21, rested in Lucy's arms. Mabel, the male mascot cat whom Lucy had named, sat at her feet. Lucy told the reporter that Mack and Mabel were lonesome now that Mike was gone. They used to play with Mike, especially when he was trying to sleep. The dog loved sleeping on his back, and the cat and monkey would run around and jump all over him. Although Mike didn't always reciprocate in their playfulness, he would never nip at the other two animals or try to harm them in any way. Even when Mack nipped at the dog's legs the way Mike bit at the horses' legs when they didn't get into their harnesses quickly enough, Mike never hurt the monkey. Sure, he'd often chase the monkey up a rope and growl at him; but eventually Mack would come down the rope, and Mike would go back to sleep. "He wasn't mad at all," Lucy told the reporter. "He was only bluffing."

Although Mike spent most evenings sleeping—or trying to sleep—on the top floor of the engine house, he was a hobo dog at heart, spending his days traveling to Captain Fox's house on East Forty-Third Street or to other firehouses as far away as the Bronx. One of his favorite firehouses to visit was Engine 44 on Seventy-Fifth Street. Every time he made his way there, the men would call Engine 21 to let them know they had the dog. Then they'd put Mike outside, tell him to go back home, and shut the door. One time Mike made the mistake of visiting Engine 39, where Oakie was top fire dog. Mike didn't know that Oakie was a gift from Alfred Gwynne Vanderbilt. He picked a fight with Oakie, and to prove he was just as good as a Vanderbilt dog, he stayed at Engine 39 for a few days.

When Mike wasn't tramping around Manhattan, he was a true FDNY fire dog with a passion for two- and three-alarm fires. As soon as the alarm sounded, Mike would bound down the stairs three at a time and start biting at the horses' heels. When the doors opened, he'd run ahead of the horses, barking continuously and keeping off any stray dogs trying to participate. "You ought to have seen him when one of these street dogs got in the way," Lucy said. "Mike would bristle all up and start a fight and lick the other dog and catch up with 21 before she had got to the fire. Honest, it got so the rest of the dogs wouldn't get in the way at all—they knew all about Mike."

Lucy admitted that she was still too young to go to fires, but she knew for certain that Mike always stuck close to her father when the men entered a building. "Papa is captain and goes ahead, you know. Well, Mike used to stay right by Papa and when he saw Papa start into a place, he would be right behind him. Poor Mike! His eyes were all red from being in the smoke, you know, and he had some hair burned off, but he was too quick to get much hurt. Once or twice, he was in a building when the roof came through, but he heard it first and came out on the dead run."

One of Mike's other favorite activities was singing. According to Lucy, whenever anyone in the firehouse started playing a harmonica or whistling, Mike would sit up on his hind legs and sing. "The men in the house called Mike the barytone—that means some sort of singer," Lucy explained. "He really sang awfully well—for a dog, of course—but the men in the house would laugh at him. But that didn't make any difference with Mike—he just went up on his hind legs and sang just the same, and really you ought to have heard him sing!"

Asked about the company's plans to honor Mike, Lucy said the men were planning a fine funeral for the dog. "Papa hasn't made up his mind yet about it, but we're going to have one and all the men that can get off will be there and we will have flowers and everything. And Mack and Mabel will be there too. I am going to make some of the men carry them if we have to go far. I'd just as soon carry Mack; he don't weigh much. But Mabel, he's getting heavy."

Shortly after Mike's passing, the company got another dog, whom they named Mike II. Mack the monkey helped raised the new pup, but Mike II died of unknown causes. Mack also took ill; perhaps his heart broke after losing his two canine chums. Mrs. Sarah Pope, the widow of Fireman John Pope (who died in the line of duty) and a matron for the company, tried to nurse the monkey back to health, but he couldn't hang on. He died sometime prior to December 1910.

Incidentally, in December 1910, Mrs. Pope became the first woman in the history of the FDNY to be honored with a "long and faithful service decoration." The members of Engine 21 presented her with a department Maltese cross in solid gold in commemoration of her service as a matron for twenty years.

Ladder 52: Sport and Pete

Sport was a fire dog who loved to sing and do backward somersaults. Pete was an old bay horse who loved to eat apples. The two friends shared a home in the two-story brick and brownstone firehouse of Ladder 52 at 894 Bedford Avenue in Brooklyn.

Sport wandered into the circa-1891 firehouse in 1905. Cold, hungry, and bedraggled, the mud-covered, brown-and-white-spotted mutt of about nine months old showed every sign of living a hard life on the streets. Driver James J. "Crackerjack" Murphy took pity on the puppy and fed him leftovers from his breakfast. All the firemen loved the little dog, but Sport chose to adopt Murphy as his master. The men voted to adopt Sport as the mascot of their company so they all could share him.

Soon after Sport's arrival, Murphy discovered his natural talents for singing. According to the *Brooklyn Times Union*, Sport could "sing a solo or join in a duet like an operatic star—almost." Master and dog would sing together, Sport sitting on his hind legs on a chair, throwing his head back, and swelling out his throat to hit the high notes. Like every professional, Sport would look for an encore and continue singing if his audience seemed pleased. He also sat up and sang every time the alarm sounded.

One of Sport's best friends was Pete, the company's center horse, who was described as an "old-timer" at the firehouse. After every fire, Sport would give Pete a kiss and tease him by hanging on his bridle. Pete loved apples, and Sport would do whatever it took to ensure that his friend received his fair share of them. One day while dining at the home of Fireman Michael Roach, Sport received an apple. The dog didn't eat the fruit but watched it carefully and growled if anyone attempted to take it from him. When it was time to go back to the firehouse, Sport carried the apple carefully in his mouth and gave it to his equine buddy.

In addition to singing and doing somersaults, one of Sport's greatest tricks was climbing ladders. He once climbed a series of three ladders at a fire—thirty, eighteen, and twenty-two feet high—but he had to be carried back down. In Murphy's opinion, Sport was the "greatest thing in the United States"—even greater than President Theodore Roosevelt.

Engine 109: Spot and Big Tom

Four blocks to the west of Ladder 52 was the home of Engine 109 at 159 Taaffe Place. This company had a mutt named Spot who had also lived a hard life prior to joining the FDNY. Spot was best friends with Big Tom, one of the company's most popular horses in 1908.

Spot joined the company in 1907, after slinking into the firehouse with his back hunched and his tail between his legs. The men didn't think the dog would amount to anything, but he did have a spot of coach dog in him, and this appealed to the driver. Feeling sorry for him, the men adopted him as their company mascot. (One fireman told the *Brooklyn Citizen*, "He looks as if he didn't amount to shooks, but he's been hanging 'round; s'pose we adopt him.") They assumed that his former master had been cruel or that he had experienced a frightening incident and that all he needed was some time and initiative to get over his fears.

Spot was terrified at first—whenever the alarm sounded, he'd tremble and hide—but he loved the horses and gave them tons of attention, which won the hearts of the firemen. Although Spot was afraid of any stray dog that passed by, he felt safe with his equine friends. When a neighborhood canine bully tried to enter his territory one time, Spot ran into Big Tom's stall. The bully then made the mistake of following Spot into the stall. Big Tom showed his teeth and struck out with his front hoof. The other dog turned on Big Tom, which incited Spot to protect the horse as a mother bear would defend her cubs: Spot threw himself on the invader and gave him such a licking that the dog's owner had to take him to the animal hospital. Spot's victory gave him the courage of a lion, and from then on, after word got around, he was the terror of all the dogs in the neighborhood. No dog ever dared to come near the firehouse when Spot was around.

Spot's crowning glory came during a fire in a tenement building at 81 Taaffe Place in October 1908, which had started in the cellar and spread up the dumbwaiter shaft to the third floor. According to a fireman named Billy, all the rooms and corridors were filled with smoke, but everyone thought that the tenants had gotten out safely. Spot kept barking frantically and tugging at Billy's coat, dragging him toward the stairs. Billy followed the dog's lead and stumbled over Mrs. Leonard Welman and her six-year-old son, Eddie, who were both semiconscious in their third-floor apartment. Billy was able to save the mother and son, but he refused to take credit for the heroic act. "Spot did it," he told the press. That night, Spot was rewarded with a shower bath, a large round of congratulations, and a medal.

Engine 107: Whiskers and Minnie

In 1911, Engine 107 was one of the largest companies in the FDNY. Although most engine and ladder companies at this time had about twelve or fourteen members, respectively, Engine 107 had nineteen members. The company was this size because it was a high-pressure company comprising a hose wagon and an engine equipped to connect to the new high-pressure hydrants in downtown Brooklyn. Engine 107 occupied a circa-1865 firehouse at 245 Pearl Street, between Concord and Tillary Streets (now Concord Village). This firehouse, described in 1892 as "an old but a substantial three-story brick building," had previously been home to Volunteer Engine 7 of Brooklyn's volunteer fire department. When Engine 7 was established under the paid Brooklyn Fire Department in September 1869, many of the men from the volunteer company transferred over. In addition to the nineteen firemen, led by Battalion Chief Henry P. Kirk and Captain George O'Shea, the company had seven horses in 1911: Old Bill and Henry K. (both driven by Chief Kirk), Ben Mack, Willard, Dynamo, Walnut B., and Ago. Whiskers the Scottish terrier and Minnie the cat completed the family.

Whiskers joined the company in 1909, after deciding that life as a fire dog was the best option for a stray dog always on the run from dog catchers. Whiskers was reportedly the only fire dog in the FDNY capable of climbing a fire escape, and he was invaluable for keeping away tramps, stray cats, and other dogs. He was also skilled at making sure the men responded quickly to every alarm. Whenever a nighttime alarm sounded, Whiskers would run upstairs and jump on the men's beds to wake everyone up. Then he'd run back downstairs to snap and bark at any horse not responding fast enough to meet his satisfaction. Although he'd only follow the engine for a block to urge the horses to go faster, he faithfully guarded the firehouse until the men and horses returned.

Minnie was the queen of the firehouse, having joined the company in 1905. The black cat was in mourning on the day a reporter from the *Brooklyn Citizen* visited the firehouse in 1911. Several months earlier, she had given birth to one kitten. The kitten, named

Tom, "was her pride, her joy, her all." But sadly, Whiskers was not paying attention to Tom when the little kitten walked in front of the apparatus as the alarms began sounding. The engine ran over Tom, killing him instantly. As the men buried Tom behind their firehouse, Minnie "tearfully watched the last rites, which were very impressive," according to the members of the company.

Four years later, in December 1915, Whiskers's life ended when he slipped under the wheels of the heavy engine while responding to a fire at 83 Plymouth Street. Many neighborhood children came to pay their last respects to the faithful fire dog. The members were undecided at the time whether to bury Whiskers with honors or have him stuffed, as was popular during this period.

Ladder 105: Jack and Tom

Another popular fire cat and dog duo of Brooklyn was a young Dalmatian named Jack and an elderly gray tiger cat named Tom, attached to Ladder 105 at 648 Pacific Street. Jack joined the department well after Tom did, in 1931, when he was a "chubby, weak-kneed puppy." He immediately stirred up trouble for the firemen with the local merchants—the dog was a hoarder with a penchant for canned vegetables, ketchup bottles, toilet-paper rolls, and fresh produce. He also assumed that all those items at the neighborhood produce stands or at the Great Atlantic & Pacific Tea Co. at Dean Street and Sixth Avenue were just for him. He'd chow down as much swiped produce as he could get away with, and then he'd steal a few bunches of asparagus or radishes for his human pals. Sometimes he'd also grab a few cans of food to store in his favorite corner of the firehouse. When the storekeepers threatened to press charges, Captain Michael McCaffery could hardly believe that the dog was a thief—until he found a pile of canned vegetables and toilet-paper rolls in Jack's corner. The men soon realized that their dog was just trying to be useful. They started sending him to the White Horse Tavern with a list tied to his collar; the proprietor would make the sandwiches listed on the note, put them in a bag, and give them to Jack to bring to quarters.

The press described Jack as a perfect gentleman who not only attended fires but also escorted Tom to the alarms. Both cat and dog would wait their turn to mount the truck, and then they'd share a coat, with Jack acting as a bolster for Tom in wintry weather. Although Tom stayed outside with the apparatus, Jack would enter burning buildings with the firemen. If ever a fireman made a rescue with Jack at his heels, Jack always received credit—he was credited with twenty-two rescues during his career. Jack also received a medal from the SPCA for saving the life of child who had been hanging out in the driveway when an alarm came in. The little boy "probably would have been bowled over" had Jack not dashed out and pushed him aside.

At the firehouse, the two mascots shared almost everything, save for the dog bones, which the firemen gave Jack to reward him for his fine behavior, and the lap of Fireman George Callahan, which was Tom's domain. In fact, Jack and Tom were practically inseparable until May 1933, when a hit-and-run driver struck Jack and left him in the gutter. The men rushed Jack to the Ellin Prince Speyer Animal Hospital, where the vets treated him for two broken legs. Tom moped about the firehouse while his pal was away receiving extended treatment at the Bideawee Home and then convalescing at the home of Fireman Arthur Sartain. The cat didn't cheer up until his friend returned home. Asked about the hit-and-run driver who almost killed the company's dog, Captain McCaffery said angrily, "The guy who did that is one of those thugs who's so low he can walk underneath a flivver without bending his knees and on stilts, wearing a high hat."

In April 1934, the cat and dog were separated again when Jack landed in the Brooklyn SPCA shelter after an attendant picked him up in Prospect Park on a no-license charge. Apparently, Jack was wearing his collar with a plate inscribed with the words "United Veteran Uniformed Firemen's Association," but he had lost his license tag a few days earlier. The attendant, Thomas Nielson, noticed that Jack acted up whenever a fire engine passed the shelter. Nielson began calling Brooklyn fire companies to see who would claim him. A few days later, Jack was back with his friends at Ladder 105 and ready for action—with the lady dogs, that is. As Captain McCaffery told a reporter for the *Brooklyn Times Union*, "Jack is a Lothario and his official position in the truck quarters seems to give him prestige with dogs of the opposite sex." Although Jack's days of running to fires more than a few blocks away were over, Tom didn't seem to mind. He was just ecstatic to have his best friend back home where he belonged.

Sadly, the two best friends had to separate for good about a month later, when Fireman Sartain retired to a new home in Oakland Beach, Rhode Island, taking the dog with him. Callahan went to visit Jack and Sartain, and upon his return, he told the *Daily News*, "Believe it or not, Jack has adopted the volunteer fire company at Oakland Beach as his very own. The dog just can't get the smell of smoke out of his hair."

Engine 8: Mike, Tom, and Jerry

Mike was no ordinary fire dog. In fact, he was no ordinary Dalmatian. Not only did he take home the first blue ribbon ever awarded to a fire department Dalmatian at the Westminster Kennel Club show at Madison Square Garden in 1910, but he was also the son of Oakie and Bess, two of the most famous fire dogs in the history of the FDNY. Mike was no doubt destined for greatness as a full-blooded FDNY fire dog.

One of several noble pups born in 1908, Mike partnered with Driver David M. Lynx. Shortly after Mike was old enough to start training for his position, the department transferred Bess to a quieter station house to recover from injuries she had sustained from running into burning buildings. As Bess no longer needed her Third Avenue surface-rail pass, Lynx escorted Mike to the office of Receiver Frederick Wallington Whitridge to see if he would transfer Bess's pass to her son.

Now, Mike was not one for acknowledging anyone who wasn't wearing a fireman's uniform. But according to Lynx, he jumped right up on Whitridge's lap and smiled at him "just like a politician asking for a favor." Although the meeting left Whitridge covered in mud and dog hairs, he gave Lynx permission to transfer the pass to

Mike, saying, "It's the only pass of the kind ever issued by the road, and if Mike is willing to take all the risks and not sue the company in case of accident, I guess we'll transfer the pass to him."

The special pass was engraved on a silver plate attached to Mike's collar, which also held a tiny brass fire helmet. All the conductors received instructions to honor this pass, which allowed the fire dog to ride on the front platform of all Third Avenue cars. Mike used the pass to go home with one of the men for dinner or to visit other fire companies on the Upper East Side of Manhattan. According to one newspaper, he often rode the car on his own and went wherever his appetite led him. When he reached his destination, he'd trot to the rear of the platform, bark once and wag his tail, and wait for the conductor to stop the car and let him off. Sometimes he'd also catch a streetcar to return to the engine house if he was too lazy to walk home after a fire.

The national press often celebrated the large happy family at Engine 8. In addition to Mike, who received the most publicity due to his status, the family comprised a large gray horse named Jerry, a black cat named Tom, three other horses named President, Pat, and Miguel, and three turtles. Although Mike was friendly with President and would often lick the horse's lips after President had a drink of water, it was Mike, Tom, and Jerry who were inseparable and loved doing everything together. Passersby often laughed at Jerry, who enjoyed rolling in the street during his afternoon exercises while Mike and Tom watched with delight. The trio also loved sugar, and there were always plenty of neighborhood children around to supply them with the treat. Jerry also reportedly knew that the engine driver, Frank Leonard, kept lumps of sugar in his coat pocket. He'd poke his nose in the pocket and help himself to a few lumps for himself and his two friends.

At night, the three animals always slept in Jerry's stall. Mike would put his head on Jerry's neck, and Tom slept on Jerry's back. Jerry fussed over his small friends in the stall and would always lie down carefully so as not to crush them. If an alarm came in at night, Tom would slide off Jerry, jump out of the way, and supervise the harnessing of the horses. (Sometimes, the men would have to pull Tom off Jerry's back when the cat was in a deep sleep.) Then he'd go back inside for another catnap until his friends came home. One time, Tom tried to ride on Jerry's back as he raced to a fire. He held on for a few seconds but fell to the ground while the horses were turning a corner. He wasn't badly hurt, but after that episode, he had no further ambition to respond to fire calls.

Mike knew that his chief duty in life was to be a fire dog, and he took his job seriously. As soon as the gong sounded, he'd jump up and down in excitement as Jerry, Pat, and Miguel got into their harnesses. Then he'd dash out of the stall and bark for the rest of the company to hurry and get ready to roll. Sometimes he'd run two or three blocks ahead of the engine, warning away pedestrians and vehicular traffic by barking and snapping. Once at the fire scene, Mike would either stand next to Jerry or run into the buildings with the firemen, just as his mother had done. Only once during his active years of duty did Mike miss a fire call—but he had the best excuse. According to the *New-York Tribune*, on June 7, 1913, Tom was dozing under the engine when an alarm came in. He was just about to be crushed under the wheels when Mike grabbed him by the neck and dragged the cat out of harm's way. One of Mike's legs was crushed. Although the men originally thought that he'd lose the leg, he eventually healed enough to stay on duty.

On another occasion, Mike came to the rescue of his friend Jerry. The dog must have sensed that Jerry was about to lose his job when he noticed that the horse was falling asleep on the scene. Jerry would run fast enough to the fire, but as soon as the engine was in operation and Lynx threw a blanket over the horses, Jerry would drop down in the gutter in his harness, roll on his side, and fall fast asleep before Lynx and Fireman Dennis McNamara could come around to get him up. Even Captain Joseph C. Donovan didn't know what to do about Jerry's sleeping sickness, but Mike had an idea. For the next few nights, the dog remained outside with the horses and began nipping Jerry on the knees as soon as he started to kneel. Sometimes he'd nip him ten times in half an hour; but eventually the trick worked, and Jerry stopped falling asleep on the job.

In addition to Mike, Tom, and Jerry, Engine 8 also had three turtles. Nosey, the oldest and largest of the turtles, had joined the fire service fifty-five years earlier during the volunteer era, even before Engine 8 organized in the Relief Hose 51 firehouse in 1865. According to Captain Donovan, the turtle got his name for always nosing around the horse stalls and the fire engine. On more than one occasion, the men had to haul him out from under the wheels before responding to a call, wasting precious seconds from their response time. To celebrate Nosey's anniversary with the company, the men held a celebration in the rear yard of the engine house. They relieved Jerry and Mike from duty for the day and encouraged them to spend their time at the party. Tom and the other turtles also received invitations to celebrate. The firemen said that the event "gave the old shell-backed veteran something to remember as long as he lives."

Although Jerry and Tom were his best fire department pals, Mike's best canine friend was his next-door neighbor, Jerry, an ordinary mutt attached to what was then the Twenty-Ninth Police Precinct (present-day Seventh Precinct) at 163 East Fifty-First Street. Jerry arrived at the police station on March 4, 1909, with a woman who had found him outside starving and shivering. Captain John J. Lantry accepted the dog, and the men named him Jerry in honor of the station's doorman (they were originally going to call him Bill Taft in honor of President William Taft's inauguration that day, but the vote went to Jerry).

One of the dogs' favorite activities was taking the ferryboat from East Fifty-Third Street to Blackwell's Island (now Roosevelt Island). If it was warm, they'd go swimming to cool off. Sometimes they would stay there for two or three days, but they always returned to their respective stations. When it came to the job, though, Mike and Jerry were all business. Jerry would accompany the policemen on patrol or ride along with the patrol wagon that picked up the prisoners for night court, and Mike would ride along with the fire engines. The two never switched jobs or mixed pleasure with business.

On March 15, 1914, Lieutenant Alonzo Weiss (aka Wise), the master of Bess, told a reporter that he hoped the Engine 8 driver would see that Mike got a comfortable retirement home after motorized vehicles replaced the horses. "Any son of Bessie and

Oakie is worth that at least," he said. Sadly, Mike never lived to see the horses retire. Just nine months later, on December 4, 1914, the engine struck Mike while responding to a small fire at Fifty-Seventh Street and Park Avenue. His hind legs were crushed, giving the men no other option but to humanely put him down.

Engine 8 would acquire several more popular Dalmatians who captured the media's attention from the 1920s to the early 1940s, but Mike's passing marked the end of a romantic era for the FDNY. The motorization of the fire department was well on its way—and happy families were on their way out.

HISTORICAL HOOK

In February 1910, Mike and his mother Bess appeared at the annual bench show of the Westminster Kennel Club at Madison Square Garden. Mike, exhibited by Driver Lynx, took the first-place blue ribbon for best-looking dog in the class, and Bess, exhibited by Fireman Weiss of Engine 39, took second place. There were only two other FDNY dogs in the running that year, which was the second year the fire department Dalmatians were invited to take part in the annual show.

Due to a rule change, the FDNY Dalmatian event did not take place again until 1941, when the fire-dog contest was one of two extra events that the Westminster Kennel Club added to provide something special for "those who are not so much interested in the fine points of show competition as they are in any and all dogs." That year twenty-five firehouse Dalmatians—primarily from Brooklyn and Queens—competed with their masters for three trophies awarded for smartness, obedience, and alertness. These choice dogs had been selected from eighty Dalmatians in a preliminary competition, which caused considerable rivalry around the firehouses.

In the months preceding the show, as the *New York Daily News* detailed, "The black-and-white bow-wows got the works. Their beautifying rivaled a glamor gal's. Those with hefty figgers were dished out less food. They were washed and brushed like never before in their careers. They were walked miles for better streamlining. Their not-so-dainty nails were manicured. Some even got tips from their anxious masters on proper show posture."

King, the singing Dalmatian of Engine 311 in Queens, took first place with his master, Fireman George F. Donnelly. King, who began his career with Engine 302 in 1938, lived with the Donnelly family and received his daily workouts from ten-year-old James Donnelly, who classified King as "not a bad looking dog." Although King did not so much howl or hum a single bar for the judges, his good looks and behavior earned him the silver cup. Bonnie, handled by Fireman Richard Garrett of Ladder 158 in Queens, took second place, and Patches, owned by Fireman Joseph Mechler of Ladder 142 in Queens, came in third. Specky of Brooklyn's Ladder 107 received an honorable mention for never missing a fire during her career.

The following year, Fire Commissioner Patrick Walsh organized an FDNY Dalmatian dog show in the yard of the department's School of Instruction on East Sixty-Eighth Street. The purpose of the show was to select the department's best Dalmatians for the Westminster Kennel Club Show. On February 12, 1942, the chosen Dalmatians participated in a parade featuring the large Fire Department Band led by Chief George Briegel, the staff of the Fire Department School of Instruction, and members of the Firemen's Auxiliary. Joseph Gould Remick, the governor of the New York Stock Exchange, and Dr. Samuel Milbank were the two judges for the firehouse dogs. Smokey, owned by Fireman William Smith of Manhattan's Ladder 7, edged out King to win the first-place trophy. One uniformed reporter for the *New York Daily News* snidely commented that "probably most of the other 18 'fire dogs' were named Smokey, too."

The Brooklyn Kennel Club gave the Dalmatians another chance to shine at its annual show in December 1949 and again during a special exhibition in December 1950. In 1949, only 7 of the 250 companies invited to participate entered the competition. Representing Brooklyn were Spanner of Engine 228, handled by Fireman George A. Ouchterloney; Luke of Engine 250, shown by Fireman Alfred A. Fredholm; and Queenie of Engine 249, exhibited by Fireman Joseph F. Fessler. Manhattan's two contenders were Prince of Ladder 5, shown by Fireman Leonard Smith; and Bess of Engine 36, with Fireman Roland Kahan. Speck and his handler, Fireman Harry P. McConville of Engine 50, represented the Bronx; and Staten Island was represented by Prince and his handler, Fireman George F. Groce of Engine 163. The press did not report on the winners of either event.

═══

6

Lifesaving Horses and Mascots

When Battalion Chief James Devanny's horse saved the life of a child in September 1905, the public attributed the remarkable act to "just good common sense." Perhaps the *New York Times* should have suggested that it was good horse sense, or rather, good fire-horse sense, that saved the boy's life.

According to the story, the chief was driving up Ninth Avenue at a gallop in response to an alarm when a four-year-old boy stepped out from the sidewalk in front of the rapidly approaching buggy. John Monihan, the driver, didn't see the boy until the horse was about four feet from him. At such short distance, there was no time for Monihan to pull the horse up or pull him to the right or left. All he could do was shout at the boy and hope for divine intervention. The horse took the wheel, so to speak, and leapt clear over the boy. Although the wheels of the chief's buggy passed dangerously close to the child, the boy dropped to the ground at the same time the horse jumped, avoiding injury. Chief Devanny told the press that his lifesaving horse would get extra oats and several lumps of sugar before bedtime.

Chief Devanny's horse was fortunate in that he did not get hurt when he made this sudden and dangerous move to leap over the child. Split-second decisions involving pedestrians and galloping fire horses were a common occurrence in Old New York, and often the horse suffered a career- or life-ending injury. Even though chief's horse didn't intentionally enter this life-or-death situation, he took a substantial risk to save a child—and he deserved every extra lump of sugar he got that night.

Just as fire horses did not receive any training for avoiding collisions with humans, lifesaving fire dogs were not trained to rescue people from burning buildings. A good fire dog had an instinctive desire to save not only the humans who were close to him or her but also any human—or animal—in distress. Fire-dog rescues were typically intentional rescues—those in which the dog entered a burning building because he could smell trouble. In addition to having great noses, fire dogs reportedly had the advantage over the firemen with regard to height. One news article published in 1911 suggested that dogs were especially suited for the hero role because they were closer to the ground and could thus stand more smoke than the firemen could. In a time when there was no self-contained breathing apparatus and firemen were called "smoke eaters" for good reason, this ability to spend more time in a burning building and ascend to upper floors allowed the dogs to rescue those victims who may have otherwise lost their lives.

Oftentimes the victims were babies or children, but many FDNY canine heroes saved the lives of their two-legged partners. Others came to the rescue of their natural enemy: civilian cats. Fire horses could also be lifesavers, although like Chief Devanny's horse, they were more likely to be unintentional heroes forced to make last-minute decisions. Black Beauty of Engine 131 in Brooklyn, for example, spread his legs at the last second after a child had fallen in front of the oncoming engine. Retired FDNY fire horse Dan was also an unintentional lifesaver, albeit his heroic deed lasted more than five years: Dan was one of many New York horses who produced the equine tetanus serum used to save thousands of soldiers during World War I.

Engine 203: Chief

In 1936, Chief, the veteran fire dog of Brooklyn's Engine 203, won medals of honor for heroism from the New York Women's League for Animals and the ASPCA. *Dog World Magazine* also awarded him with an international diploma of honor and inducted him in the Dog World Canine Hall of Honor for saving several lives. He also won an Animal Hero Medal from the New York Anti-Vivisection Society for his "heroism, intelligence and loyalty." Although he despised all the neighborhood cats, Chief received all these accolades for saving felines. According to *Dog World Magazine*, Chief's actions to save cats' lives were "unparalleled in canine history."

Taken in as a stray one winter night in 1929, when the five-year-old black-and-tan mutt walked into the station and curled up near a steam pipe, Chief served ten years with Engine 203 at 533 Hicks Street. During his years of service, Chief demonstrated many acts of bravery and heroism. He rode with the company to every fire and was always the first to leap off the engine and run into a building to scout for victims. He even had his own special-made leather turnout coat, helmet, and raincoat. Chief could recognize all the bells and signals, and he knew exactly which signal meant that his company was responding to a call (he never made a mistake). On fire scenes, Chief would supervise the firemen and alert them if he knew something was wrong. Having mastered climbing the seventy-five-foot extension ladder, he'd run up the ladder if that's what it took to warn his fellow firemen.

Described as "part hound, part Flatbush terrier, but every inch a hero," the brave fire dog always barked until his two-legged partners responded whenever he found a victim in need of help. Like a true firefighter and not a mere fire buff, Chief received numerous injuries from broken glass and falling debris, burns from scalding water, and bruises from falling off the fire engine—he was even run over twice (once by a chief's car and once by a passenger car). But he also had fun times, especially when he got to toll the bell on the engine by working the rope with his paws or visit with one of the firemen in his home on Long Island during summer months.

One of Chief's many heroic rescues took place during a small blaze at a tenement house in which the fire escape had broken. Firemen Schenck and Carlton had fallen into a smoke-filled basement, but no one saw the accident happen. Chief didn't see it either, but he could sense trouble. Barking furiously, he dashed into the building. Recognizing the barking command, the firemen followed Chief into the basement, where they found Schenck and Carlton lying unconscious. Chief spent a month in the animal hospital after this successful rescue.

Chief was twelve years old and a six-year veteran with the FDNY when he made his eighth heroic rescue, on February 2, 1935. On that day, he put his disdain for felines aside to do his duty. Using his self-imposed skills to search every building for victims, Chief was able to save two kittens in desperate need of a hero. According to the press, Engine 203 had responded to a reported structure fire at a three-story building at 161 Union Street. The building had a stationery and cigar store owned by Mrs. Escole on the ground floor and apartments on the upper floors. Upon the company's arrival, neighbors told the men that the building was empty and everyone had made it out safely. Chief ignored the humans. Trusting his nose, he made a dash for the burning basement. Singed and nearly overcome by smoke, he emerged from the basement four minutes later with one of Mrs. Escole's kittens in his mouth. He laid the feline survivor at the feet of Battalion Chief John G. Pfann. He then gave a short warning bark and ran back into the basement. Once again, he came back to the street carrying another kitten in his mouth. He refused medical attention until he had licked the kittens clean. Then he watched as a firefighter placed them inside a large, flannel-lined fireman's hat. Turning toward the amazed bystanders, the fireman said, "He's the greatest bit of dog-flesh you people ever saw. He's been a hero many times before. He's got no pedigree, but he sure is a thoroughbred." Knowing that the kittens were safe, Chief reported to the department surgeon for treatment. When the men returned to the firehouse, they rewarded him with a large, marrow-filled meat bone. He spent more than a week in the animal hospital for his extensive burns.

The preserved mount of Chief, the lifesaving mascot of Engine 203, is on display at the New York City Fire Museum. (Photograph provided courtesy of the New York City Fire Museum)

Our cat-saving hero came through one more time on November 10, 1936, when a fire broke out in the basement of a four-story brick apartment building at 308 Hicks Street. It quickly spread to the upper floors and roof through a dumbwaiter shaft. Ten people were in the building when seventeen-year-old Adela Gomez ran screaming into the hallway on the second floor after smelling smoke. Sixteen-year-old John Bermudez was with his mother, sister, brother, sister-in-law, and baby nephew in their top-floor apartment when they heard the commotion. As the family started descending the stairs, John noticed a stray cat running in the opposite direction toward the top floor. The boy was determined to save the cat. His mother protested, but the teenager darted upstairs. During a search of the building, the men of Engine 203 and Ladder 118 found John unconscious on the stairway between the third and fourth floors. As they were leaving the building with the boy, Chief emerged from a hole in the roof. He was a bit singed and carrying the cat in his jaws.

"You won't believe it," said Deputy Fire Chief David Kidney, "but [Chief] came out of the smoke holding the cat by the nape of the neck with his jaws." The cat had lost a few of its nine lives, but it survived. The men of Rescue Squad 2 tried to revive John for an hour, but the young would-be hero did not make it. Mrs. Ambrosio Lorenzo, wife of the building's owner, told the press that the cat was just a stray that had wandered into the house one day. "It was no one's particular pet," she said, "although John was very fond of it."

Although Chief was a sixteen-year-old senior citizen in 1939, he probably had a few more good years left as an active fire dog when his life abruptly ended on November 9. While playing in front of the firehouse, Chief was struck by a hit-and-run driver. People in the street called out for help, and a group of children followed the fire dog into the firehouse and told Lieutenant Matthew F. Rogers that the car had kept going. Instead of waiting for help to come, Chief dragged himself back inside and tried to jump up on the engine seat. Missing the seat, he landed on the running board, where he curled up and died. In commemoration of Chief's many acts of bravery and heroism, the members of Engine 203 hired a taxidermist to mount their treasured fire-dog mascot. They kept him in a place of honor on a pedestal with all his medals at the firehouse until the company disbanded in 1974. The mount is now on display at the New York City Fire Museum.

Engine 225 and Engine 36: Pansy and Happy

Chief was not the only FDNY fire dog who received rewards for saving cats. A few years before Chief made his saves, Pansy of Engine 225 at 657 Liberty Avenue in Brooklyn received accolades for making her first rescue in May 1931—she raced into a burning building and chased out a cat. Although Pansy officially belonged to Police Emergency Squad 14 attached to the Liberty Avenue police station (the men had found her almost dead the previous summer and used an oxygen tank to revive her), the dog was a fire buff who answered all alarms with the nearby firehouse. Following the cat rescue, Special Agent George J. Salzer of the SPCA presented Captain John H. Doherty with a free license for Pansy. The firemen told the press, "When there are more and better rescues to be made, Pansy will make them."

Another cat-saving hero was Happy, attached to Engine 36 at 1849 Park Avenue in Manhattan two decades earlier. On February 26, 1910, the company responded to a fire on the top floor of a tenement building at 2162 Fifth Avenue. During the fire, caused by an overturned oil lamp, Happy ran into the building with the firemen. He seized a cat by the nape of its neck and carried it outside. Hundreds of people cheered when the dog placed the cat on the sidewalk. According to the men, the cat had protested vigorously at first and even scratched Happy on the nose, but the dog overlooked this indignity as he performed his duties. Back at headquarters, Happy refused to confirm the scratching part of the story. The cat did not confirm or deny overturning the lamp.

One year later, in December 1911, when Happy was now a veteran with six years in the department, he performed a dramatic rescue at Adolph Finkenberg's furniture warehouse at 2287 Third Avenue in Harlem. This time, Happy didn't run into the building with the firemen—he ran up the building. While standing near a hose cart, the dog heard Fireman Thomas Norton's cry for help. Norton and two other firefighters had been caught in a backdraft in the rear of the third floor and were forced to flee. The smoke was so dense that they lost their way back to the window where they had raised an extension ladder.

To the astonishment of the spectators, Happy darted to the ladder, gave a few short yelps, and began to climb as fast as he could. Firemen on the street "stopped to marvel at the dog's agility and to wonder why he should risk his life by the dizzy climb." Higher and higher he scrambled, until he reached the open window. As he began barking furiously, a small breeze blew the thick smoke away, allowing the people on the street to see the forms of three firemen framed in the window, fighting for air. Several firemen ran up the stairs and helped the men make their way down. According to published reports, Happy had taught himself how to climb ladders and even put on a demonstration that shocked Chief Edward Croker. The men had always considered it just a good trick, but Happy no doubt inherently knew that someday the trick would save a few lives.

HISTORICAL HOOK

On May 29, 1897, the pet cat of Mr. and Mrs. Patrick W. Gallagher at 237 West Sixtieth Street got into an altercation with a stray cat that had entered through an open window. The cats began chasing each other around a table, on which stood a kerosene lamp. One cat jumped on the table, overturning the lamp. The lamp exploded, spreading flames across the floor. One of the cats caught fire and began running around the room before jumping out a window. As smoke filled the hallway, the residents of the tenement building started rushing out, causing chaos that reporters detailed in a manner one would now consider inappropriate. According to a *New York Sun* reporter, Mrs. Johnson and Mrs. McIlvaney, who lived in the back rooms behind the Gallaghers, tried to make it down the stairs at the same time. Both women were "stout and short of breath," and they became wedged together on the first-floor landing. The two women began engaging in their own cat fight, both refusing—or unable—to budge. Finally, "after some difficulty," the firemen were able to separate the women. In the end, the fire caused only about $100 worth of damage. As the *New York Times* reported, "The only other damage was to the tempers of Mrs. Johnson and Mrs. McIlvaney."

Prior to the age of electricity, newspaper stories with headlines such as "Cats Set a House Afire" and "Playful Dog Overturned Lamp" were a dime a dozen. Animals occupied a prominent place in the annals of the FDNY, with dogs, cats, horses, mice, and even pet fish listed as the direct or indirect cause of many fires in the city. One of the most common causes of fires was an overturned kerosene lamp, courtesy of the household pet. Arsonists also used cats and dogs to set lamp-based fires by tying a cat's tail to a lamp and setting the feline free or tying a piece of meat directly over a lamp and releasing a hungry dog into the room. Rats and mice often nibbled the matches used to light these lamps—rodents were so notorious for their connection with fires that they were reportedly listed as "incendiaries" in official reports. Horses and cows kicked over lanterns, and even goldfish took the blame when the sun generated enough heat on their fishbowls to set nearby inflammable materials on fire.

Fortunately for the citizens of Old New York, in a time when there were no smoke alarms or carbon monoxide detectors, there was no shortage of

The FDNY had to commandeer as many workhorses as possible during the Great Blizzard of 1888. (The Miriam and Ira D. Wallach Division of Art, Prints and Photographs: Picture Collection. "The blizzard of 1899." *The New York Public Library Digital Collections*)

four-legged civilian heroes who sounded the alarm with barks, scratches, howls, and bites when lives were at risk. By warning humans of fires and gas leaks in residential buildings and offices, dogs and cats saved hundreds of lives and prevented thousands of dollars in property damage.

Civilian horses also played a role in fire suppression, although unlike the fire horses, they rarely garnered publicity. For example, when the FDNY had to commandeer as many workhorses as possible during the Great Blizzard of 1888, the horses received minimal credit in the press. And in Staten Island, where there were still about five hundred volunteer firemen divided among eleven companies as late as October 1913, the law required that all civilian horses be paid for their time in service with the volunteer companies. When the volunteers had to seize teams of horses from brewery wagons or nearby livery stables, workhorses that were "a bit too fat for fire horses" got the job done and pulled the apparatus. Unfortunately, the newspapers ignored these unsung equine heroes.

Engine 3: Zeke, Mike, and Baby

The most petted and praised horses in all of New York on January 19, 1899, were Zeke, Mike, and Baby, the well-trained, intelligent horses who were the pride of the firemen of Engine 3 at 417 West Seventeenth Street. According to a story in the *New York Times*, the engine was responding to a fire at 344 West Fourth Street when, while rounding the corner of West Thirteenth and West Fourth Streets, the front axle broke. The jolt threw Lieutenant Daniel P. Fitzmaurice and Engineer J. J. Mulligan to the ground. The two firemen escaped with only slight injuries. Driver John Rooney, who had been strapped to his seat, fell with the engine, landing under the hoofs of the galloping horses. Instead of dragging the engine, the horses sensed the danger of what had just happened. All three came to a sudden and full stop, leaving Rooney unharmed. The lifesaving horses munched on sugar treats the rest of the day.

Engine 131: Baby

Like Baby of Engine 3, Baby of Engine 131 at 107–109 Watkins Street in Brooklyn also saved the engine's driver in a similar way in 1912. While responding to an alarm, D. William Gobel was suddenly jerked from his seat. He fell right under Baby's hoofs. The large black horse threw his weight backward, successfully stopping the engine. When Gobel stood up, Baby rubbed his nose affectionately across the fireman's face. Baby's lifesaving act was officially reported at Fire Headquarters. A *Brooklyn Daily Eagle* reporter surmised that the horse would retire on a pension and spend the rest of his life in a shady green meadow, "where he can dream of clanging gongs, of breakneck runs and of loyal friends in the thrilling days of the department."

Unfortunately, Baby was killed in the line of duty on February 26, 1914, when a grocery truck plowed into the three-horse team. The engine, driven by William Shaffer, was plunging down a snow-covered Sutter Avenue when the driver of the grocery wagon lost control. A sharp edge of the truck tore into Baby, who had to be dispatched on the scene.

Engine 258: Nellie

Nellie, the fox terrier mascot of Engine 258 at 136 Eighth Street (now Forty-Seventh Avenue) in Long Island City, Queens, was another fire dog who was a knight in shining armor for felines. On August 11, 1926, the company responded to a small fire at the American Fibre factory at 540 Van Alst Avenue (Twenty-First Street). As the engine pulled up to the hydrant, Nellie, as was customary, jumped off and ran toward the building. She disappeared for a brief time, but then suddenly emerged from the basement carrying a kitten by her teeth. After one of the firemen took the kitten from her, Nellie started back toward the basement. She was coughing and unsteady on her feet from the smoke, so the men held her back. When the fire was out, the building's janitor went into the basement and returned with a basket filled with five more kittens. Women in the crowd rushed to take the kittens, promising to give them each a loving home. One woman took a bright-red hair ribbon from her hair and tied a bow on Nellie's collar.

HISTORICAL HOOK

Long Island City was chartered on May 4, 1870, with the merging of old Astoria village and the villages of Ravenswood, Hunters Point, Laurel Hill, Blissville, and Dutch Kills in the Town of Newtown. At one time, there were more than twenty volunteer fire companies serving the new municipality, some of which had been in service since the 1840s and 1850s (including the Astoria Hook and Ladder Company and Protection Engine Company). Under the volunteer system, every company was equipped with hand-drawn apparatus. Although the companies were strategically positioned across the city, allowing for quick responses to even the outlying districts, the primary water supply was limited to wells and cisterns; even after the city established a public water system, the hydrants were few and far between.

On February 1, 1891, the Long Island City Fire Department transitioned to paid firefighters. Prior to this time, the department had comprised five engine companies (Jackson 1, Protection 2, Franklin 3, Hunter 4, and Washington 7), seven hose companies (Mohawk 1, Empire 2, Hope 4, Jackson 5, Union 6, Steinway 7, and Tiger 8), and three hook and ladder companies (Astoria 1, Live Oak 2, and Friendship 3). The city also had at its service five fireboats owned by the Newtown Creek Towing Company. The new paid department could afford to purchase only five apparatus with horses, which created an understaffed department that was inadequate for the city's population and frequent multiple-alarm calls at oil works and lumber yards. By May 1897, the department had just six steam engines and one truck, manned by one chief and thirty-six men who were not paid nearly enough to work as hard as they did to protect the large city. Mayor Patrick "Battle Axe" Gleason was all but ready to abolish the paid system and call back the volunteers—his plan was to keep two paid men at each house to care for the horses and drive the apparatus and then use volunteers to fight the fires. Fortunately for Long Island City, he didn't have to take such action. In January 1898, the fire departments of Brooklyn and Long Island City merged with the FDNY.

At the time of the merger, the Brooklyn Fire Department had fifty-seven engines and fourteen ladder trucks, so Long Island City's Engine 1 and Ladder 1 were renumbered Engine 58 and Ladder 15 to avoid confusion with the Brooklyn apparatus. This, however, muddled the numbering for the Manhattan companies, which also had an Engine 1 and a Ladder 15. The solution came on November 1, 1899, when the department added one hundred numbers to every engine and fifty numbers to every truck in Brooklyn and Queens—thus creating Engine 158 and Ladder 65 in Queens. Once again in 1913, the FDNY added another one hundred numbers to engines and fifty numbers to trucks in Queens. Engine 158 became Engine 258, and Ladder 65 became Ladder 115.

The days of Long Island City's horse-drawn vehicles began winding down in November 1921, starting with the ladder trucks in the Eighth Street, Jackson Avenue, and Steinway Avenue companies. Chief Albert Reid of Battalion 45 predicted that by January 1922, every company in the battalion would have turned in its horses for motor apparatus. As the *Brooklyn*

Steinway Hose No. 7, founded by William Steinway, had a hand-drawn wagon built in 1875 at the Steinway & Sons piano factory for use in Steinway Village (Astoria), Queens. (Photograph provided courtesy of the New York City Fire Museum)

Times Union put it, "The famous fire horse, the delight of every boy and the admiration of many men and women, will not be seen in Long Island City after the first of the year. . . . Progress makes its demands, even upon the fire horse, but he will long live in the hearts and memory of the generation that has seen him."

Ladder 29: Maggie

Like the battalion chief's horse who saved a child by making a split-second decision, a similar lifesaving tale involving a young girl and a fire dog named Maggie took place one night in February 1908 in the Mott Haven section of the Bronx. One of the firemen of Ladder 29 explained what happened that night when the company received an alarm at the intersection of East 138th Street and Brown

Place: "When the gong tapped that night, Maggie, who was sitting on the desk, jumped down in a jiffy and began barking loudly at Bill, Saul and Major—them are the three big gray horses that pull the truck, you know—as they came running from their stalls. The heavy truck was going along at a good speed. Jim Sommerhaze was driving. Maggie was running ahead barking loudly as if urging the three big grays on faster."

Responding west from the firehouse at 898 (now 618) East 138th Street, the truck had only a few blocks to go to reach the scene of the fire. When the apparatus reached St. Ann's Avenue, a young girl started crossing the street. Fireman Andy Degnam, who was on the side step, began ringing the bell, but the little girl froze in the path of the speeding truck. Maggie dashed ahead of the horses and grabbed the girl by her dress, dragging her across the street just in time. "Well, that's just the kind of a dog she was, mister," the fireman told the *New York Sun* reporter. "She seemed to know when danger was approaching."

Only three months later—and at the exact same intersection—Maggie tripped and landed under Major the horse. Before Maggie could get back on her feet, the truck wheels ran over her, killing the canine hero on the very same spot where she had saved the young girl's life.

Engine 3: Rover

In Jules Verne's *Around the World in Eighty Days*, published in 1873, the British gentleman Phileas Fogg makes a wager with his fellow members of the Reform Club that he can travel around the world in eighty days. Fogg and his French valet set out from London on October 2, 1872, determined to return to the club on December 21, 1872.

Perhaps the balloonist William Ivy Baldwin had this story in mind when he made a $20,000 wager with a London man in 1896. The conditions of this wager were that Baldwin had to start on a journey without any money and, except for waterways, walk across two continents and return to New York within eighteen months with $2,000 in cash. Baldwin's plan was to use a hot-air balloon as needed over the waterways and earn a living by playing half a dozen musical instruments. Baldwin didn't have a French valet, but he did have a lifesaving Newfoundland dog named Rover, whom he borrowed from Driver George L. Molloy of Brooklyn's Engine 3 at 533 Hicks Street.

Rover was a fearless and intelligent dog who joined the company in 1891. Some of the men called him Gulliver because of his size, and he answered as readily to Gulliver as to Rover. He was a pro at his job, always staying about a block in front of the engines, ready to bark furiously at any pedestrian or animal who dared get in the way. His skills proved especially valuable the time he saved a little girl from certain death in 1895. According to the *Brooklyn Daily Eagle*, the engine was responding to a fire when the tot wandered into the street just as a trolley car came whizzing by near the corner of Smith and Fulton Streets. Rover ran to the child and was able to use his size and weight to push her backward out of harm's way.

By March 1895, Rover was getting reckless on fire calls. The men were certain he would meet his end while performing his duties. While they trusted their three fine horses (Paddy, a large iron-gray horse who drew the hose cart; Sam, a glossy black horse; and Pete, a gray horse who drew the engine), they didn't trust their reckless Rover. The company had at this time three other fire dogs—Bob, a Gordon setter owned by the former chief engineer Thomas F. Nevins; and two English coach dogs named Frank and Nell—so perhaps it was an easy decision to allow Rover to travel in a balloon with Professor Baldwin. Not only would Rover be safer in a hot-air balloon than running along the fire horses, but the other three dogs could easily cover for him while he was off seeing the world. The press reported that if Rover completed his globe-trotting adventure, Baldwin would return him to the firehouse to finish out his years as a stay-at-home fire dog. There was no additional press coverage of Baldwin and Rover, but if the dog did return to the firehouse, the men no doubt bragged about Gulliver's travels.

Ladder 35: Gyp

Gyp (aka Spot) was a Dalmatian who regularly brought good luck to Ladder 35 at 142 West Sixty-Third Street. On August 16, 1915, the company's canine talisman saved the life of his master, Captain George F. Ricketts. That evening, the men had been called out to a fire at the Mason-Seaman Transportation Company, a four-story brick garage and shop for taxicabs at 622 West Fifty-Seventh Street. The smoke in the building was especially rancid, because the fire had started in the top-floor shop, which was filled with rubber tires and rubbish. As Gyp stood across the street watching man after man stagger from the building, choking and gasping for breath, he whined and paced nervously back and forth. He knew it was against department rules for dogs to go to the fire floor, but like most firefighters, the rules meant nothing when lives were at stake. And so, when Gyp didn't see his master exit the building, he knew he had to act fast. Checking to make sure Chief John Kenlon wasn't looking his way, he sprinted across the street. After snarling and snapping at the man guarding the door into which Captain Ricketts had disappeared earlier, he bounded for the stairs.

Quickly but quietly, Gyp made his way through the dense smoke to the top floor. There, Captain Ricketts and Firemen John Kelly, Thomas O'Toole, and Harry Gardiner were breaking down the walls of a small enclosure within the machine room from where the worst of the smoke was coming. A sudden blast of smoke sent the men staggering backward. In the ensuing chaos, the men lost their captain. But then they heard Gyp barking; his sobs told them he had found his master. Following the sounds, Kelly stumbled over Captain Ricketts and grabbed him. The other men helped him drag the unconscious captain into another room. As the smoke eaters of Rescue Squad 1 carried the four men downstairs to the sidewalk, Gyp tumbled down behind them. Before leaving the building, he sprang for the guard who had tried to stop him from entering and saving his master. It took several firemen to pull the angry dog off the man.

Dr. Harry Archer resuscitated Kelly, Gardiner, and O'Toole on the scene and sent the captain to Roosevelt Hospital. "Gyp, coughing at every bound, set out in pursuit of the automobile and camped in the hospital for the night." Doctors expected a full recovery for Captain Ricketts (according to records, he did recover).

HISTORICAL HOOK

One day in January 1918, Chief Kenlon remarked that there were too many fire alarms coming in for the men at Ladder 35, Engine 74, Ladder 22, and Engine 56. It's not that the fires were too much work for the men, but the calls were interfering with the men's knitting. Yes, knitting. A reporter from the *New York Sun* set out in search of a good yarn.

"By hen be danged!" Fireman Patrick Murphy of Engine 74 exclaimed. "Here I've started five times to stitch the last three rows to this helmet, an' by the holy greased pole I've been interrupted every time. Now, look a' that," he told the reporter while grabbing a ball of drab-colored yarn from the yards of yarn covering the floor. "By the grace of hivin I've lost me count! They can't even let a fireman knit in comfort."

Fireman Murphy was one of many firemen from the four companies who had volunteered to knit wool military helmets for the US soldiers stationed in France during World War I. Each man had consented to knit one helmet a month for the boys of the Rainbow Division as part of an effort led by Mrs. M. J. Warren of the Rainbow Division Welfare Association. Mrs. Warren explained how she got the idea to employ firemen as volunteer "red wagon needle workers":

> I started out on the theory that men are better knitters than women. Mrs. Charles G. Stirling, president of the Welfare Association, told me she needed fifty volunteer knitters. I said I would get them. I didn't know where—then. But I strolled up past Engine 74 and saw a fireman come out. That was John Hastings. I asked him if he thought the men would consent to learn knitting so as to do their bit. He thought they would. I went in and spoke to the desk man. He was rather startled, but offered to let me put it up to the men. I did, and they agreed.

The first four men to sign up for knitting classes were Firemen Nixon, Walsh, Murphy, and Becket at Engine 74. At Ladder 35, Firemen Charlie Lazzaro and Jimmy Fitzpatrick took up the knitting needles (Lazzaro's wife and daughter fell to the floor laughing when he brought his knitting project home), and one fireman from Ladder 22 said he would even knit on the subway if a few other men would join him. Mrs. Warren said purling was one of the hardest stitches to teach the burly men, and they often bent the needles by applying too much pressure; but they seemed to enjoy mastering new tricks. "You know those men get so interested that they hate to leave to answer alarms," she said. With a request for more than one thousand knit helmets, Mrs. Warren expected that the firemen would be purling for a long time.

Engine 25: Barney

Barney may have been the pet of Driver James J. Campbell, but every man in Engine 25 valued and adored the four-year-old Dalmatian known for his "almost human intelligence." Fireman William Steele was especially attached to the dog; in fact, he owed his life to Barney.

Barney was born in the engine house at 148 East Fifth Street in 1892. As soon as he could walk, he began training for his important role. In addition to barking furiously as the engine started out and running alongside the horses, he took guard over the tender, growling and flashing his teeth when anyone tried to come near. The firemen said that Barney even responded to every still alarm; if it turned out to be a major fire, he'd tear back to the firehouse barking wildly to spread the news. Should the engine receive a call while Barney was making his daily visit to the meat market, he'd drop his basket of meat and go along.

Barney earned his keep by responding to calls and guarding the tender, but it was no doubt his lifesaving actions at 29–31 First Avenue on November 11, 1896, that earned him a special place in each man's heart. During a fire in the wine cellars of Engel, Heller & Co., Fireman Steele became overcome by smoke. There were no accountability tags back then, so after the men extinguished the small fire, they started to leave. Barney refused to go with them, and when his barking and whining failed to get their attention, he seized one of the firemen by his coat and dragged him back to the building. Thinking that their dog had discovered more fire in the cellar, they followed him into a corner, where they found Steele unconscious. Barney, satisfied that he had done his job, let the men complete the rescue and returned to his guard duties.

In July 1899, Barney lost one of his eyes when someone accidentally struck him with a pitchfork while he was sleeping under straw. Shortly afterward, he was blindsided while running beside a new horse being broken in by Campbell. The horse kicked Barney, who died about two hours later. The men said that they would have his body stuffed and placed in the firehouse.

Fireboat *George B. McClellan*: Peggy

During the late nineteenth and early twentieth centuries, a city full of people formed close-knit communities along New York City's waterfront in wintertime. They didn't live in the city proper but in small cabins on coal barges moored at various docks in Manhattan and Brooklyn. Throughout the spring, summer, and fall, these coal barges dotted the Great Lakes and large rivers of Upstate New York. But at the first signs of winter, the captains would go in search of a haven for their boats and their families who lived on board with them. As the *New York Times* described these floating colonies in 1905, "A merrier, happier colony is not to be found in New York than the tenants of the cabins of the canal boats."

In the winter of 1926, a fleet of thirty to forty coal barges laden with fifty thousand tons of coal were moored together and anchored for the season at the foot of East Ninety-Sixth Street. The fleet comprised two lead boats: the *J. J. Reynolds*, led by Captain Jim MacLennon, and the *R. T. Davies*, with Captain Frederick Graves at the helm. Behind them, lashed together three abreast, were the other barges. Approximately eighty men, women, and children made up this small barge community, which was just south of the FDNY fireboat *George B. McClellan*, docked at East Ninety-Ninth Street.

On Christmas Day, the families dressed in their best and gathered for holiday celebrations. Several dogs, including Fanny of the *R. T. Davies*, Sandy of the *J. J. Reynolds*, and Peggy of the *George B. McClellan*, shared friendly back-and-forth banter throughout the festive day. But that night there was a sleet storm accompanied by strong gale winds. While the families were sleeping in their cabins, the moorings that tied the fleet together and held them to the shore slipped. One newspaper reported, "So suddenly and without sudden motion did this occur, that not a soul on board of any of the barges was awakened." With the detached fleet of barges caught up in the surge of Hell Gate in the East River, a tragedy was in the making. One wrong move could have meant sudden death for the sleeping families.

Fortunately, there were two occupants in the barge colony who were wide awake: Fanny, a crossbreed Airedale and shepherd, and Sandy, a crossbreed Airedale and Alaskan husky. When the boats broke loose, Sandy growled and sank his teeth into the bedclothes of Captain MacLennon, who was sleeping on his bunk. On the other lead barge, Fanny went onto the deck and started barking and growling as the barges began heading east toward the rocks of Hell Gate. Three blocks north, Lieutenant John Hughes and his crew of sixteen men on the *George B. McClellan* were sleeping below deck. Peggy, a fluffy white spitz dog who served as fireboat mascot, was sleeping on a comfy coat. Hearing Fanny's barks for help, she woke up and sprang from her bed. She leaped through a partly open hatch and landed on the boat's icy deck. Looking out through the darkness, the little dog began to answer Fanny's staccato yelps for help. Barking at the top of her lungs, Peggy aroused Hughes and the other men. They knew that something must have been very wrong for their mascot to sound as if someone were murdering her.

Lieutenant Hughes was the first to respond to Peggy's barks. At the sight of him, Peggy doubled her efforts, changing her barks to deafening howls as she faced the danger. Hughes leaned over the gunwale and aimed his light at a ghostlike fleet of barges drifting toward the treacherous rocks and currents of Hell Gate. On the *R. T. Davies*, Captain Graves began shouting along with Fanny's howls for help. Members of the coal-barge families ran from their cabins and joined in the barking and shouting. Soon they heard the long, shrill blast of the fireboat, followed by many short blasts summoning other ships for help.

Back on the fireboat, two pilots were ready for action at the wheel. Other men tossed a line to the foremost barge just as the cluster of boats moved swiftly toward the piers of Hell Gate Bridge. Using clever maneuvering and full power, Hughes attempted to herd the boats into the center of the stream. But the fireboat was no match for the coal-laden barges. Fortunately, Captain John Jones, commanding the tugboat *Frank A. Furst*, heard the blasts and responded to the fireboat's distress signal. The tug and fireboat pressed against the *J. J. Reynolds* and, through combined effort, pushed the heavy mass away from Mill Rock, a dangerous whirlpool, and the upper end of Welfare Island (present-day Roosevelt Island). Despite the gale winds, Hughes managed to fasten a line to the *J. J. Reynolds*. Captain Jones steamed down river toward the end of the runaway barges and tossed a line onto the anchor barge to secure that end. Together, the fireboat and tug maneuvered the heavy boats in the wind-freshened currents. Once the caravan reached the Brooklyn shore, a dredge with a crew of three men joined the rescue party.

With the barges finally secured to a pier at Greenpoint and along the Newtown Creek, the men and women drank hot coffee in their cabins while offering Peggy "choice dainties from their galley cupboards." While the barge captains thanked their human rescuers for saving them in the nick of time, others offered a prayer of gratitude for Peggy for responding to Fanny's howls for help. Fanny and Sandy received juicy chunks of steak for their reward, but it was Peggy who received the most praise in New York. She had proven that a small FDNY mascot could be a lifesaving hero.

"Engine 54": Harry

When Coney Island's Dreamland amusement park on Surf Avenue opened to the public in May 1904, the most popular of the many disaster-simulation attractions at the resort was a stunt spectacular called "Fighting the Flames." The large attraction, which the press called a "mimic fire," simulated a major conflagration at a six-story hotel in which a cast of firefighters in full uniform (many of them retired from the FDNY) used extension ladders to rescue guests trapped on the collapsing roof while other guests jumped into nets to escape the flames shooting out the windows. In addition to hundreds of paid human actors, the show also featured elephants: one elephant turned in the fire alarm, and another elephant dragged up a ladder for an impending rescue act.

The attraction was a huge crowd-pleaser among the paying spectators, who each paid a quarter to sit in the large, fifteen-hundred-seat amphitheater and watch the complete progress of the fire, from the moment the firemen were awakened in their beds by the alarm to the time they returned to the firehouse with their horses and apparatus. The show began with a marching band leading a parade through a city square. Moments later, a man would come running from the hotel screaming "Fire!" at the top of his lungs. The sleeping firemen would awake in the two engine houses, tumble into their clothing, and slide down the polls as the harnesses dropped onto the horses. Within a few seconds, the city street filled with fire engines and ambulances, and a large crowd gathered to watch the firemen in action. The *Brooklyn Standard Union* summarized the show as follows: "The fire features are thrilling. High jumping into the life net from each floor and the roof of the hotel is fraught with danger. Tongues of flame lick the front of the hotel, surrounding the jumpers as each one makes the desperate leap to safety."

In July 1904, FDNY Chief Edward F. Croker spent an afternoon at the fire attraction. After watching one performance from the amphitheater as a spectator, he inspected the apparatus and horses—including the three horses that drew Engine 54—and then took charge of the firefighting forces for the remainder of the shows that day. Many of the actors had worked under Croker before retiring, and they all enjoyed working with him again at the mimic fire. "Boys, you did well, and I will see that you are all placed on the honor roll for promotion," Croker told the men after the last flames had been extinguished. After saying good-bye to his old friends, the chief checked out the newest novelty attraction at Dreamland: "The Baltimore Fire," in which a model of the city of Baltimore, which had literally burned down only five months earlier, went up in flames every hour on the hour.

"Fighting the Flames" at Coney Island's Dreamland included an entire block of fire-ravaged buildings, dozens of firemen, and hundreds of spectators. (Library of Congress, Prints & Photographs Division [LC-DIG-det-4a17580])

"Fighting the Flames" was so popular in its first year that promoters expanded it in 1905 to include an entire block of fire-ravaged buildings with a crowd of six hundred spectators and more than one hundred firemen led by Chief Sweeney. Sweeney's Dreamland fire department was equipped with four engines, including Engine 54 (from a former volunteer company organized in 1895 at 56 Gravesend Neck Road), and one ladder truck. In addition to people jumping into nets, the 1905 show featured a rescue involving a fireman climbing down from the roof headfirst with a woman on his back.

On June 18, 1905, seven-year-old Anna Ryan of Coney Island was nearly crushed by Engine 54 while playing with other young performers in the fire show. It was Harry, one of the three white horses drawing the engine, who came to her rescue. According to numerous reports of the incident, the driver had given a warning shout as the engine approached the crowd, giving everyone adequate time to move aside for the fast-moving apparatus. Although the adults moved quickly, the noise and turmoil of the show had mesmerized the children, causing a delay in their response. Anna completely froze directly in the path of the responding engine, petrified with fear. People in the audience stood up and gasped, expecting to see the child crushed to death. The driver didn't see Anna, but Harry did. When the engine was about ten feet from the girl, Harry swerved to the left, nearly throwing the other horses off their feet. The sudden movement turned the front wheels of the engine just enough to avoid a serious accident. Those who witnessed the thrilling spectacle stood up and cheered. (Only three weeks earlier, a performer named Ralph McLean was killed during the show when he fell from a rope while sliding from the top of the hotel.) As one newspaper noted, the incident with Engine 54 "was not part of the programme, and the action of the horse was unrehearsed—just simply a bit of intelligence on the part of the well-trained animal." Anna's mother told the press that this would be the first and last time her daughter performed in the fire show. Harry received lots of loving attention and extra oats with lumps of sugar as his reward.

Sadly, poor Harry, who became the favorite pet of the fire brigade and children after his heroic deed, died only two months later. The grieving firemen buried their beloved Harry with honors. Little Anna served as the chief mourner. The following year, the park replaced the fire spectacle with "The Destruction of San Francisco," which simulated the great earthquake that had taken place only a month before, on April 18, 1906.

Ironically, Dreamland stood atop the burned ruins of Coney Island's infamous Bowery, a sixteen-block neighborhood of dive saloons and cheap dance halls that were all destroyed in a fire in 1903. Only eight years later, on May 26, 1911, Dreamland sustained a similar fate after workers in the "Hell Gate" boat-ride attraction accidentally kicked over a bucket of hot tar. Deputy Chief Thomas Lally turned in the department's "last resort" 2-9 alarm (the alarm telegraph ticked off nine long taps twice), in which every apparatus in Brooklyn south of Bergen Street responded—this was only the second time in the history of the department that the 2-9 had been issued. By the next day, however, largely due to the failure of Coney Island's high-pressure water system, there was little left of Dreamland but a nightmare of ashes and rubble.

HISTORICAL HOOK

One extremely popular attraction at Dreamland was the Lilliputian Village—also inappropriately called Midget City—which was a fully functional miniature town along the park's west promenade modeled after fifteenth-century Nuremberg, Germany. (The site of the village was at the present-day parking lot between the Cyclone roller coaster and New York Aquarium.) The tiny town was home to about three hundred little people recruited from circuses and dime museums all over the United States. Everything in the village, from the vehicles to the restaurants, houses, taverns, and furniture, was built to scale. The villagers lived on-site and performed their own circus, opera, and theater acts. They even had a beach with lifeguards as well as their own police and fire departments, complete with a miniature steam-powered fire engine and two ponies to pull it to an hourly simulated fire.

When Dreamland burned down, the Midget City Fire Department sprang into action with the real FDNY firefighters. After having responded to more than two thousand fake fires over the years, it was now time to fight a real fire with their miniature steam engine. While the park burned all around them, their efforts to save their tiny town were all in vain, albeit one unconfirmed report said that they were able to save their tiny firehouse.

Dreamland's Lilliputian Village had its own small-scale fire department and police department featuring miniature horses and apparatus. (Postcard image courtesy of the Greater Astoria Historical Society, https://astorialic.org/)

Engine 15: Roderick McNulty

Roderick McNulty was a Dalmatian attached to Engine 15 at 269 Henry Street in the 1890s. The company occupied the former engine house of Americus Engine Company 6 of the volunteer fire department, of which William Marcy Tweed was not only a founding member but also its foreman for two years. It was in this firehouse that "Boss" Tweed launched his notorious Tammany Hall political career.

Like all good fire dogs, Roderick McNulty's primary job was running ahead of the horses, bossing them on to go faster by barking and biting at their legs. His greatest achievement, however, took place in January 1897, at a small fire in a tenement house at 311 Henry Street. Roderick ran into the burning building and found an unconscious child in a smoke-filled bedroom. His barks alerted the

This dog collar may have belonged to Roderick McNulty, but it was more likely worn by an earlier canine mascot of Americus Engine Company 6 of the city's volunteer fire department. (Photograph provided courtesy of the New York City Fire Museum)

firemen, who were able to carry the child outside. Credit for saving the child's life was given to Roderick.

Roderick never made the news again. However, on October 10, 1923, the company's black cat mascot, Tommy, appeared in the *New York Daily News*, sliding down the pole.

Ladder 9: Jack

Jack was a bona fide fire dog, but the ten-year-old Dalmatian was also "a professional tramp." That's because in his early days, before he became a hero, Jack wasn't completely loyal to his official company, Ladder 9. Sure, Jack stayed close to his men and the truck at every fire scene, but once the chiefs began releasing companies, he'd choose whichever one packed up and returned to quarters first. In this way, Jack visited about every firehouse in the city, from the Battery to the Bronx. Though he didn't have a license, Jack was never at risk walking home from other quarters: dog catchers had strict orders from the Bergh Society (SPCA) to give him free rein. They could easily distinguish Jack from other Dalmatians because he was "much larger and fatter and also handsomer than the majority of that clan." Following his visits, the tramp fire dog would return to the Ladder 9 firehouse at 209 Elizabeth Street "and slink into his home like a culprit."

Described as a "stocky-built dog with jet black head and saddle," Jack joined the company in 1891, after walking into the firehouse with complete confidence. Jack was not only a vagabond but also a big eater, sometimes chowing down eight meals a day at Michael F. Lyons's restaurant at 259 Bowery. The restaurant had a fire bell over the door, so no matter what Jack was eating or how delicious it was, he would always bolt for the door as soon as the gong rang. He sometimes knocked over patrons who were not familiar with the fire dog.

Lyons's restaurant was a popular rendezvous during the Bowery's halcyon days, so no doubt Jack came to know many movers and shakers. One of the most prominent patrons during Jack's reign was Police Commissioner Teddy Roosevelt, who ate his meals at

Lyons's restaurant when he was carrying a big stick at police head-quarters on Mulberry Street (his favorite dish was sliced roast beef with vegetables, pie, and a mug of ale). Roosevelt served as police commissioner from 1895 to 1897, so one can be fairly certain that Jack hobnobbed with the future president while they were both dining at Mike Lyons's place.

Unlike other patrons who had to pay for their meals, Jack dined at Lyons's restaurant for free as his lifetime award for saving the life of a veteran volunteer fireman. The rescue came during a fire on December 20, 1895, at Military Hall, a historic meeting hall, ball-room, and lodging house with a ground-floor saloon at 193 Bowery. According to the *New York World*, Policeman Farley of the Eldridge Street police station had discovered the fire in George Groveling's saloon at 3:15 a.m. When Ladder 9 arrived at the four-story build-ing one minute later, Foreman Charles W. Kruger and Fireman Pat Hanberry (the axe man) could hear shouts coming from the lodg-ing rooms upstairs. They broke through the front door and rushed through the saloon toward the stairs, but the thick black smoke drove them back. As the building's janitor and another man came hurrying down the steps, Jack began howling. He bounded up the stairs and into a large dance hall. There he found James Hogan—also known as the Bowery Wonder (because everyone wondered what he did for a living)—asleep on a bench.

Here's what Hogan, a Civil War veteran and former fire laddie, told a reporter about the fire and his rescue:

> Right on top of me, snarling and growling, was a big fat dog, roll-ing me over and over. The room was pitch dark and full of smoke, and I thought I was done for and on the other side of eternity. Just then a flame shot up a few yards away, and it was only then that I was able to take in the situation. The house was afire, and the dog had been trying his level best to make me understand it. I jumped to my feet, but for the life of me I wouldn't have known which way to run if it hadn't been for the pup. He's a corker, he is. He just took my sleeve between his teeth and began pulling me in the direction of the flames. I made up my mind that the pup was sent by Providence, and so I followed him right clean

through the blaze and the smoke, and he led me safe and sound to the street.

After Jack and Hogan reached the ground floor, the firemen hustled Hogan outside and poured a tub of ale over him to cool him off. When a reporter sought to interview the dog, the men told him to go to Lyons's place, where he'd find the dog in the kitchen eating "a luxurious dinner." Although Jack declined to talk about his good deed, the men of Ladder 9 were more than willing to praise him, believing that the dog was the reincarnation of a long-gone fire vamp. Lyons rewarded Jack for his lifesaving heroics by giving his employees a standing order to feed the dog at no charge. From then on, Jack cut back on his hobo ways so he could stay close to the Bowery and his daily free meals.

On August 17, 1899, four years after saving Hogan, Jack met his death while responding to what turned out to be a false alarm at Bleecker Street and Broadway. According to reports, Driver Kerrigan had just swung horses Tom, Mike, and Jim onto Prince Street to avoid a street fair on Elizabeth Street. Jack was not expecting the sudden turn, which caused Jim to kick him, sending the dog rolling in the street. Before Jack could get up, the wheels of the four-ton ladder truck ran over his neck, killing him instantly. Kerrigan told a crowd that had gathered around the lifeless dog, "Well, he's a veteran, and he lost his life in the same way many another fireman did, turning out for a false alarm." The men told grieving visitors that they'd have his body stuffed and placed in the firehouse to honor his eight years of service and thirty-five hundred calls.

One New Yorker who was especially touched by the death of Jack was Jefferson Seligman, a New York banker whose wealthy family took great interest in the fire department. He began searching for the perfect Dalmatian, which he presented to Ladder 9. The firemen named their new dog Swipes and immediately began training him in the art of four-legged firefighting and lifesaving.

Engine 44: Wag and Fritz

Wag and Fritz were father and son Dalmatians of Engine 44 at 221 East Seventy-Fifth Street. Fritz, a gift to the company from Miss Montgomery of Merrick, Long Island, in 1903, was older and wiser, but it was the younger dog who knew all the new tricks. Wag could hold a pipe in his mouth, sit on his haunches, and pretend to be a smoker. He also knew how to say his prayers by bowing his head and placing his paws over his eyes (when someone said "Amen," he'd uncover one eye and blink). One of the greatest tricks he ever performed, though, was the night he used his nose to save a freezing puppy in the snow.

As Fireman Charles H. Ehrhardt told the story, he was taking Wag for the dog's bedtime walk one night in March 1907. Suddenly, Wag stopped short and began investigating a snowbank with his nose. Ehrhardt, thinking that the dog had discovered some old bones, continued walking on. A minute later, Wag caught up with him and placed a neat little parcel at his feet. When Ehrhardt untied the parcel, he found a baby pug, cold and wet and shivering with fear. He brought the puppy to the firehouse, wrapped him in a blanket, and placed him in a warm bed. While Ehrhardt was making the little pug comfortable, another fireman ran out to buy a nursing bottle and milk. As the men cared for the pup, Wag looked on with paternal pride, as if the baby pug were his own offspring.

Sadly, the puppy never lived long enough to become a fire dog. Although he recovered from the cold exposure and had a great appetite, "he just up and died," one fireman said. A few months later, Wag's original master, who had only temporarily given Wag to Engine 44, joined the New York Athletic Club. The club had a country home at Travers Island on the Long Island Sound, and the man wanted to bring his dog there. So, Wag left the city behind and moved to Travers Island, where he "smoked" his pipe and said his prayers for all the up-and-coming Olympic athletes. His old man, Fritz, stayed at Engine 44, where he continued the risky tradition of running into burning buildings with hopes of saving lives.

Fritz continued running to fires until 1912, when old age and years of injuries from hot roofs, cinders, and sparks kept him on the sidelines. Fireman John Eagan found him dead in his sleep beside Jerry, his equine pal, on March 17, 1913. His body, covered by a fireman's full-dress jacket and service helmet, lay in state in the firehouse, where hundreds of children came to say good-bye to the favorite firehouse mascot. With special permission from Deputy Chief Thomas J. Hayes, Firemen Patrick Golden and Rudolph Schwamberger took the remains of Fritz to a pet cemetery, where they placed a special monument on the grave.

Engine 53 and Ladder 1: Lucy

Born in the Highlands of Scotland in 1902, Lucy was a Gordon setter described as "a lean dog with black and tan markings, long ears, and large, intelligent eyes." Shortly after her birth, she became a US citizen and a proud fire dog with Engine 53 at 175 East 104th Street. During her first two years of service, Lucy never missed a call. On one of those calls, she saved a human life by running into a burning room and finding a crying infant. Using her teeth, Lucy was able to carefully seize the infant and carry the baby out of danger. Although Lucy survived, she received extensive burns and nearly succumbed to smoke inhalation. For her valiant efforts, she received a beautiful token, which she wore on her elaborate collar.

Lucy may have learned to seize the toddler with her teeth by practicing with her dinner pail. Every day at dinnertime, Lucy would place the handle of the small pail in her mouth and carry it to a neighboring hotel, where the kitchen workers would give her scraps of food. Lucy would then carefully carry the tin pail back to the firehouse, where she'd wait until her master, Lieutenant Collins, placed a newspaper on the floor where she ate her meals.

In June 1905, Collins transferred from the East Harlem firehouse to Ladder 1 at 26 Chambers Street. Lucy didn't take well to the move, as she preferred the quieter setting uptown and missed all the children she had played with there. The first day of her transfer, while Collins was away, she bolted from the firehouse and ran back to Engine 53, five miles away. When she didn't find Collins there, she went to his house and waited for him. When Collins returned home, he found the faithful dog sitting on the doorstep. Lucy eventually came to accept her new city home with Ladder 1 and resumed her full duties as an FDNY fire dog.

Engine 55: Smoke

When the Sixty-Ninth New York Infantry Regiment (aka the Fighting Sixty-Ninth or the Irish Brigade) arrived on the firing line in France during World War I, it had a mascot dog by the name of Smoke. The famous regiment, which had formed in New York City initially as a state militia unit during the Civil War, drafted the dog with consent of the members of Engine 55 at 363 Broome Street. The firemen had allowed the regiment to borrow their life-saving mascot to show their appreciation for the enlisted soldiers. Smoke was taking a summer break with Fireman Joe Horack at his home in Long Island when the special request came from Private Michael Dineen.

Smoke, described as "a Dalmatian veteran with no more pedigree than a hornet," joined the company in 1913 after wandering out from a haze of smoke at a fire on Mercer Street. Having raised him from a puppy, the members said they'd miss him while he was overseas, especially when turning out for alarms in the East Side tenement district or the West Side waterfront. In September 1917, they gave their dog an honorable discharge from the FDNY with a banquet and reception at the Sixty-Ninth armory building.

As a member of the Sixty-Ninth Regiment, Smoke was expected to bring the same good luck to the military men as he did for Engine 55. He received training to emulate the German sheepdog in bringing food and water to the wounded men in the field. The men believed that Smoke would be just as successful at saving lives on the front line as he was on the fire scene. Not only was Smoke fearless when it came to rushing into a smoke-filled building, but the intelligent dog was adept at guiding his comrades to unconscious firemen. According to the *New York Sun*, Smoke had an outstanding reputation in the FDNY, having saved the lives of several firemen in Engine 55 and other companies. He was also a great guard dog: in

1916, he was the guest of honor at a firemen's banquet after taking down a thief who had tried to enter the firehouse.

HISTORICAL HOOK

Before diphtheria toxoid became widely available in the early 1930s, diphtheria was one of the most common causes of death for children. The acute bacterial disease often spread quickly through schools, causing its young victims to slowly suffocate as the bacteria grew into a thick film in the throat. Until some retired FDNY fire horses and other retired working horses came to the rescue during the World War I era, there was little doctors could do to help a child with respiratory diphtheria, save for tracheotomies and intubation to counter the suffocation.

By the late nineteenth century, German and French scientists led by Professor Frederick Loeffler had discovered that by inoculating animals with small doses of toxin harvested from lab-grown bacteria, the animals would build up immunity against diphtheria infection. In 1890, researchers learned that serum made from the blood of immunized animals contained an antitoxin that, when injected, cured human patients suffering from diphtheria. However, to produce adequate amounts of antitoxin for human use, scientists needed large animals with lots of blood. Researchers tried cows and donkeys, but horses turned out to be the least affected by the injected toxin. Led by the efforts of chief bacteriologist Dr. Hermann Biggs, the New York City Health Department took a lead role in the cause, establishing a facility in 1906 in Otisville, New York. Here, the blood of horses—including retired FDNY horses—was drawn to provide a local source of both diphtheria and tetanus antitoxin serum for doctors.

One of the horses who took part in this pioneer program was Dan, a fire horse who had retired from the FDNY in 1912 when a motorized vehicle took his place. Dan retired to the city's 175-acre tuberculosis sanatorium farm in Otisville, where he supplied enough diphtheria antitoxin and tetanus serum to treat at least one hundred thousand European soldiers fighting on the front lines during World War I. Dan was one of twenty horses on the farm employed to produce the antitoxins for distribution to allied nations and to New York City hospitals. Up to the start of the war, most of the serum produced was for diphtheria antitoxin, as there was little need for tetanus antitoxin in the city. But soon after the war started, the demand for tetanus antitoxin on the battlegrounds increased. Dan became "a lockjaw serum plant," turning out many quarts of serum for use during the war.

According to Dr. William H. Park, then head of the city's health department, as many as four hundred thousand wounded soldiers had received

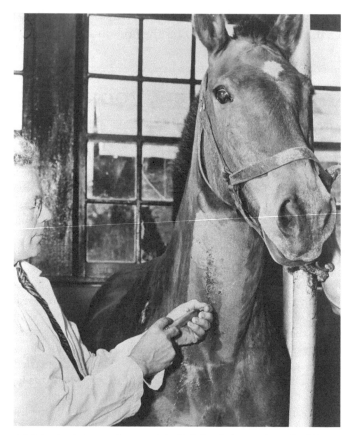

A biologist injects a horse with diphtheria bacteria at the New York City Department of Health serum and vaccine farm in Otisville, New York, in 1944. (Library of Congress, Prints & Photographs Division [LC-USZ62-136363])

the tetanus antitoxin, resulting in thousands of lives saved. He explained that Dan and the other horses "suffered almost nothing" save for some minor pain and grogginess and perhaps a shortened life span. Other than providing their blood, the horses did not have to perform any other work on the farm, and they all received excellent care. "The example of the horses at Otisville was a consummate example of service which no human ever excelled," Dr. Park said.

By 1929, under Dr. Daniel Poor, the farm had about one hundred horses dedicated to producing diphtheria, tetanus, meningitis, and pneumonia equine serum. According to the *Brooklyn Daily Eagle*, there was not one horse that had not saved thousands of children from premature death. Old

Faithful, another pensioned FDNY horse, had saved at least twenty thousand New York City children with the serum he produced.

The health department continued to produce antitoxin for many years after World War II, with commercial companies taking over from the 1950s to the 1980s. A biotech company purchased the Otisville facility in 1987; one stipulation was that the heroic horses would have a good life on the farm until they died of old age.

Engine 12: Jack and Jim

When a reckless boy with a blazing broom caused the wreckage of a fire engine on Kent Street in January 1898, the two black horses pulling the Engine 12 apparatus saved the lives of several Brooklyn firefighters simply by staying still.

On the night of the accident, Assistant Foreman Bryan O'Rourke of the fireboat *David A. Boody* was in charge, having relieved Assistant Foreman Thomas Kane and Foreman Thomas Cleary, who were both off duty. John F. Judge was the driver, and sixty-year-old Michael Delaney was the engineer. When an alarm came in for a chimney fire on Greene Street, O'Rourke, Judge, and Delaney jumped on the engine, the harness snapped over Jack and Jim, and the horses began pulling the heavy vehicle toward Kent Avenue, then a deeply rutted road from heavily laden sugarhouse wagons.

As the horses strained to pull the engine down Kent Avenue, they came upon a group of boys encircling a bonfire. One of the boys began swinging a burning broom over his head. The blazing handle came off and flew directly between the two horses. Both horses bolted in opposite directions, causing the engine's front wheel to turn into a deep rut, which sent the engine crashing on its side. O'Rourke was tossed from the engine, but Judge and Delaney were pinned beneath the overturned vehicle. Jack and Jim were also thrown to the ground. The heads of both men were just inches from Jim's iron-shod hoof.

According to the *Brooklyn Times Union*, Jack and Jim demonstrated "remarkable intelligence" by their actions following the accident. "Neither scarcely moved and had they followed out the general impulse of animals in such circumstances and began kicking, Judge would have had his brains strewn about the street." Judge spoke calmly to the horses, "who whinnied a response to his well-known voice." Jack and Jim remained quiet and still until the firemen released them by cutting them free from their entangled harnesses. All three firemen were injured and attended to by Department Surgeon De Long and Ambulance Surgeon Schaefer of the Eastern District Hospital. News accounts varied, but some physicians predicted full recoveries for the injured men.

Sadly, one of the horses of Brooklyn Engine 38, which was also responding to the chimney fire, was killed on Leonard Street when he had to stop suddenly to avoid hitting a woman who was crossing the street with a child in her arms. The sudden stop threw the horse to the ground, causing the engine to crush him to death. The woman had become paralyzed with fear when she saw the engine coming at her; had she kept on walking, the life of the lifesaving horse would have also been saved.

Engine 111: Tip

On May 16, 1907, Brooklyn Battalion Chief John Howe, in the quarters of Engine 111 on Clymer Street, received an unusual letter. The letter was from a well-known woman who asked for "the privilege of decorating with flowers the gravesite of Tip" on Decoration Day (Memorial Day). Tip, who started life as a dirty and shabby stray dog, had for two years been an honorary member of Engine 111, where he earned an admirable record for making every call with old Ted, the veteran horse, and saving several lives. The loyal fire dog had lost his own life a few weeks earlier when the company was returning from a basement fire in a tenement at Harrison Avenue and Walton Street. During a near collision with another vehicle, the engine's wheels rolled over Tip, breaking one of his legs and crushing his body.

One of Tip's most memorable saves came on May 2, 1906, at a cellar fire at 292 Wilson Street. Tip ran into the smoke-filled cellar, where he found the unconscious bodies of Firemen Taylor and Robinson. He ran into the street and snatched the coat of Lieutenant Isaac Ludgate, leading him into the cellar. For this rescue, Tip received a silver collar. Another rescue took place in December 1906, when Tip dragged an unconscious child from a burning hallway.

Tip's sudden passing caused much sorrow throughout the neighborhood. To honor the faithful pup, the men buried Tip in the rear of the engine house (now a private residence). They inscribed the following on the small marble headstone: "Here Lies the Body of TIP. A brave dog, who gave his life to save others. Died April 29, 1907."

Several New York newspapers reported on the death of the Engine 111 fire dog. The *New York Times* referred to the dog as Kip, the *Brooklyn Daily Eagle*, *Brooklyn Standard Union*, and *New York Evening World* called him Fly, and the *New-York Tribune* called him Tip. Somewhere in the backyard of 166 Clymer Street, perhaps, an old marble slab bears the heroic dog's true name.

7

Line-of-Duty Deaths

> If New York had a special cemetery for the dead four-legged
> heroes, as Paris does, it would undoubtedly be full of eloquent
> monuments.
>
> —"Animal Mascots of Police and Firemen Aid to Stop
> Thieves and Save Lives," *New York Evening Telegram*,
> December 3, 1911

In Riverside Park, on a hillside facing the Hudson River at One
Hundredth Street, the Firemen's Memorial offers a peaceful place
to rest or meditate. The memorial, designed in 1912 by the architect
Harold Van Buren Magonigle and the sculptor Attilio Piccirilli,
was unveiled at the conclusion of a fireman's parade on September
5, 1913; fifty-seven young girls whose fathers had died in the line
of duty participated in the ceremony. The memorial comprises a
grand staircase, a balustraded plaza, a fountain basin, and a central bronze monument flanked by two marble groups symbolizing
"Duty" and "Sacrifice." The monument features a massive bas-relief
of three galloping horses drawing an engine. According to the *New-
York Tribune*, the image is based on a photograph of fire horses
responding to a fire; the actual photo "is even more graphic," as only

The Firemen's Memorial and tablet for fallen fire horses in Riverside Park.
(Photograph by the author)

one hoof of the three horses was on the ground when the camera
caught them in action.

The monument is attributed to Bishop Henry Codman Potter,
who suggested that a memorial be erected in honor of the firemen who lost their lives in the line of duty. During the funeral for
Deputy Fire Chief Charles Washington Kruger, who was killed in a
fire at 217 Canal Street in 1908, Bishop Potter observed that while
there were many memorials to public and private citizens, there
were none "to our brave citizens who have lost or will sacrifice their
lives in a war that never ends." In May 1927, the American Society
for the Prevention of Cruelty to Animals added a second tablet to
memorialize the fallen fire horses. The bronze panel reads, "This
tablet is dedicated to the horses that share in valor and devotion
and with mighty speed bore on the rescue."

Just as countless firefighters have made the supreme sacrifice
while trying to save life and property, many brave working animals
and mascots of Old New York lost their lives performing their
honorable duties. Many of these line-of-duty deaths came during
intentional rescues, such as when a fire dog entered a burning

building and used his formidable nose to save a victim. But all too often, an unintended rescue, in which a split-second decision meant life or death, cost the life of a four-legged firefighter. When horses participated in such decisions, the driver's life was also in jeopardy. Sometimes the driver had to sacrifice himself or the horses to save a civilian's life.

In January 1930, a veteran fireman spent time reminiscing with a reporter for the *New York Sun*. He recalled the death of Jim Calman, the driver of Engine 24, who lost his life one Christmas morning when he had to abruptly steer his horses off the roadway to avoid hitting a woman and child who had crossed the engine's path. The veteran told the reporter, "Many a good man laid down his life to save others while driving, and hardly a day went by that you didn't read of a driver being hurt and horses killed when they'd swing their teams into 'L' pillars, curbs or something, to avoid running down some pedestrian who got in their way. Women and kids would often become frozen with fear right in the path of a company, and unable to move."

In addition to curbs and elevated ("L") railroad pillars, trolley cars also presented a danger to the fire horses and their drivers. Although not all trolley accidents resulted in a fatality, they often shattered the horse's nerve, making him untrustworthy, or caused injuries that prevented the horse from obtaining the speed required to respond to emergencies. Injured horses were humanely dispatched or put on the auction block alongside the old horses who were no longer able to perform their duties.

The fire scene was also dangerous for those horses placed too close to a burning building. On January 31, 1901, the men of Engine 21 tried in vain to save their three white horses, who were standing next to a seven-story cigar-box factory at 401–419 East Thirty-First Street. As the paint on the engine wheels blistered and the hair on the horses' backs began to burn, Captain Roan "Barney" Conklin and Firemen John Flynn and John Gillespie secured overcoats from people in the crowd and placed them on the horses' backs. The horses struggled to escape, but they were paralyzed with pain and fear. When they finally broke free, they plunged madly down

Of all the four-legged firefighters, fire dogs who ran ahead of the horse-drawn apparatus—like this dog of Engine 235 in Brooklyn—were the most vulnerable to line-of-duty deaths. (Courtesy Municipal Archives, City of New York)

First Avenue and became entangled about a lamp post. One horse was so severely burned that the men had to shoot him; they also worried that the other horses would not recover.

Of all the four-legged firefighters, fire dogs were the most vulnerable to line-of-duty deaths. The biggest threat, however, was not fire but the horses' hoofs and the apparatus wheels. To be sure, many dogs were seriously injured at fires, but getting to the fire was more dangerous than working on the scene alongside the men. "That is the way most fire dogs finish, by getting run over by the engines of their own companies," a battalion chief told a reporter in 1912. "It is impossible to keep them from in front of the horses, and sometimes they will become tired, or perhaps lose some of their vigor as they grow older, and a single misstep means that they go under the wheels."

A reporter for the *Buffalo Commercial* explained it this way:

> A false step in front of the galloping horses and one of their heavy hoofs is likely to strike him down and then the driver feels the sickening horror of the heavy wheels going over his beloved pet. Sometime as the engine leaves the house the dog will miscalculate the space between the wheels and the door jam, only to have his life crushed out. Again, one of the horses will harbor an enmity against the dog and he will wait for a chance to cripple or kill him with a kick. . . . The oldest dog in the service today has seen at most not more than five years of active life, and on an average some fire company in the department is mourning one of its canine pets at least once in every three months.

Even the fire cats were not immune from line-of-duty deaths; many lost at least one life, if not all nine lives, by accidentally eating a poisoned rat or taking a catnap in front of the apparatus at an inopportune time. And tragically, some fire cats and dogs were also victims of cruel humans who poisoned their food, tossed them from buildings, or otherwise hurt them. Not every death made the news, but no doubt, many a beloved fire cat or dog is resting in eternal peace at a pet cemetery or under a hidden stone in the backyard of an old city firehouse. What follows are the final tales of just a few faithful FDNY animals who lost their lives while serving the citizens of Old New York.

Engine 14: Chappie, Peter, and Chops

Chappie was a pedigree bull terrier who called Engine 14 at 14 East Eighteenth Street his home. According to the *New York Sun*, Chappie came of the best blue blood in England, having arrived in the United States with William Waldorf Astor, the son of John Jacob Astor III and Charlotte Augusta Gibbes. Astor presented the dog to the company in 1889.

Everyone in the Eighteenth Ward knew and loved Chappie, described as a forty-five-pound white bull terrier whose "ferocious looks utterly belied him." Chappie loved children, but he was especially attached and loyal to anyone wearing a fireman's uniform. He could not tolerate police uniforms and thus would always lose his temper when a policeman was in sight. (Reportedly, an officer had used his stick on Chappie, which is why he spurned the police.) On one occasion, when Chappie was alone in the firehouse, Police Commissioner James J. Martin dared to come inside. Chappie didn't allow him to leave until the firemen returned.

Chappie was in his glory when responding to fire calls. As soon as the alarm gongs started ringing, he'd cock his ears and wait to see if he had to report to duty. He understood the signals and wouldn't stir if the alarm denoted a fire outside the company's boundaries in the Flatiron District. When the gongs sounded a fire for Engine 14, Chappie would race around with "an absurd energy" as soon as the doors opened, playfully snapping at everyone, tumbling over himself, and incessantly barking to rush everyone along. He'd bound ahead of the galloping horses, furiously barking and springing up between their legs. Spectators would close their eyes, expecting to see him get trampled. But he'd always come racing out from under the flying hoofs and lead the procession once again, biting and barking and urging the horses on. Once on the scene, Chappie would calm down and sit on the driver's seat, comfortably wagging his stubby tail as he watched his friends at work. Sometimes he'd bark a few times to encourage them.

During Chappie's three short years with Engine 14, he sustained several injuries. He broke his leg and lost part of his tail while leading the horses, and he often received bruises from the horses' hoofs. But nothing could stop him from doing what he loved most. One time when Chappie was sick, the men tied him to the oaken staircase in the firehouse and rushed to the fire, thinking he was secure. As they rounded a corner, they heard children shouting. There was Chappie, running alongside the horses with a rope around his neck—the other half of the rope was still tied to the staircase.

One fateful night, as the engine was responding to a box alarm, Chappie broke his paw in two places. The firemen bandaged him and placed him on the sick list. Still determined to respond to every call, he joined the engine the following night when it responded to a fire on Broadway at Ninth Avenue—he ran to the scene on three legs. On that call, Chappie got underneath the horses and went down. As he tried to right himself, either the engine pan or the pumps caught him in the back and crushed him to the pavement. The firemen cried as they carried their maimed mascot back home.

Dr. Thomas D. Sherwood, a veterinary surgeon, diagnosed Chappie with a fractured spine, broken leg, and several internal injuries. At first the firemen wanted to put him down, but they later decided to try to save him. They rigged a canvas hammock on two billiard cues, from which they suspended the injured dog above an open dry-goods box. Dr. Sherwood took great interest in the case, calling several times that day. There was hope at first, but Chappie suffered greatly in his suspended position. The men tried to make him as comfortable as possible in a pile of straw. They also gave him opiates to help ease the pain. Chappie died on March 23, 1892. Shortly after his death, cats Peter and Chops took over as the chief mascots of Engine 14.

Chops was one of several kittens whose mother cat had been rescued by Engine 14 following a large parade during the 1884 presidential campaign. He was a white cat with a few spots, a chopped-off tail, and a hearty appetite. According to the firemen, Chops "was a Catholic cat and liked fish on Fridays." He and his good chum Peter, a jet-black cat who also had a stubby tail, loved to perch on the desk blotter and rub themselves against the horses' legs—the horses never dared move for fear of hurting them. But while Chops was a domestic cat who was content to stay at the firehouse, Peter was a more adventurous feline who excelled at catching rats in nearby hotels and other establishments. Peter was also an expert acrobat who could slide from the second floor to the engine floor whenever the firemen tossed him onto the brass pole.

One of Peter's favorite places to visit was the millinery firm of Aitken, Son & Co. on Eighteenth Street and Broadway. Here he could practice and finesse his hunting skills among the stacks of lacy bonnets and velvet hats. According to the firemen, Peter would wait until everyone had left the establishment at night, and then he'd jump to a window and enter through the open transom. Whenever he was successful, he'd bring a rat back to the firehouse, lay it on the floor, and meow "until someone appeared and expressed appreciation of its prowess by a caress." Unfortunately, Peter's love of rats cost him his life. He devoured a poisoned rat and was in "death spasms" when he arrived at the Bergh Society (SPCA) shelter, where he took his last breath.

Chops met his death a month later while wearing his fire boots, so to speak. According to the men, Chops was sleeping on the company's tender when an alarm rang out for a fire. As the tender picked up speed at Broadway, Chops woke up to discover he had been caught napping. Determined to return to his post, the cat jumped from the tender. According to the men, "He turned a somersault as he fell, rebounded as he struck the pavement, shot under the tender, and a wheel ended his life."

On the night of an impromptu memorial service for Peter and Chops, the firemen shared their memories of the deceased felines with a reporter from the *New York Times*. According to the story, the following two blotter entries, recorded by Foreman Charles H. Shay, "were entered in sorrow, as they chronicled the end of two favorite Grimalkins":

July 22, 1896, 5:00 a.m.: Peter, cat, transferred to Bergh Society.

August 25, 1896, 11:25 a.m.: While responding to an alarm for Station 343, Chops, cat, jumped from seat of tender at Broadway and Eighteenth Street, and was killed by being run over and having neck broken.

During the memorial service, Fireman Joe De Size and Engineer A. W. Melvin received orders to choose a burial spot and prepare a proper funeral so the men could pay their last respects. The reporter concluded, "The members of the company will be disconsolate until they get a new pet. A likely kitten straying in the neighborhood . . . will probably be snapped up. It will certainly find there all the comforts of a good home as long as it lives."

Engine 51/151: Cinders, Nellie, and Dewey

Six months after organizing under the FDNY in January 1898, the men of the new Engine 51 at 47 Washington Avenue in Brooklyn were desperate to find a canine mascot. In two months, they had lost six dogs, including one who died in the line of duty. They were hoping seven was the charm.

Their first dog was a fox terrier named Cinders, whose brief and promising career was cut short when the engine ran him over on the way to a fire. His successor, also named Cinders, had an intense dislike for trolley cars. One day the little dog dashed in front of the Flushing Avenue car and got hit by the fender. He hobbled back to the firehouse, where he stayed until he healed. Then he walked out, never to return to the job. A few weeks later, a lean and hungry dog whom the men named Hobo entered the firehouse. Fireman R. Collins trained him well, and it looked as if he would be their dog. But then a few sailors from the nearby Brooklyn Navy Yard took the dog on their ship and headed toward Manila Bay.

Tag, another fox terrier, was next in line to try out for the mascot position. He was a favorite from the start and took to firefighting as naturally as if he had been born in the firehouse. One day, a horse stepped on his paw. Tag decided that he wasn't cut out for the work and disappeared. His replacement was Dewey, named for Commodore George Dewey, the heroic admiral of the Navy who led the United States to victory during the Spanish-American War. Dewey applied for the position on July 8, 1898. Someone stole him a week later.

In 1899, under General Order No. 2, the bad-luck Engine 51 on Washington Street became Engine 151. Unfortunately, the name change didn't bring the company any good luck with regard to animal mascots. After losing their seventh dog within a few months in 1898, the company finally adopted a feline mascot. They named the black cat Dewey, in honor of their last dog. They also inherited a Dalmatian named Nellie, who was a true fire dog. Dewey and Nellie were a perfect fit for Engine 151. At last, the company had two reliable mascots who both enjoyed responding to fire calls.

On February 19, 1901, the company received a call at 447 Kent Avenue. Mrs. Kate Campbell had caught fire after a kerosene lamp exploded in the apartment. The young bride and new mother was preparing her husband's dinner when she slipped and dropped the lamp on the stove. The explosion set fire to her clothes, sending her running and screaming down the stairs to the street. An ambulance transported her to the Eastern District Hospital, where she succumbed to her extensive injuries.

With the Campbells' kitchen now engulfed in flames, neighbors called in a box alarm, sending Engine 151 to the scene. Fireman Raab had the engine, and Fireman Hunter had the water tender. Dewey was taking a nap outdoors, stretched out in front of the firehouse, when the call came in. Nellie was overseeing the horses and took her position to the right of the team. As the tender pulled out of the firehouse, Dewey looked up but wasn't quick enough to get out of the way. The wheel of the tender ran over him, killing him instantly. Meanwhile, Nellie ran alongside the horses, barking all the way. Just as the engine turned at South Ninth Street and Kent Avenue, she became tangled in the legs of one of the horses, sending the wheels of the engine over her. There was absolute gloom in the firehouse following the tragic passing of both mascots.

Ladder 58: Chief

On November 20, 1901, a fire of suspicious origin started on the third floor of a four-story brick factory building at 18–20 Johnson Avenue in Brooklyn. The floor was occupied by Barnett & Flannel, manufactures of children's clothing. Fifteen minutes before the flames were discovered, someone turned in an alarm. A few minutes later, all the women employed at the firm evacuated the building. When firemen arrived on the first alarm, they couldn't find any fire. While the men were returning to quarters, a second alarm came in. Ladder 58 at 112 Siegel Street was one of the companies to respond.

As the ladder truck was turning from Leonard Street into Johnson Avenue, Chief, one of the horses, slipped on a streetcar track.

He fell to the ground, breaking his left foreleg. The men had no choice but to humanely dispatch him on the scene. The firemen continued responding on foot, carrying their ladders to the fire about a block away. They were able to contain the fire to the third floor, saving Isadore Gerber's sweatshop on the top floor and the Bedford Carpet Cleaning Company on the ground and first floors.

The death of Chief, a favorite horse, caused much sorrow. One fireman remarked, "He died like many of our comrades. His was a fireman's death."

Incidentally, the scene of this fire was just east of the intersection of Johnson and Union Avenues, where present-day Engine 216 and Ladder 108 share quarters with Battalion 35. This section of Johnson Avenue was renamed Firefighter Daniel T. Suhr Place in 2002, in honor of the Engine 216 firefighter who lost his life during the World Trade Center attack on September 11, 2001. Suhr, who was struck by a fallen body, was the first reported FDNY fatality on that horrific day.

Ladder 16: Socks

When Socks first joined Ladder 16 at Fire Headquarters at 159 East Sixty-Seventh Street in July 1900, the little puppy developed a habit of stealing the firemen's stockings and carrying them down to the cellar, where he'd chew them into shreds. Thus, the greyhound-Dalmatian mix earned his name.

Socks loved children and women, but he had a strong aversion to strange men. Many distinguished guests who came to Fire Headquarters—including Teddy Roosevelt and the Crown Prince of Siam—tried to befriend the dog, but Socks wanted nothing to do with esteemed dignitaries. Socks also disliked the horses of Engine 39, which shared quarters with Ladder 16. Whenever an alarm came in for both companies, he'd dash up to the engine and nip their legs. Perhaps the tragedy that befell Socks on December 16, 1902, was their payback.

On that day, both companies were responding to a fire on Second Avenue. After nipping at the Engine 39 horses, Socks fell back with the ladder truck before taking a shortcut to get ahead of the engine again. He slid across the engine's path, and big Rob, one of the horses, sent him spinning on his back. One of the wheels went over him, leaving him helpless in the street. Driver Joe Finger, Sock's caretaker, was able to turn his team just in time to avoid running over the dog again. Policeman Wilkesman dispatched the dog on the scene.

The men held a funeral for Socks outside Fire Headquarters on December 17, 1902. Almost everyone in the building turned out to pay their respects "with all the honor due a member of the department who had met death in the performance of his duty." The men put him in a little pine coffin with the inscription, "Socks—A Third-Grade Fireman Who Might Have Been Chief." Then they took the coffin to the East River, where they watched in sorrow as it sank to the bottom.

Four years later, on Christmas Day 1906, Finger made the ultimate sacrifice when he drove his truck—he was then with Ladder 29 in the Bronx—into a street curbing on St. Ann's Avenue to avoid running down a little girl.

HISTORICAL HOOK

During the horse-drawn era, several wealthy New Yorkers donated expensive coach dogs to the FDNY to show their appreciation for the firemen. Socks, for example, was the third fire dog gifted to Fire Headquarters by Henrietta Hellman Seligman. The first dog, Starch, was run over in October 1901. The second dog, a $600 Dalmatian puppy, fell down a coal hole shortly thereafter. The following day, Mrs. Seligman's coachman delivered Socks to the firehouse.

Mrs. Seligman was the wife of the late Jesse Seligman, a prominent New York banker. Seligman was one of eight brothers who opened a banking house at 21 Broad Street in 1865. The brothers devoted much of their attention to the national debt incurred during the Civil War and in short time were recognized as some of the brightest bankers in the country. Jesse Seligman was also one of the city's most prominent philanthropists, donating both time and money to causes such as the Hebrew Orphan Asylum, Metropolitan Museum of Art, and American Museum of Natural History. When he died in April 1894, his wife and six children inherited his estate.

One of the causes near and dear to Mrs. Seligman and her children was the FDNY. In 1902, a reporter for the *Buffalo Commercial* wrote, "Whenever a fire company in the department wishes a dog, the family of Jesse Seligman always is ready to supply one, and that a fine Dalmatian hound. The Seligman family takes the keenest interest in the fire department, and this is one of its methods of expressing that interest substantially."

Several members of the Seligman family resided on East Sixty-Ninth Street, so the nearby Fire Headquarters was a frequent recipient of Dalmatians. In addition to the three dogs gifted to Ladder 16, Engine 39 received a Dalmatian named Joe from Jefferson Seligman in July 1900. Jefferson Seligman also donated a Dalmatian named Swipes to Ladder 9 in October 1899 upon reading about the death of their Jack, who was killed when the truck ran over him two months earlier. A year later, he presented another dog named Jack to Captain Friel of Engine 8 in honor of the bravery they displayed during the Windsor Hotel fire in 1899. Thinking that the dog was an imported animal of great value, the men bedecked the dog with an expensive collar. Unfortunately, they soon learned that Seligman's assistant had unknowingly purchased the dog from a thief, who had stolen Jack from a livery-stable keeper on Sixth Avenue. Hearing of the theft, Seligman presented the company with another dog from a more reliable source in April 1900. Seligman told the press that he intended to make similar gifts to other fire companies. "The dogs made good pets for firemen and might be useful at fires," he said. He was correct.

Engine 115: Mike

Mike had only seven months of active duty with Brooklyn's Engine 115 at 88 India Street when he lost his life to the heavy hoofs of the horses and heavy wheels of the tender in April 1903. Mike was a faithful companion, a gallant fire dog, and a great friend of the neighborhood children, who loved nothing more than watching the canine fire laddie prancing ahead of the company and nipping at the horses to shift them into faster gear. On the night of his death, Mike was dozing peacefully when the gong broke the silence. For more than a block, he headed the whistling steam engine, barking encouragement to the horses. As the engine approached Java Street, he slipped and fell. The driver struggled to evade him, but it was too late. The men carried Mike's body back to the firehouse and buried him with full honors in the presence of the children who had loved him. The call that had summoned Mike to his death was a false alarm.

Ladder 14: Fire, Chief, Smoke, and Spot

In the spring of 1904, the manager of Keith and Proctor's Theatre at 209 West 125th Street rescued a small kitten from some boys who had tied a can to its tail. He presented the kitten to Driver John McManus of Ladder 14, which was located near the theater at 120 East 125th Street. The kitten, named Smoke, made friends with Fire and Chief, who were the coach dogs of Battalion Chief John Lawlor. Soon, the feline had mastered the pole and was a regular fire cat. But one day during the dog days of summer, the two dogs went into convulsions and died. An autopsy showed that they had been poisoned. A week later, on August 15, 1904, the cat also stumbled into the firehouse and died. An autopsy revealed that she had also ingested poison. Chief Lawlor asked the police to assist him in finding the person who poisoned his pets.

In addition to Smoke, Ladder 14 also had a Dalmatian named Spot, who joined the company when he was a puppy in 1902. On June 17, 1908, the company received a call for a fire in a tenement building at First Avenue and 117th Street. According to the *New York Times*, "Spot was on his feet in a flash, down the stairs, and out on the sidewalk, awaiting the coming of his three friends, the horses, whose approach it has been his delight for almost all his six years of life to herald joyously all the way to any fire." Fourteen men jumped onto the truck, with McManus taking the reins. Assuming people's lives were in danger, Lawlor told the men to hurry.

"Tenements. Lose no time," he ordered. As the horses strained to draw the heavy truck, Spot barked ecstatically, "whirling and circling like a sunset-mad swallow." The center horse struck Spot, sending the truck over the dog's body. The men of Ladder 14 "howled a not pretty word or two," but they had to continue to the fire. Battalion

Chief O'Connor, whose buggy left after the truck, stopped to check on Spot. He ordered him taken back to the firehouse, where he died a few minutes later.

"And this a damn cellar fire," McManus told a reporter after receiving news of the dog's death. "Damage fifteen cents, and . . ." McManus stopped to walk around, brokenhearted and unable to complete his thoughts.

Engine 54: Jerry

On May 17, 1904, an explosion of illuminating gas on the third floor of a tenement house at 516 West Fifty-Third Street took the life of one woman and injured two other women who had been searching for the gas leak using a lit match as a light source. Jerry, a favorite fire horse of Engine 54 at 304 West Forty-Seventh Street, was killed going to the explosion.

While responding to the alarm, the engine just missed colliding with a delivery wagon. In an attempt to avoid the collision, Driver John B. Keenan nearly ran over two young girls. He avoided them by running his team against the "L" pillar at Ninth Avenue and Forty-Seventh Street. The broken engine tongue struck the large white horse, completely disemboweling him. Jerry died instantly. Keenan, a lieutenant, and the engineer were thrown to the pavement and severely bruised. Police arrested the reckless driver of the delivery wagon.

Engine 76: Joe

A split-second decision saved the lives of three children on December 6, 1904—but cost the life of the hero fire horse. The young boys had just left Public School No. 179 and were throwing snowballs in the street. Engine 76, stationed at 105 West 102nd Street, had just turned out on an alarm, and the three horses were galloping toward Amsterdam Avenue. Just as the engine reached the avenue, Driver

Edward Rittle saw the children. He made a desperate effort to stop the horses, but he couldn't stop quickly on the snow-covered pavement. The children paid no attention to his warning shouts.

Engine 76 was a new company, having formed only eight months earlier, on April 15, 1904. So Joe, the nigh horse, was still inexperienced. But somehow the horse sensed the impending danger. He reared up and leapt to one side, carrying the other horses with him. The engine rolled by, just missing the children by a foot. Joe fell and slipped about fifteen feet down the slippery road, landing on the downtown tracks of a trolley-car line. The motorman on the approaching car couldn't stop until Joe was wedged underneath. Joe broke his leg, which at that time was a death sentence for a fire horse. While the firemen stood with their caps off in reverence, a policeman quickly put an end to the equine hero.

Engine 19: Tom

For ten of Tom's many years in the FDNY, he was attached to Engine 19 at 355 West Twenty-Fifth Street. Specifically, he was one of the two horses assigned to the water tender. On July 2, 1905, his long career ended while saving the life of a ten-year-old girl. That night, the company received a call at Ninth Avenue and Nineteenth Street. Just as the tender turned onto Ninth Avenue, Ida Schmitz started to cross the street. Driver John Kirschner, realizing that he'd have to make a sacrifice to save the girl, gave a fierce tug of the reins, turning Tom straight into an "L" pillar. As the tender came to a sudden stop, Tom's head jerked sharply over the pole, breaking his neck. The girl ran away, frightened but unhurt.

HISTORICAL HOOK

In 1867—one year after Bellevue Hospital put the first ambulance into service for humans—the SPCA began running the first ambulance for injured horses. Until 1906, the FDNY relied on the SPCA ambulances to transport their horses to the department's horse hospitals. Due to numerous delays, however, many valuable horses who might have benefitted from more accessible transportation did not survive.

On July 28, 1906, Deputy Fire Commissioner Hugh Bonner announced that the FDNY now had its own horse ambulance. The white ambulance, which cost $1,000, was drawn by a pair of white horses selected specifically for speed and endurance to make long runs. The ambulance was based at the department's veterinary hospital and training stables at 133–135 West Ninety-Ninth Street in Manhattan. This three-story brick building had been erected in 1889 for the New York Police Department. By 1892, it had been turned over to the FDNY for training and providing medical care for the department horses assigned in Manhattan, the Bronx, and Staten Island. Battalion Chief Shea was the supervisor in charge of the hospital and training stables during the late nineteenth and early twentieth centuries.

During Chief Shea's reign, more than one hundred horses received medical treatment each year, and about sixty horses were stricken from the rolls and reported either as "died in discharge of duty" or "condemned because of unfitness." The hospital was also where the old and unfit horses were sold to the highest bidder on the auction block, "to end his days in front of a truck or a coal cart—the reward of a big city for gallantry displayed in action."

In addition to the main hospital on Ninety-Ninth Street, the FDNY had a branch hospital for horses at 199 Chrystie Street, which was the former quarters of Lafayette Engine 19 of the old volunteer department. Prior to 1892, this three-story building, which had also served as quarters for Ladder 9 from 1883 to 1889, was the department's main horse hospital. During the 1880s, there were about 240 horses in the department, some of which had been in service since 1865. Under the care of Foreman Haviland, about a dozen horses were regularly on the sick list in need of treatment for distemper and sprained legs. "You see they run these horses for all they are worth, because each foreman wants to get to the fire first," Haviland told a reporter in 1881. "It's hard on the horses and men, too. Most of the horses sent here get well after treatment and rest." After the department established the new hospital uptown, the branch hospital served the great number of horses attached to those companies with three-horse hitches in Lower Manhattan.

For the horses of Brooklyn and Queens (including the volunteer companies in Queens), the department had a horse hospital and training center at St. Edwards and Bolivar Streets near the northwest corner of Fort Greene Park in Brooklyn. As with the Manhattan facility, the Brooklyn branch also served as an auction site for retired and unfit horses.

The large complex occupied a three-story brick and limestone building constructed in 1897 for the Brooklyn Fire Department on the former site

The FDNY hospital and training stables at 133–135 West
Ninety-Ninth Street, 1915. (X2010.11.9688, Museum of
the City of New York)

of the Union Engine 5 firehouse (volunteer). For many years, as far back
as 1870, this former firehouse had functioned as a makeshift veterinary
hospital, but by 1897 the two old sheds serving as a hospital were unfit for
use. The new building comprised three sections with an entrance door for
each. On the right side was a "thoroughly equipped engine house" and a
corps of firemen who not only trained the horses but were also available
to respond to emergencies should their services be required. The door on
the left led to a large storage room and repair/paint shop supervised by
Battalion Chief Patrick Nevins; the center door led to the veterinary and
training stables and forty-two horse stalls (which the sick horses shared
with a mascot goat named Teddy), as well as the offices of the veterinary
surgeon Dr. Edward M. Heard and the stable foreman James Brennan.
During the early part of the twentieth century, Brooklyn and Queens had
more than four hundred horses, and fully one-half of them would require
care from Doc Heard every year.

In 1915, when maintaining a facility for fire horses in Manhattan was no longer feasible, the building on West Ninety-Ninth Street was surrendered to the Sinking Fund Commission. The city's Department of Street Cleaning Stable L moved into the building, and all remaining veterinary care took place in Brooklyn. The Brooklyn facility served as temporary headquarters for the Auxiliary Volunteer Corps of the Fire Department during World War I and later as a youth center for St. Michael–St. Edward Church. The building survived demolition under a Title 1 Slum Clearance Project in 1954, when Fred F. Trump built Kingsview Homes on the site, but in 1974 the building was replaced with a twelve-story structure now serving as a rehabilitation and nursing center for humans. The former Manhattan facility is now the site of the Happy Warrior Playground.

Engine 131 and Ladder 70: Rocks

Rocks, a Brooklyn brindle bulldog, was one of the few fire dogs who had the honor of serving as a mascot for both an engine company and a ladder company at the same time. His companies were Ladder 70 and Engine 131 at 107–109 Watkins Street.

On December 22, 1907, while the company was responding to a chimney fire at Blake Avenue and Osborn Street, Rocks lost his footing in a hole as he was running ahead of the three horses. Before the driver could swerve the horses, the heavy wheels rolled over the dog. The men picked him up and continued to the fire as per protocol. After extinguishing the small blaze, the men hurried back to the firehouse with Rocks. There, the dog died in the arms of Captain James Mooney of Ladder 70. The men said that they planned on burying Rocks in a neighboring backyard in a box made by one of the firemen.

Engine 107/207: Bang and Whiskers

In August 1907, the members of Brooklyn's Engine 107 at 245 Pearl Street mourned the loss of their pet cat, Bang, who joined the company when just a kitten. Although Bang spent much of his time sleeping on the driver's seat, he was the house watchman's companion and was just learning how to use the pole. Bang was poisoned, the men thought, by eating a large rat. Fireman Watson did all in his power to save the beloved feline.

Eight years after Bang's passing, the men of what was now Engine 207 rescued a Scotch terrier from dog catchers who were chasing him. Whiskers lived a wonderful life at the firehouse, dining daily at his favorite restaurant and learning how to climb fire escapes. On December 28, 1915, the company was responding to a fire at 83 Plymouth Street when Whiskers slid under the wheels of the heavy engine. Members of the company were undecided whether to bury their faithful mascot with honors or have his body stuffed.

Engine 7: Christian

Five Dalmatian puppies were motherless following the death of Christian, who was killed by a hit-and-run driver in front of 100 Duane Street in September 1908. Christian was presented to Fireman Christian Maher of Engine 7 in 1906 and was always an active fire dog when she wasn't tending to her puppies. Following her death, the men told a reporter that they would keep two of her puppies and give the other three to Deputy Chiefs William Guerin and Frederick W. Gooderson and Battalion Chief B. J. Galvin. When Maher heard that the driver of the truck may have deliberately run over Christian, he said that he would "make trouble" if it turned out to be true.

Ladder 21: Larry

On April 11, 1909, several little girls were playing in front of 502 West Thirtieth Street when Ladder 21, with three horses at a full gallop, bore down on them. With only an instant to react, Driver John Jordan threw his horses to the sidewalk. His action saved the children from a crushing death, but it cost the life of Larry, the company's big brown horse. The horse broke his right hind leg, leaving the men with no choice but to end his life with a bullet. The company had been responding to a fire in a watchman's shanty on West Thirtieth Street.

Engine 58: Jim and Jerry

When Driver Jerry Monahan of Engine 58 at 81 West 115th Street had to make a quick decision to save a life, it nearly killed him, both mentally and physically. Sadly, his decision caused the death of Jim, a large gray horse with five years of service—and the company's favorite.

On September 1, 1909, while making a run to a fire at 229 East 110th Street, Monahan saw a truck drawn up beside the curb just as he swung onto the street. The truck driver was trying to back his horse, which was rearing out of control. Monahan knew that if he didn't take drastic measures, everyone's life would be in danger, including his own. Putting all his weight on the right rein, he swung Jim straight into an "L" pillar, causing the horse's head to violently strike it. The truck came to a sudden halt on top of Jim's lifeless body, saving its driver. Monahan was thrown from his seat, but he escaped injury. The other men on the tender jumped in time to save their lives.

About six years after Jim's passing, the men acquired a Dalmatian named Jerry. The dog, who never missed a fire during his six years of service, died from heart-related conditions in May 1921. The men had sent the distressed dog to the Ellin Prince Speyer Animal Hospital, accompanied by the Reverend Joseph Ives, chaplain of the department, and a letter asking that everything be done to make his passing easy. Following Jerry's death by electrocution, they placed his body in a box draped with the American flag, and all the children in the neighborhood gathered to say farewell to their old friend. One little boy nicknamed Charlie Chaplin refused to leave the firehouse until Captain Joseph Boner buried the dog "with military honors" late in the afternoon. The *New York Daily News* published a photo of the funeral the following day.

Engine 46: Nick

Nick was a large black horse who took the center position for the three-horse team of Engine 46 at 451 East 176th Street in the Bronx. He joined the company in 1904, when much of the Bronx was still rural—the three-story brick firehouse was surrounded by frame houses and stables, and many of the roads were not yet paved.

In November 1909, the company was responding to a fire in a defective flue at 3827 Third Avenue. The heavy engine, driven by John Doran, was making good speed over the fresh-paved Washington Avenue when the offside horse caught his shoe in a sewer lid. The shoe was wrenched off, dragging Nick to the ground. Doran sustained many injuries when he was thrown from the driver's seat, and it took him a few minutes to get his wits together. He crawled to Nick and cradled the horse's head in his lap until medical help arrived. Although Doran needed urgent care, it took the other men time to convince him to let go of the gravely injured horse. Nick had to be dispatched on the scene. Doran was taken to Fordham Hospital, where doctors said he had a moderate chance of recovery (according to records, he did recover).

Engine 125 and Engine 166: Spot and Sport

For many years, it was Spot's responsibility to clear the road for the apparatus of Brooklyn's Engine 125 at 657 Liberty Avenue. His life ended abruptly on August 13, 1904, when he fell under the wheels of the engine while going to a fire that destroyed a two-story frame house at 409 Milford Street. The men of the company, as a token of affection for their friend and coworker, erected a tablet at the head of his grave bearing the inscription, "Killed in the Performance of His Duty."

Spot's replacement, Sport (aka Chief), may have been a little dog without pedigree, but he had a big heart and a tremendous devotion to his master and constant companion, Fireman Thomas

McNamara. Although he lived at McNamara's home in East New York, he shared every evening vigil at the firehouse with McNamara and delighted in running ahead of the engine to fires. He was a faithful friend whose joy for living disappeared when his master lost his life in the line of duty.

Sport's master was a veteran fireman with forty years of service in the department. When he was transferred to the new Engine 166 at 211 Beach Eighty-Sixth Street in 1905, he was one of the oldest active firemen in the FDNY at the age of sixty-two. On January 23, 1907, Engine 166 responded to a smoldering fire in a frame cottage. As McNamara was groping his way down a hallway in search of a baby, a backdraft sent the flames and smoke full upon the veteran fireman. The men carried McNamara's lifeless body to the street, but the ambulance surgeon could not revive him. All Sport could do was lick his friend's hands and yelp piteously.

Following McNamara's death, Sport remained at Engine 166, but he stopped responding to fire calls and became despondent. In March 1909, he accompanied one of the firemen to his old home in East New York. On the return trip back to Queens, Sport jumped off the train as it was leaving the station and disappeared into the crowd. One week later, he returned to Engine 166, where the men rejoiced in his homecoming. No one knows what he did while he was gone, but perhaps he searched his old neighborhood with hopes of finding McNamara. Seven months later, on October 13, 1909, he died in his sleep. Although his was not a line-of-duty death, Sport no doubt died of a broken heart from losing his best friend to the red devil.

Ladder 15: Smoke and Gaby

Smoke was the prize collie dog of Ladder 15 at 73 Water Street who earned his name by dashing into smoky buildings alongside the men. One of the biggest fires he ever experienced was the fatal Equitable Life Building fire in January 1912—he spent several weeks in the hospital for smoke inhalation following that historic conflagration. Four months after the Equitable fire, Smoke lost his life while responding with the ladder company to a fire at West and Rector Streets. The truck, driven by John Corey, had just turned the corner at Battery Place when a dog ran directly into the path of the horses. Smoke, seeing the other dog in trouble, ran out in front of the horses and butted the mutt out of the way, only to fall victim to one of the horses' hoofs. The crack stunned Smoke, sending him under the wheels of the truck. "He died a hero," Corey told a reporter. "We brought him to the firehouse, and he'll be buried with honors, believe me."

In 1914, ten years after Smoke died, Ladder 15 received a small white dog from the Broadway actress and silent film star Gaby Deslys. The men named the adorable lap dog Gaby, and soon she became a favorite FDNY mascot. Gaby served during the early years of the motorized department, but she rode on the truck when the men responded to calls. She was faithful in this duty until February 11, 1920. That was the day Miss Deslys died following an operation for a throat infection she had contracted during the influenza pandemic. Following the starlet's death, the firemen told the dog that her namesake had passed away during surgery. From that point on, the little dog stopped answering alarms. Instead, she paced the floor and ignored the efforts of the twenty men who tried to interest her with extra bones and milk.

On March 27, 1921, Gaby walked outside the firehouse and stepped into the road. A truck came along, and Gaby ran under the wheels. She didn't bark or utter a cry of pain. Some of the men believed that the dog had refused to move from the path of the truck. She knew that her former mistress was dead, and therefore she decided to also end her life. Captain Bill Purdy assigned Fireman Gardella and a few other men to a funeral detail for Gaby. The men placed her in a little casket and took her by ferry to Staten Island, where they laid her to rest.

Engine 17: Rex

The canine mascot of Engine 17 wasn't a handsome dog; in fact, the press described him as "a bull with heavy jowls and legs which spoke of strength and not beauty." But for four short years, he guarded the firehouse at 91 Ludlow Street and kept his friends safe.

In July 1912, Engine 17 was responding to a fire with its team of two horses, including a new roan horse who was difficult to handle. Rex ran alongside the new horse, barking when it was time to make a turn and doing his best to show the green horse how to answer an alarm. The large roan was slow in answering to the reins, and when the engine came to a corner, he hurled his body to one side, dragging the engine after him. The wheels of the vehicle passed over Rex, killing him instantly. The firemen buried their dog "with all the honors due a hero."

Ladder 3: Jimmie

Jimmie, the feline mascot of Ladder 3, had a penchant for sleeping on the tillerman's high seat on the truck or in the tool basket between the footboards. One day, sometime prior to 1912, Jimmie was curled up asleep in the high seat when the ladder company received a call. When the tillerman hopped into his seat, he slung Jimmie over his shoulder, where he remained perched all the way to the fire scene. From then on, Jimmie went to numerous calls crouched across the tillerman's knees or curled up in the basket. The cat always stayed with the truck at the scene and never entered the buildings.

Poor Jimmie met his death when he made the mistake of jumping off the truck on the way to a fire. Soon after the cat's death, construction workers began doing excavating work opposite the quarters of Ladder 3 and Water Tower 2 at 108 East Thirteenth Street. It was the rainy season, and about five feet of water had collected in the hole. One day a kitten fell into the water-filled hole. A fireman rescued the kitten from drowning and brought her to the firehouse, where she was warmed, dried, and fed. Once the little cat was well, a fireman gently dropped her over a fence at the rear of the firehouse. The yard where the kitten landed belonged to a restaurant facing Twelfth Street, which the men thought would be the perfect home for a cat. But the next day, the kitten returned to the firehouse, whereupon the men adopted her as the company's new mascot.

Engine 40: Fan

Fan, a white and tan fox terrier, had only been a member of Engine 40 at 153 West Sixty-Eighth Street for two weeks when she met her premature death on May 5, 1913. As the company was responding to West End Avenue, an automobile crossed the engine's path at West Sixty-First Street. Fan was just doing her job clearing the way when the vehicle struck her.

Fan, who belonged to Captain Elmer Mustard, had been a favorite among the men and the horses. "And the toughest part of all," said Captain Mustard, "it was only a false alarm. Somebody saw the reflection of the fire in Weehawken and thought the wharves on the New York side were burning. They pulled the box at Eleventh Avenue and Fifty-Ninth Street and Fan was the first one out of the door."

Engine 115: Dan

In the debris of a broken wall that had once been part of the three-story frame building housing the Lignum Chemical Company at Meeker Avenue and Varick Street, Fire Chaplain Thomas McGronen knelt on smoldering boards to administer the last rites of the church to Firemen Jeremiah Looney and Walter Weatherow of Brooklyn's Ladder 106. The men had been rescued from under a pile of smoking embers following a series of explosions, which had blown out a section of the wall. They both went to St. Catherine's Hospital, where Looney succumbed to his injuries a few days later, on November 28, 1913. (According to department records, Weatherow survived.)

Smoke and flames were pouring from the structure when Engine 115 came flying down Meserole Street, going as fast as its three horses could manage. Ahead of the racing horses was Dan, the

Dalmatian of Driver Dan Gallagher. Just as the engine was rounding the corner at Manhattan Avenue, Dan hesitated a fraction of a
second to make sure the engine was still following him. One of the
horse's hoofs struck him, followed by the heavy wheels. Gallagher
watched in horror, but he stuck to his horses and continued racing
toward the smoke and flames. There were people whom he had to
help save.

Fortunately, the blaze, caused by spontaneous combustion,
began at the noon hour, when all fifty employees were at lunch. The
police had also evacuated all the neighboring tenements, which the
firemen were able to save. On their way back to quarters, the firemen picked up Dan's body and brought their deceased canine companion home. The men told the press that the dog would receive a
fireman's burial.

HISTORICAL HOOK

On October 5, 1914, one year after this fatal fire, Fire Chaplain McGronen
passed away at the Holy Family Hospital following an emergency gallstone
operation. About one hour before he died, the fifty-two-year-old chaplain,
who had served with the FDNY for eleven years, told a fire commissioner,
"I have reported for the last time!" Almost 250 firemen, as well as numerous battalion chiefs other fire officials, attended the funeral mass at St.
Ambrose's Church. The Fire Department Band played "Nearer, My God, to
Thee" as the chaplain's body was carried from the church. Every firehouse
along the route of the funeral procession was draped in mourning out of
respect for the chaplain.

The chaplaincy of the FDNY dates to March 28, 1899, when Fire Commissioner John J. Scannell appointed the department's first two honorary
chaplains. The two Manhattan-based chaplains, Rev. James Le Baron Johnson of Grace Church and Rev. Father William Smith of the Church of the
Fathers of Mercy, also received the rank of battalion chiefs, albeit without
any compensation. The following official statement of the FDNY appeared
in the *Brooklyn Daily Eagle*:

> The new chaplains will furnish their own equipment. This in each case
> will consist of a uniform, costing $80; a gold battalion chief's badge,
> costing $100; and a horse and buggy, $500. They will have fire alarm
> instruments in their sleeping apartments, and will be summoned just as

is a regular fireman. They will be kept informed, however, as to whether the call is of a nature likely to require their presence. If it is they will both be ready to respond. A fireman who has been incapacitated for active work by injuries received in the line of his duty will be assigned as driver to each chaplain.

Following news of the appointments, reporters and members of the public were quick to express their opinions on Commissioner Scannell's appointments—some of which hinted that Scannell was a member of the corrupt Tammany Hall political machine. One reporter for the *Brooklyn Daily Eagle* questioned why the FDNY hadn't appointed any clergy from Brooklyn. As he observed, the fact that the chaplains had to serve without salary and furnish their own equipment would probably be a deterrent for the poorly paid Brooklyn clergy interested in the position; however, an appointment to a chaplaincy in the fire department would be considered more desirable than one to a military regiment liable to be called on during wartime. One critic questioned why the New York Police Department

Father Mychal Judge was a Franciscan friar and Catholic priest who served as a chaplain from 1992 to 2001. He was killed while serving at the World Trade Center, becoming the first certified fatality of the attacks on September 11, 2001. (Photograph by Octavio Duran, OFM, provided courtesy of the Franciscan Friars of Holy Name Province)

hadn't supplied its force with chaplains. He also suggested that chaplains be appointed for "theaters, race tracks, boxing shows, baseball matches, and even the Democratic Club itself." Another critic noted that Commissioner Scannell had recently given Miss Helen M. Gould a gold fire badge as a "small token" of his respect and yet was charging the chaplains $100 for the same badge.

The two chaplains received their first baptism of fire less than a week into their appointments, at an early-morning blaze at the Colonial Boarding Stable at 249 West 124th Street in Harlem. With Rev. Johnson driving his own horse and wagon (which he had to summon from a livery stable on Twelfth Street) and Rev. Smith seated next to him banging the gong, the men raced up Eighth Avenue, making the five-mile distance in thirty-eight minutes. The flames spread to three rear houses on West 125th Street, but all the tenants managed to make it out safely through the smoke and heat. Twenty-six horses died in the fire, but fortunately no human victims required the chaplains' spiritual administrations.

During the fire, the chaplains spoke with a reporter from the *New York Sun*. Rev. Smith said that he found his new duties exhilarating and was certain he'd become more accustomed to the duties even though it would mean a loss of sleep. Rev. Johnson said that his first fire had been an exciting one. According to the reporter, both men remained at the fire for a while and seemed to enjoy being up and about so late. The stables were a complete loss; the A. H. Meter Pabst Harlem Music Hall and Restaurant building (extant) was constructed on the site in 1900.

Engine 272: Sport

Sport, the mascot of Engine 272 at 135-16 Thirty-Eighth Avenue in Queens, was killed on April 6, 1914, when the wheels of the engine passed over his body, killing him instantly. Sport was the son of Madge, owned by Battalion Chief William Clark, and a prized male Dalmatian owned by James A. Macdonald of Jamaica Avenue. He was still a young pup and had only recently won first prize in the puppy class at the Sheepshead Bay Kennel Club show when he lost his life.

Ladder 12: Smoke

Smoke, a descendant of the famous Oakie of Engine 39, joined the FDNY in 1910 and served with Ladder 12 at 243 West Twentieth Street, where he was born. He was an intelligent dog with kind brown eyes "and a tongue that seemed a mile long when he insisted upon kissing everyone right on the mouth." There was no haul too long and no pace too fast for Smoke, who, according to the men, "could smell his way to a fire in Iceland." Smoke loved running with the company's trio of gray horses, and while he was inconsolable for some time after they retired, he also enjoyed the new motorized apparatus—it encouraged him to run even faster.

The men of Ladder 12 had a good record with few accidents, even though they had gained notoriety as a reckless group of fire eaters "by taking risks that ordinarily would have meant sure death." They attributed their good luck to Smoke's presence. It was no surprise, then, that things began going horribly wrong when Smoke disappeared for six weeks in December 1916 (he was possibly chased out of town by the two hundred cats living in the new Seventh Avenue subway trenches and terrorizing the Chelsea neighborhood at this time).

Two days after Smoke's disappearance, Captain Larry McGuire was diagnosed with a broken shoulder blade. Shortly thereafter, Battalion Chief George L. Ross, who made his headquarters in the firehouse, came down with rheumatism and had to use a crutch. And then there was an explosion in the Helmuth Printing building on West Eighteenth Street, which severely burned Lieutenant George Hauser, Fireman Hugh Bonner (son of the late Chief Bonner), and Fireman Patrick Mulroy. When the company received news that the SPCA had located a black and white dog with a license numbered 1277 in a bakery shop at Second Avenue and Seventy-Second Street, they celebrated in the street. As the SPCA agent walked toward the firehouse with Smoke, "a series of staccato barks and the roars of deep throated men created joy currents that shot into the air from a spot midway between Seventh and Eighth Avenues, on Twentieth Street, and drove the sulkiness from the skies."

Smoke ran away again in March 1917, when the large cat colony chased him through the neighborhood (according to one reporter, "only six of the countless number of black spots on Smoke's once smooth coat had been recovered within a radius of half a mile of the fire house"). The tormented dog didn't stay away long, but by this time, his luck was running out. In April 1917, the company responded on a third alarm to a chemical-factory fire at Bleecker and Bank Streets. Poisonous fumes struck down man after man, and three times Smoke led rescue parties to the unconscious victims. When the valiant dog left the building for the third time, he fell unconscious in the street, overcome by chlorine gas. The battalion chief took Smoke to quarters, but homemade remedies were of no help. The next day, Smoke awoke with bloodshot, glazed eyes and began growling at the men. The men chipped in for a private ambulance to take Smoke to the Ellin Prince Speyer Animal Hospital, but even the veterinarians couldn't help him—they had to euthanize Smoke with chloroform. When news of the final decision reached the firehouse, many of the men of Ladder 12 cried. Plans were made to erect a monument over his gravesite.

Engine 39: Whoopee

In the quarters of Engine 39 at 157 East Sixty-Seventh Street, the "4-4-4-4" bell that signaled the end of a fire sounded for Whoopee, the tiny Dalmatian pup who had learned in five short months of life to count the gong strokes. The firemen thought it fitting that the gongs sounded just as she died, cradled in one of the men's arms.

Whoopee wasn't yet a bona fide FDNY fire dog, but she had already gotten a taste for firefighting by teething on several rubber boots and chewing on new uniforms. She had also mastered all the intricacies of the fire-alarm system and knew how to distinguish the number of beats assigned to her company. She often misjudged the count, which would cause the men to laugh (and cause Whoopee to drop her head in shame), but she never missed springing to the back step of the engine when it was time for Engine 39 to respond.

On October 14, 1929, an alarm came in while Whoopee was napping on the sidewalk across the street. Without pausing to look for traffic, she darted across Sixty-Seventh Street and ran into a taxicab. The impact broke her back. As Whoopee took her last breath in the arms of a fireman, the ticker from headquarters announced that a fire in a nearby district was out and companies were returning to quarters. Pooch, the Dalmatian of the neighboring Ladder 16, was inconsolable following the death of his best canine friend.

Engine 8: Rex, Rex II, and Rex III

The most popular Dalmatian to run with Engine 8 was Bess, who joined the company on East Fifty-First Street in 1908 and was the first dog in the history of the FDNY to have a pass for the Third Avenue streetcar line. When the company replaced its horse-drawn apparatus with motorized vehicles in 1912, Bess refused to respond to calls. She eventually retired with her master, Lieutenant Alonzo Weiss (aka Wise), to Engine 274 at 41-20 Murray Street in Queens.

Although Bess was the media darling of Engine 8 in the early twentieth century, the company had three more popular Dalmatians who captured the media's attention from the late 1920s to the early 1940s. Their names were Rex, who joined the company in 1927, Rex II, and Rex III. The first Rex was a gift from Mrs. Joseph Choate, wife of the late US ambassador to Great Britain. He rode to all the fires on the motorized vehicles and guarded the apparatus at night. A photo of him grabbing the steering wheel of the fire engine, published in the *New York Daily News* in September 1929, offers proof that he was quite comfortable riding the motorized rigs; in fact, the men told the reporter that they believed Rex could drive the truck if someone started it and switched gears for him. In May 1935, Rex was chosen to be the official mascot for the FDNY baseball team in its annual game with the New York City Police at the Polo Grounds. He died from pneumonia at the Ellin Prince Speyer Animal Hospital on November 19, 1936.

Rex II followed in Rex's paw steps, but tragically, he succumbed to fatal injuries at a fire in July 1938 when the truck ran over him.

The firemen buried Rex II at the Bideawee Pet Memorial Park in Wantagh, Long Island. He had for his hearse a Wantagh fire engine, on which the men placed his velvet-lined coffin on a hose reel.

Rex III joined the company shortly after his predecessor's death and shared mascot duties with Sparky, a large Tuxedo cat. Rex III went out on almost every alarm, riding on the rear step; if he missed a call, he'd crawl into a corner, looking thoroughly ashamed of himself for his dereliction of duties. On August 3, 1941, Rex III missed the truck, and the company responded without him to a call on Third Avenue. Hearing the sirens of Engine 21, which was also responding, Rex III tried to redeem himself and ran into the road to hitch a ride with that engine. The front axle struck the loyal dog, breaking his back and killing him instantly. Engine 21 couldn't stop, so the poor dog's lifeless body remained in the street until his company returned. When Sparky saw that her canine pal had died, she ran to the basement, mewing plaintively. The firemen told reporters that they would have their mascot cremated.

Engine 283: Clown

In 1934, two sisters from Huntington, Long Island, presented Brooklyn's Engine 283 with a Dalmatian after reading about the death of Smokey, the company's previous canine mascot. Even though the horses were long gone from the FDNY, Clown still performed the job of clearing the way for the apparatus; he took special pride in warning the children of Public School No. 175 whenever the engine headed that way. He was also eager to master new tricks. One of his favorites was catching a biscuit that the men would toss down from the second floor. Biscuit time became his favorite part of the day, and the better he got, the more people would come to watch and cheer him on.

Clown shared the firehouse with Spot, a lady Dalmatian who never missed a fire unless she was busy being a mother (one time she gave birth to ten puppies). Clown was also the beloved beau of Jill, the Dalmatian mascot of Ladder 120 on Watkins Street, whom he would visit every day. According to Captain Henry J. Keil, the

The men of Engine 73 and Ladder 42 in the Bronx erected this monument following the burial of their dog Lady in 1953. The monument also honors their dogs Boots and Buckeye, who were buried just five months apart in 1950. Several other fire dogs, including Cappy of Engine 65 and Rex II of Engine 8, are buried at the Bideawee Pet Memorial Park. (Photograph provided courtesy of Bideawee)

dog didn't have an enemy in the world. Observed one reporter, "The firemen loved him, as they would have loved human children of their own. Small wonder that each member of the company looked on him not merely as a mascot but as a friend!"

On July 22, 1939, two little girls ran into the firehouse shouting, "Someone just threw Clown off the roof!" Captain Keil ran outside and found the dog with his legs broken and a stab wound under his left front leg. Someone had stabbed him with an ice pick and then tossed him from the roof of the three-story tenement at 212 Bristol Street, next to the firehouse. Clown passed away before the neighborhood veterinarian arrived. The firemen notified Detective John Connors of the Liberty Avenue police station, who launched an investigation. He said whoever killed Clown must have had a "depraved mentality."

The men were devastated about the loss of their dog, especially since he was one of the last Dalmatian firehouse dogs of that generation in Brooklyn. Arthur L. Amundsen, assistant superintendent of the SPCA in Brooklyn, assigned Agent Thomas Midwinter to investigate the dog's murder. Captain Keil, with tears in his eyes, said that the men were offering a $100 reward to find the fiend who killed their beloved mascot. The men scoured the neighborhood, but they never found the culprit. "If the killer had fallen into their hands," a reporter noted, "there would have been little left for the police to do, after the firemen were done with him."

Two weeks after Clown's murder, Robert G. Roberts, a dog breeder and master of Rockwood Hall Riding Academy in North Tarrytown, presented the company with a three-month-old Dalmatian. The men named him Clown II. The puppy was skilled at chewing clothes and running away in terror when the alarm sounded, but the men hoped he'd one day walk in Clown's shoes. They would be big Clown shoes to fill.

Epilogue

Following the death of Rex II in 1938, Mrs. Grace Carrera, the wife of John Carrera, superintendent of the Bideawee Pet Memorial Park, authored a poem in the fire dog's honor. Although Mrs. Carrera dedicated the poem to the Engine 8 dog, the words apply to every FDNY horse and mascot of Old New York—whether their story was told or not.

> The eighth alarm has rung, old boy;
> It's the first time you didn't answer.
> You've taken from our hearts the joy
> You gave us with playful banter.
> We've ridden together in all sorts of weather;
> The sun on our coats—the wind in our hair.
> You've answered your last alarm,
> And so will we all one day.

ACKNOWLEDGMENTS

Although most of the stories in this book are taken from old news articles, many of the "Historical Hook" accounts come from the books in my home library. As a volunteer firefighter with an interest in New York City history, I have collected numerous books on the history of the FDNY. One of my favorites is the classic *Fire Fighters and Their Pets* by Alfred Michael Downes, who served as the secretary of the FDNY from 1904 until his death in 1907. Downes's book was published in December 1907; he reportedly received the first copy only a few days before he died. Another favorite of mine is Kenneth Holcomb Dunshee's masterpiece, *As You Pass By*. I came across Dunshee's work while doing research for this book, and what a find—I was blown away! Dunshee, who was associated with the firefighting museum of Harold V. Smith on the twelfth floor of the Home Insurance Company at 59 Maiden Lane, explores the history of Old New York and its volunteer fire department through amazing tales, hundreds of old photographs, detailed street maps and map overlays, and gorgeous illustrations.

In writing this book, my intention was not to replace these iconic works but rather to complement them with a comprehensive study of the horses and mascots that served in the FDNY during the late nineteenth and early twentieth centuries. Many people assisted me in this endeavor, but I'd like to give a special shout-out to Sean Britton, curator of collections at the New York City Fire Museum, who not only welcomed me into the cellar of the museum to search for photos and check out the old horse harnesses but also let me hold the helmet and bagpipes of FDNY firefighter Dennis Smith, who had died only one year earlier, in January 2022. I have read several of Smith's books—I've read *Report from Engine Co. 82* three times—so that was a special treat for me.

I'd also like to thank retired FDNY firefighter-turned-author Paul Hashagen, FDNY historian Gary Urbanowicz, and Brent DeNure, publisher of *Vintage Fire Truck & Equipment Magazine*, for agreeing to review the book; Wayne and Lucy Crossman of the Connecticut Firemen's Historical Society for finding a few great old photos; my neighbor Michael Darcy, who lent me a leather-bound journal filled with hundreds of handwritten and typewritten orders for the FDNY from 1895 to 1899; Assistant Commissioner Kenneth Cobb of NYC Municipal Library and Archives for providing access to archived photographs; my mom, Marge Gavan, who always offers to proofread my work; my husband, Joe Ebler, for spending countless nights looking at me with my face buried in my laptop computer; and Rutgers University Press executive editor Peter Mickulas, who discovered me and embraced my proposals to write about the history of Gotham through animal stories. Finally, special thanks to all my brothers and sisters of the Warwick Fire Department for listening to my old fire stories and being a family to me for all these years.

NOTES

═══════

INTRODUCTION

1 *the Fire Department of the City of New York (FDNY) permitted firemen:* On June 1, 1982, the title "fireman" was officially changed to "firefighter." That year, following a lengthy court battle, the FDNY was required to hire eligible female firefighters. All the stories in this book take place at least thirty years before the title was changed; therefore, all the men in this book are referred to as "fireman" or "firemen." Sources: Anna Merlan, "Progress: The FDNY Now Has as Many Female Firefighters as It Did in 1982," *Village Voice*, June 4, 2014; Paul Hashagen, *A Photographic Journey through the Firehouses of the Fire Department City of New York* (Evansville, IN: M.T., 2014), 13.

1 *one dog, one cat:* "Adventures of Fire House Dogs and Cats," *New York Sun*, March 17, 1912.

1 *"it would probably be":* "Animal Mascots of Police and Firemen Aid to Stop Thieves and Save Lives," *New York Evening Telegram*, December 3, 1911.

1 *"A gentler phase of the fireman's life":* Alfred Michael Downes, *Fire Fighters and Their Pets* (New York: Harper and Brothers, 1907), xii.

3 *"from hero worshipping small boys":* "Firemen Boast Pole-Sliding Cat, Dog Mascot That Counts Signals," *Brooklyn Daily Eagle*, July 17, 1932.

3 *"There were pets among them":* "Old Fire Horses as Wise as Serpents," *New York Sun*, January 4, 1930.

3 *"Loyalty and courage were two":* "The Fire Horse, First Aid to Melodrama, Will Soon Respond to His Last Alarm," *New-York Tribune*, January 4, 1920.

3 *about 90 dogs and 120 cats:* "The Unofficial Members of the Fire Department," *New York Press*, July 10, 1903.

3 *about 1,500 horses:* "Names Now for Fire Horses," *New York Sun*, April 9, 1911.

1. FIRE HORSES

Page

5 *Young boys called runners:* Andrew Coe, *F.D.N.Y.: An Illustrated History of the Fire Department of New York on Its 150th Anniversary* (New York: New York City Fire Museum, 2015), 15.

5 *The volunteers also used:* Paul Hashagen, *Fire Department, City of New York: The Bravest: An Illustrated History 1865–2002* (Paducah, KY: Turner, 2002), 26.

6 *"the introduction of horsepower":* Augustine E. Costello, *Our Firemen: The History of the New York Fire Departments from 1609 to 1887* (New York: author, 1887), 424.

6 *"no good after that":* Costello, 424.

6 *Apparently, the squabble:* George William Sheldon, *The Story of the Volunteer Fire Department of the City of New York* (New York: Harper and Brothers, 1882), 439.

6 *James Gulick billed the city comptroller $863.75:* Costello, *Our Firemen*, 94.

6 *Other reports from the volunteer era:* Sheldon, *Story of the Volunteer Fire Department*, 87, 162.

6 *Horsepower eventually caught on:* Hashagen, *Fire Department, City of New York*, 26.

6 *Public hearings to address:* "Public Meeting Relative to the Recent Fires," *New York Daily Herald*, January 31, 1840; "Reform of the City Government," *New York Daily Herald*, December 25, 1842.

7 *the city was able to cut its fire-related losses:* Coe, *F.D.N.Y.*, 36–37.

7 *"In the future":* This order from Acting Chief Croker is one of hundreds of handwritten and typewritten orders from the Fire Department City of New York pasted into a leather-bound journal titled "Special Orders 1895, 96, 97, 98, 99." This journal, which I had the privilege of reading in full, is in the collections of Michael Darcey, retired firefighter, Engine 28/Ladder 11.

9 *"no expense should be spared":* "Fire Horse Almost Strangled," *New York Times*, July 3, 1898.

9 *Driver John Biggers was making a turn:* "Three Horses Go Over a Thirty Foot Wall," *Brooklyn Daily Eagle*, August 7, 1901; "No Pensions for the Horses," *New York Sun*, October 5, 1902.

9 *"as good as ever":* "Fire Horse Dan Made to See Again," *New York Times*, July 3, 1907.

9 *New horses (called green horses):* "Green Horse Causes Much Excitement," *Brooklyn Standard Union*, May 28, 1905; "Fire Horses Run Away," *Brooklyn Citizen*, May 28, 1905.

11 *"but they might just as well":* "Fire Horses Didn't Wait; Started for Blaze Alone," *Brooklyn Daily Eagle*, June 28, 1910.

11 *"A fire-horse . . . never forgets":* Alfred Michael Downes, *Fire Fighters and Their Pets* (New York: Harper and Brothers, 1907), 101.

11 *The injured man was treated:* "'Pete' Was Mistaken," *Brooklyn Daily Eagle*, February 5, 1911.

12 *the blaze was minor:* "Balky Fire Horses," *Brooklyn Citizen*, February 6, 1901.

12 *it took about thirty minutes:* "Fire Horses Stop to Rest," *New York Times*, January 22, 1913.

12 *He kicked over whatever:* "The Horse Breaks Lose," *New York Times*, January 22, 1896.

12 *There were no injuries:* "Schrieber's Boy Out on Top," *New York Sun,* November 23, 1903.

12 *"The city had grown great":* "The Fire Horse, First Aid to Melodrama, Will Soon Respond to His Last Alarm," *New York Tribune,* January 4, 1920.

13 *Jim was a large strawberry roan:* "Jim, the Veteran Fire Horse, Saved from the Auction Mart," *New York World,* November 20, 1897.

13 *During his long FDNY tenure:* "Old Fire Horse Honored," *New York Times,* November 20, 1897.

13 *A pole plunged:* "Breaking in Fire Horses," *New York Sun,* July 24, 1881.

13 *"the three Jays":* "Jerry Badly Hurt," *New York Evening World,* December 23, 1889.

14 *Jim and Jack achieved fame:* "Old Fire Horse Honored."

15 *"pluck, strength and ambition":* "Jerry Badly Hurt."

15 *Engine 33 responded:* "Jerry Badly Hurt"; "Fire in a Hotel Kitchen," *New York Times,* December 23, 1889; "Life in the Metropolis," *New York Sun,* December 23, 1889.

15 *The veterinarian told the men:* "Jerry Is Laid Off," *New York Sun,* December 2, 1889.

15 *Calls for the second:* "Veteran Fire-Horse," *Buffalo (NY) Morning Express,* December 28, 1896.

15 *His last day of duty:* "Jim, the Veteran Fire Horse, Saved from the Auction Mart."

15 *Captain Nash sent Jim:* "Old Jim of the NY Fire Department," *Boston Globe,* November 30, 1897.

16 *In a letter that Captain Nash penned:* "Old Fire Horse Honored."

16 *"There was never a horse connected":* "Old Fire Horse Honored."

16 *"I appeal to the board":* "Old Fire Horse Honored."

16 *"an affection for the horse"; "like a little child":* "Old Jim of the NY Fire Department."

17 *Fire Board President:* "Old Jim of the NY Fire Department"; "33's Old Jim Horse," *Chicago Daily Inter Ocean,* November 26, 1897.

17 *"He will feel strange"; "You know, an old horse":* "Jim, the Veteran Fire Horse, Saved from the Auction Mart."

17 *Jim was the only FDNY fire horse:* "No Pensions for the Horses."

17 *close to two thousand workhorses:* "New York's First Work Horse Parade," *New York Times,* May 19, 1907.

18 *"to show men that it pays":* "A Parade of Nags," *Anaconda (MT) Standard,* May 10, 1907.

18 *For the fire department teams:* "Workhorses Get Some Glory," *New York Sun,* May 31, 1907.

19 *The last workhorse parade in Manhattan:* "Workhorse Has His Day; Dog Heroes, Too, Extolled," *New York Sun,* May 31, 1914; "Dogs Get Honors with Workhorses after Big Parade," *New York Evening World,* May 30, 1914; "Horse Has His Day, but Dogs Steal It," *New York Tribune,* May 31, 1914.

20 *Joe Hoss began working:* "No Pension for the Horses."

20 *Old Charley, a large bay horse:* "'Old Charley' Is Dead," *New York Times,* August 25, 1900.

20 *Big Jim, the pure white horse:* Downes, *Fire Fighters and Their Pets,* 102–103.

21 *"and assume an expression":* Downes, 110.

21 *Charley fell ill:* "'Old Charley' Is Dead."

21 *Joe was condemned:* "No Pensions for the Horses."

21 *the city finally enacted:* "Fire Horses' Pension Act in Force," *New York Times,* July 3, 1907.

22 *But in the second decade:* "Firemen Take Pride in Traveling Library," *Brooklyn Daily Eagle,* January 21, 1912.

22 *"a treasure house of knowledge":* "Firemen Take Pride in Traveling Library."

23 *"The first box aroused keen delight":* "Firemen Take Pride in Traveling Library."

23 *"The men who used to spend hours":* "Firemen Take Pride in Traveling Library."

23 *Tom, the big white horse:* "Why Tom Is a Pet," *New-York Tribune,* October 6, 1901.

24 *"We use up an awful lot of patience":* "Why Tom Is a Pet."

24 *"He's always eager":* "Why Tom Is a Pet."

25 *experienced horsemen selected horses:* "Fire Horses Wise as Men," *New York Sun,* April 15, 1888.

25 *a rate of $250 per horse:* "Making a Brain for a Gallant Fire Horse," *New York Times,* March 6, 1904.

25 *All green horses:* "Fire Horses Easy to Train," *New York Sun,* July 5, 1908.

25 *About sixteen hands:* "Training Fire Horses," *New York World,* March 21, 1895.

25 *"An animal with what we call":* "Training Fire Horses."

25 *"dig his toes"; "peculiar terrors":* "Training Fire Horses."

26 *"a fire horse needs to be":* "Training Fire Horses."

26 *there was not a more dependable:* "Fire-Horse Saves a Child's Life," *New York World,* January 3, 1897.

27 *When workers demolished:* "Four Engine Camps Out," *New York Sun,* May 19, 1893.

27 *"wonderful masculine instinct":* "Fire-Horse Saves a Child's Life."

28 *"seemingly pleased":* "Fire-Horse Saves a Child's Life."

28 *"Giddyap, Dan!":* "Must Rename Fire Horse," *New York Times,* March 10, 1910.

28 *The assigned names:* "Names Now for Fire Horses," *New York Sun,* April 9, 1911.

28 *the number was stamped:* "Training Fire Horses"; "Fire Department Horses," *New York Sun,* January 17, 1897.

28 *"When a fireman gets to know a horse":* "Fire Horses Easy to Train."

28 *Ladder 15 had a horse:* "Firemen's Pet Horses," *Washington (DC) Evening Star,* May 6, 1885; "The Champion Pedestrian," *New York Times,* November 6, 1876.

29 *"You are respectfully informed":* "Names Now for Fire Horses."

29 *there were only three mares:* "Six Old Fire Horses to Have a Good Home," *New York Times,* June 28, 1905.

29 *"horsey to begin with":* "Six Old Fire Horses to Have a Good Home."

29 *"after counties of the old sod"*: "Irish Names for Fire Horses," *Brooklyn Daily Eagle*, March 25, 1910.

29 *"Oh, consternation!"*: "Waldo Renames Fire Horses," *New-York Tribune*, March 24, 1910.

30 *many of the firemen would resent*: "Must Rename Fire Horse."

30 *At the top of the list*: "Names Now for Fire Horses"; "Abbott Sold for $26,500," *New Haven (CT) Journal-Courier*, December 1, 1900.

30 *Second honors went to Arrowood*: "Taxpayers to Be Shown How Money Is Spent," *Brooklyn Daily Eagle*, September 25, 1910; "Fire Show Tickles Crowd," *New York Sun*, October 4, 1911.

30 *"chunky white horse"*: "Fire Horse Twenty Years," *New York Sun*, June 10, 1900.

30 *But Jerry was unique*: "Fire Horse Twenty Years."

30 *Kelly received a commission*: Irish American Museum of Washington, DC, "James Edward Kelly," accessed August 2, 2023, https://www.irishamerican museumdc.org/online-library/article/james-edward-kelly.

31 *"Jerry was transformed"*: "Fire Horse Twenty Years."

31 *"a picture in his day"*: "Fire Horse Twenty Years."

31 *Dick had fifteen years*: "Fifteen Years a Fire Horse," *New York Sun*, November 7, 1909.

32 *The horse was named*: "Fifteen Years a Fire Horse"; "Harlem's Richard Croker, an Irish American Tammany Hall Political Boss, 1843–1922," *Harlem World*, accessed August 2, 2023, https://www.harlemworldmagazine.com/ richard-boss-croker-an-irish-american-tammany-hall-political-boss-1843 -1922/.

32 *"as if he had been following"*: "Fifteen Years a Fire Horse."

33 *"ugly-looking thing"; "whose rattle"*: "This Fire Horse Too Aristocratic," *Brooklyn Daily Eagle*, August 4, 1912.

33 *"quivering nostrils"*: "This Fire Horse Too Aristocratic."

33 *"drawing an antiquated contrivance"*: "This Fire Horse Too Aristocratic."

33 *"the bloomin' aristocrat"*: "This Fire Horse Too Aristocratic."

34 *"for the purpose of finding fault"*: "Getting Ready for a Fire in New York," *Springville (NY) Journal*, March 5, 1881.

34 *the horses could hitch up*: "Fire Horses Wise as Men," *New York Sun*, April 15, 1888.

34 *the company always had two men*: "Seeing and Believing," *New York Sun*, March 11, 1881.

34 *During the second annual event*: "Judging Four-in-Hands," *New-York Tribune*, May 30, 1884.

34 *"The New York Fire Department doesn't hitch up"; "Their ingenuity is taxed"*: "Something Like a Flash," *New York Sun*, February 24, 1881.

35 *John Rush earned the nickname*: "Firemen Grieve for Rush," *Brooklyn Citizen*, April 26, 1912.

35 *"the famous black horse"*: "'Daredevil' John Rush Dies in New York City," *Glen Falls (NY) Post-Star*, April 30, 1912.

35 *After serving time*: "Rush to Lose Place in Fire Department," *Brooklyn Standard Union*, October 21, 1902.

36 *He used his own body:* "'Daredevil' John Rush Dies in New York City."

36 *he lied on his civil service test:* "Firemen Grieve for Rush."

36 *"from the zone of great danger":* "Chief Rush Killed in Trivial Accident," *New York Times*, April 26, 1912.

36 *Chief Rush was traveling:* "'Dare Devil Rush' Killed by Fall on His Way to Lunch," *New York Evening World*, April 25, 1912.

36 *New York Chief of Police:* "Victor Runs Away Again," *New York Sun*, August 2, 1912.

36 *Father Philip McGrath:* "Firemen Grieve for Rush"; "Fire Gongs Tolled at Chief Rush's Funeral," *New York Sun*, April 29, 1912.

37 *Rush was buried:* "Firemen Mourn Brave John Rush," *New York Times*, April 28, 1912.

37 *the chief's estate was worth only $200:* "Chief Rush's Estate Small," *Brooklyn Daily Eagle*, May 7, 1912.

37 *"It seems a strange irony":* "Chief Rush Killed in Trivial Accident."

37 *"I didn't see how anybody":* "Chief Rush Killed in Trivial Accident."

37 *"There goes one of the bravest":* "'Daredevil' John Rush Dies in New York City."

38 *Victor got into trouble:* "Victor Runs Away Again"; "Fire Horse's Fifth Runaway," *New York Times*, August 2, 1912.

38 *Chief Croker took a new motorized wagon:* "Autos for Fire Chiefs," *New York World*, December 5, 1899.

38 *"every day or so":* "Chief Croker as Locomobilist," *New York Times*, March 31, 1900.

39 *"The strain on the chain":* "Fire Locomobile," *Rochester (NY) Democrat and Chronicle*, May 19, 1900.

39 *The chief used the vehicle:* "Croker's Locomobile," *Buffalo (NY) Express*, July 6, 1900.

39 *He reportedly also broke:* "Three Miles in Five Minutes," *Boston Globe*, December 29, 1901.

39 *"That red devil wagon":* "Fire Chief Croker Out Voluntarily," *New York Sun*, April 11, 1911.

40 *"demonstrated his title":* "The Official Test of the Knox Fire Truck by Chief Croker," *New York Press*, January 31, 1909.

40 *Roger was hooked:* "The Fire Horse, First Aid to Melodrama, Will Soon Respond to His Last Alarm," *New York Tribune*, January 4, 1920.

40 *a large first baseman:* Flip Bondy, "Everyone Knows the Magic of the Career HR Mark, but Babe's Run for the Record Never Quite Reached Ruthian Proportion," *New York Daily News*, March 31, 2005.

40 *the term "soft-shell crab":* "Detroit Beats Yanks Before Crowd of 32,000 Fans," *New York Herald*, May 15, 1922.

41 *To show his appreciation:* The age-old tradition of wetdowns—ritualistically inaugurating a new fire engine or truck by spraying it with water—reportedly originated during the horse era, when the men sprayed the animals with water to cool them down after a hard run. Wayne Mutza, *Engines and Other Apparatus of the Milwaukee Fire Department* (Jefferson, NC: McFarland, 2020), 22.

41 *the daily ration:* "Fire Horses Aren't on Starvation Diet," *New York Times*, October 13, 1910.

41 *"Do you realize":* "Fire Horses Aren't on Starvation Diet."

42 *Bright red, twenty feet long:* "Auto Fire Engine Passes All Tests," *New York Times*, March 17, 1911.

42 *"a large-bored shotgun":* "Auto Fire Engine Passes All Tests."

42 *"frozen tears of speedomaniac joy"; "The horse is sure gone":* "Auto Fire Engine Passes All Tests."

43 *The transition went slower:* "Day of Fire Horses Will Soon Be Over," *New York Sun*, March 13, 1913.

43 *there were still 333 horses:* "Firemen Cling to Memories of Horses That Have Passed," *New York Herald*, September 12, 1920.

43 *The last of the 8 fire horses:* "False Alarm Fire Horses' Last Call," *New York Herald*, August 26, 1920.

43 *"a final affectionate hug":* "False Alarm Fire Horses' Last Call."

43 *A new seven-ton motorized:* "Motors Supplant Last Fire Horses," *New York Evening World*, August 25, 1920.

43 *243 had been motorized:* "Firemen Cling to Memories of Horses That Have Passed."

44 *Mrs. Ellin Prince Speyer:* "Veteran Fire Horses," *New York Sun*, May 1, 1910.

44 *the law required:* "Six Old Fire Horses to Have a Good Home."

44 *"cheap horses of proved work"; "dragging a truck":* "Six Old Fire Horses to Have a Good Home."

44 *Under the Fire Horses' Pension Act:* "Fire Horses' Pension Act in Force."

44 *A few lucky horses:* "Six Old Fire Horses to Have a Good Home"; "Heroes Sentenced to Death Penalty," *New York Sun*, July 14, 1917.

44 *who once proposed to buy:* "No Pensions for the Horses."

44 *purchased six horses for $612.50:* "Six Old Fire Horses to Have a Good Home."

44 *who let the horses retire:* Eleanor Booth Simmons, "The Good Samaritan That Tired Animals Know," *New-York Tribune*, August 13, 1922.

45 *Injured or frail horses:* "Peace for Old Fire Horses," *New York Times*, June 10, 1910.

45 *One such blind fire horse:* "Ran Away with Deadwagon," *New York Times*, July 31, 1910.

45 *Samson sent a letter:* "Home for Old Fire Horses," *New York Times*, September 30, 1913.

45 *One of the horses who received:* "Pet Fire Horse Gets Life Pension," *New York Tribune*, January 20, 1915; "To Send Fire Horse to Inebriates' Farm," *Buffalo (NY) News*, January 21, 1915.

45 *all of Manhattan's last retired horses:* "Firemen Cling to Memories of Horses That Have Passed."

45 *165 fire horses:* "Old Fire Horses Gradually Going to Well Earned Rest," *Brooklyn Daily Eagle*, October 8, 1922.

46 *"Do you think they'll even remember":* "Old Fire Horses Gradually Going to Well Earned Rest."

46 *"probably the first time his name"*: "Bob's Best Days Over; Will Go under Hammer," *Brooklyn Citizen*, August 6, 1908.

46 *comprised all Brooklynite firemen*: "New Fire Engine Company," *Brooklyn Daily Eagle*, July 18, 1903.

46 *"as naturally as if he had been"*: "Bob's Best Days Over."

47 *"To fortune and to fame"*: "Bob's Best Days Over."

47 *"was the cause of more picayune bickering"*: "Fire Horses Are Shod at Traveling Smithies," *Brooklyn Daily Eagle*, May 7, 1911.

47 *"The men who are taking care"*: "Fire Horses Are Shod at Traveling Smithies."

48 *purchased twenty more*: "Last Fire Horses Doomed to Retire," *New York Evening World*, June 15, 1922.

48 *which fit in perfectly*: "Brooklyn to Celebrate Passing of the Fire Horse," *Brooklyn Standard Union*, December 2, 1922.

48 *Engine 205 was one of Brooklyn's first*: "Bud, Fireman's Pet Horse, Yearns for Return to Duty," *Brooklyn Daily Eagle*, December 24, 1922.

48 *The Brooklyn Heights engine company*: "Bud, Fireman's Pet Horse, Yearns for Return to Duty"; Brooklyn Fire Department, *Our Firemen: The Official History of the Brooklyn Fire Department, from the First Volunteer to the Latest Appointee* (Brooklyn, NY: author, 1892), 45–46.

48 *The company reorganized as Steam Engine 5*: "Men of 205 Did Yeomen Work in Drive for Loan," *Brooklyn Standard Union*, October 19, 1918.

48 *the engine company had four horses*: Brooklyn Fire Department, *Our Firemen*, 211–212.

49 *"These men of the company"*: "Last of Boro's Fire Horses Retire; 205 Engine Motorized," *Brooklyn Daily Eagle*, December 20, 1922.

49 *At 10:15 a.m.*: "Old Dobbins Makes Gallant Show in Last Run with Fire Engines," *Brooklyn Times Union*, December 20, 1922.

50 *"striking sparks from the pavement"*: "Gotham Fire Horses Answer Gong's Clang for Last Time," *Buffalo (NY) Courier*, December 21, 1922. Note: No two newspapers reporting on this story in 1922 used the same names for the five horses. Most papers called one horse Waterboy, but the names of the other four horses included Danny Beg, Bud, Penrose, Smuggler, Victory, Buck, Spartan, and Bill Griffin. The five names chosen for this book appeared in at least two major city newspapers.

50 *Then the last official fire horses*: "Last of City's Fire Horses Gallop to Their Farewell Alarm," *New-York Tribune*, December 21, 1922.

51 *"They have done their duty"*: "Last of City's Fire Horses Gallop to Their Farewell Alarm."

51 *"no more loveable character"*: "Chief Kenlon Off on Trip to Europe," *Brooklyn Daily Eagle*, July 21, 1928.

51 *"It was one of those cellar fires"*: "Smoky Joe Martin and How He Won His Name," *New York Herald*, January 7, 1917.

51 *They commissioned artists*: Stan Isaacs, "Smokey the Bear Is Just Like Tom Seaver," *New York Newsday*, February 4, 1907.

52 *He died four years earlier*: "'Smoky Joe' Martin Dies; Fire Hero, 78," *Brooklyn Daily Eagle*, October 25, 1941.

2. FIRE DOGS

Page

53 *"Her fate points the end"*: "Bessie, Mascot of the Fire Fighters, Pines in the Suburbs for Good Old Days before Motors Replaced Fiery Steeds," *New York Evening World*, March 16, 1914.

53 *the breed's evolution*: Shannon Sharpe, "The History of Dalmatians as Fire Dogs," American Kennel Club, November 4, 2019, https://www.akc.org/expert-advice/dog-breeds/the-history-of-dalmatians-as-fire-dogs/.

54 *Dalmatians were the carriage dog*: Anna Burke, "What Was the Dalmatian Bred to Do?," American Kennel Club, March 8, 2017, https://www.akc.org/expert-advice/lifestyle/dalmation-breed-facts/.

54 *Jack of Engine 17*: "Some Well-Known Fire Dogs," *New York Times*, October 17, 1897.

54 *Brooklyn's volunteer fire corps*: "Dogs of Fire Dept. Have It Easy Now," *New York Daily News*, December 1, 1940.

54 *Dalmatians found it hard*: "Dalmatian Dog Back as Mascot," *New York Sun*, August 13, 1936.

55 *When she passed in 1931*: "Dogs of Fire Dept. Have It Easy Now."

56 *"good at sniffing"*: "Seek Pooch to Protect the Firehouse," *New York Daily News*, August 12, 1936.

57 *just shy of 101 Dalmatians*: "This Firehound Used to Know Every Brewery," *New York Daily News*, September 4, 1949.

57 *"One of the most interesting subjects"*: Frank J. Kernan, *Reminiscences of the Old Fire Laddies and Volunteer Fire Departments of New York and Brooklyn* (New York: M. Crane, 1885), 661.

58 *"poor trembling brute"*: Kernan, 661.

58 *"stuffed and preserved"*: "Death of a Veteran Fire Dog," *Brooklyn Daily Eagle*, August 6, 1868.

58 *"large, sober-looking"*: "Some Well-Known Fire Dogs."

59 *what made Nell stand out*: "Clever Dogs Are Cherished Pets of New York Firemen," *Washington Post*, June 27, 1912.

60 *One of her greatest achievements*: "Clever Dogs Are Cherished Pets of New York Firemen"; "Morton Building Scorched," *New York Sun*, February 28, 1902.

60 *"without having spilled"*: "Clever Dogs Are Cherished Pets of New York Firemen."

60 *"to end her days"*: "Adventures of Fire House Dogs and Cats," *New York Sun*, March 17, 1912.

61 *Bang Go was the son*: "Fine Dogs Arrive in Town," *New York Sun*, February 17, 1899.

61 *"In fact, when we first saw him"*: "Bang Go, the Mascot," *New-York Tribune*, June 30, 1901.

62 *Spot ran on two legs*: "This Dog Ran on Two Legs," *New York Sun*, January 10, 1904.

62 *McAllister discovered smoke*: "Twenty-Four Blocks Burned in Heart of Baltimore," *Baltimore Sun*, February 8, 1904.

63 *"a graveyard of smoking black embers":* Isaac Rehert, "The Great Baltimore Fire of 1904: Two Neighborhood Girls Remember," *Baltimore Sun*, February 7, 1979.

63 *Chief Kruger alerted the Pennsylvania Railroad:* "New York Sends Firemen on a Rush to Baltimore," *Brooklyn Daily Eagle*, February 8, 1904.

64 *"There was a bigger body of fire"; "It reminded me":* "Fire Fighters Return," *New-York Tribune*, February 10, 1904.

64 *The icehouses also helped:* "New York Firemen Get Warm Welcome Home," *New York Times*, February 10, 1904.

65 *"Let Baltimore alone!":* "New York Firemen Get Warm Welcome Home."

65 *"A dog reveals the manners":* "Honors for 'Baltimore,'" *New York Times*, February 14, 1904.

65 *The collar had a plate:* "Honors for 'Baltimore.'"

65 *"or if he ain't that":* "Honors for 'Baltimore.'"

65 *the boilers on the steam engines:* "New York Sends Firemen on a Rush to Baltimore."

65 *The lack of uniform threads:* Momar D. Seck and David D. Evans, *Major U.S. Cities Using National Standard Fire Hydrants, One Century after the Great Baltimore Fire* (Gaithersburg, MD: National Institute of Standards and Technology, 2004), 7; Bureau of Standards, Department of Commerce, *National Standard Hose Couplings and Fittings for Public Fire Service* (Washington, DC: author, June 8, 1917), 3.

66 *the men adopted a resolution:* Bureau of Standards, Department of Commerce, 4.

66 *"every department commence":* Bureau of Standards, Department of Commerce, 5.

66 *It wasn't until the 1891 convention:* Bureau of Standards, Department of Commerce, 7.

66 *Uptake was slow:* Seck and Evans, *Major U.S. Cities Using National Standard Fire Hydrants*, 9, 11–12.

66 *Conlon received a puppy:* "Now Mascot of the Willett," *Anaconda (MT) Standard*, July 8, 1911.

67 *Ginger was always the first:* "Clever Dogs Are Cherished Pets of New York Firemen."

67 *"It's Ginger!" "Clever Dogs Are Cherished Pets of New York Firemen."*

67 *For this heroic feat:* "Clever Dogs Are Cherished Pets of New York Firemen."

68 *"It's the most wonderful thing":* "Prince Chen Sight Seeing," *New York Sun*, August 11, 1902.

68 *with twenty-six years:* "Ex-Chief Conlon Honored with Medal," *Fire and Water Engineering* 51 (January 1–July 1, 1912): 306.

68 *died in 1935:* "Last Salute for Ace Firefighter," *New York Daily News*, April 5, 1935.

68 *The fox terrier was still on active duty:* "Now Mascot of the Willett."

69 *None of the firemen ever confessed:* "Slid Down on the Mascot," *New York Times*, March 9, 1907.

69 *"Dear Sir":* "Get a Vanderbilt Mascot," *New York Times*, March 13, 1907.

69 *"Attired only in black and white"*: "Oakie Holds a Reception," *New York Sun*, March 15, 1907.

69 *"black where he wasn't white"*: "Oakie Holds a Reception."

70 *"did not so much as deign to notice"*: "Alfred Gwynne Vanderbilt's Gift Dog Warmly Welcomed by Firemen," *Daily Arkansas Gazette*, March 20, 1907.

70 *"Immediately upon the first tap"*: "Oakie Holds a Reception."

70 *"out on the avenue"; "You ought to know"*: "Vanderbilt Mascot Quits," *New York Times*, March 24, 1907.

70 *Oakie returned to the firehouse*: "No High Life for This Dog," *Fort Wayne (IN) Daily News*, April 5, 1907.

70 *His first mate was a Dalmatian*: "Oakie Proud Father of Five," *Knoxville (TN) Sentinel*, July 15, 1907.

70 *Bessie bit six boys*: "Dalmatian Hound Bites Six," *New York Sun*, July 15, 1907; "Fire Dog Bites Seven Boys," *New York Times*, July 15, 1907.

71 *"there are milk stains"*: "Firemen as Nurses for Puppies," *Kansas City (MO) Star*, July 20, 1907.

71 *he did save a human baby*: "Animal Mascots of Police and Firemen Aid to Arrest Thieves and Save Lives," *New York Evening Telegram*, December 3, 1911.

71 *a real working fire dog*: "Fire Dog Travels on Pass," *Lincoln (NE) Star*, August 4, 1908.

72 *"To conductors"*: "Fire Dog Gets a Car Pass," *New York Times*, July 27, 1908.

72 *Bess and Oakie had five litters*: "Bessie, Mascot of the Fire Fighters"; "Oakie, Famous Fire Dog, Proud Father of Eight," *New York Herald*, February 15, 1909.

72 *When Bess wasn't having puppies*: "Fire Dog Travels on Pass."

72 *the $10,000 gasoline-pumping engine*: "Passing of the Fire Horse," *Raleigh (NC) Times*, February 23, 1912; "Last Alarm Rings for Horses of Engine 39, Ousted by Automobile," *Buffalo (NY) Evening News*, February 25, 1912.

73 *But when the motor started*: "Scorns Auto Fire Engine," *New-York Tribune*, February 26, 1912.

73 *"howled until she gave everyone"*: "Mascot Balks at Auto Engine," *New York Press*, February 26, 1912.

73 *The men named him Chief*: "Woman Gives Dog to Firemen," *New York Sun*, October 28, 1912.

74 *"There is no telling when"*: "Bessie, Mascot of the Fire Fighters."

74 *"Now there's a dog worth loving"*: "Bessie, Mascot of the Fire Fighters."

74 *Lieutenant Weiss retired*: "Lieut. Weiss Returns," *Brooklyn Standard Union*, July 29, 1919.

74 *One of Oakie's many visitors*: "Buff Put Out of Fire House," *New York Sun*, November 29, 1909.

74 *"an honor to be held highly"*: "New York Buffs Must Keep Out of Fire Lines and Houses," *Buffalo (NY) Morning Express*, December 22, 1905.

74 *"a recognized institution"; "The buffs are not recruited"*: "New York Buffs Must Keep Out of Fire Lines and Houses."

75 *the term is derived*: "500 Fire Buffs to Meet Here with Old Rigs," *New York Daily News*, June 18, 1972.

75 *The organization dates to around 1865:* Grant Dixon, "Lights of New York: Fire!," *Nashville Tennessean*, September 13, 1927.

75 *Buffs with clout had alarms:* Dixon; "The Buffs Banished by Edict of Croker," *New York Times*, December 18, 1905; "New York Millionaires Who Make Fire Fighting a Hobby," *New-York Tribune*, February 22, 1920.

75 *Croker issued an order:* "Buffs Banished by Edict of Croker."

75 *suspended him in August 1902:* "Chief Croker Suspended," *New-York Daily Tribune*, August 20, 1902.

75 *Chief Croker said that his men:* "Fire Badges Redeemed," *New York Times*, July 24, 1906.

76 *"the prize buff":* "New York Millionaires Who Make Fire Fighting a Hobby."

76 *His fire telegraph signal:* "Being the Wife of a Famous Fire Buff Makes Life Difficult, but Interesting," *New York Sun*, January 12, 1934.

77 *"I have never missed a second"; "I do not know":* "New York Millionaires Who Make Fire Fighting a Hobby."

77 *Dr. Archer, who was appointed:* "Dr. Archer Given Post for Free Aid to Firemen," *Brooklyn Daily Eagle*, July 16, 1940; "Dr. Harry M. Archer," obituary, *New York Daily News*, May 21, 1954.

77 *"dashing out in a wild state":* "Had to Run with the Engine," *New York Times*, September 24, 1910.

77 *"recuperating went to the winds"; "and with the broken":* "Had to Run with the Engine."

78 *"There's no such thing":* Elizabeth Kolbert, "What P. T. Barnum Understood about America," *New Yorker*, July 29, 2019, https://www.newyorker.com/magazine/2019/08/05/what-p-t-barnum-understood-about-america.

78 *"Firehouse Dog Sleeps in Flat":* "Firehouse Dog Sleeps in Flat after a Blaze," *New York Evening World*, September 19, 1911.

78 *"a long, lean, smoke-eating greyhound":* "Firehouse Dog Sleeps in Flat after a Blaze."

78 *"he merely opened his blood-shot eyes":* "Firehouse Dog Sleeps in Flat after a Blaze."

79 *"he meekly dropped his tail":* "Firehouse Dog Sleeps in Flat after a Blaze."

79 *"and woe would be unto him":* "Loss of Pet Moves L.I. City Fire Fighters to Shed Tears," *Brooklyn Daily Star*, July 31, 1920.

79 *"as if sensing":* "Loss of Pet Moves L.I. City Fire Fighters to Shed Tears."

80 *Battalion Chief Albert Reid announced:* "Bid Farewell to Fire Horses," *Brooklyn Times Union*, October 22, 1921.

80 *"Instead of oats now":* "Bid Farewell to Fire Horses."

80 *trotting past the office of Piquet & Piquet:* "Dog Gives Alarm for Awning Blaze," *Brooklyn Times Union*, August 7, 1912.

81 *the company was an independent:* "Trumpet for Chief Kaiser," *Brooklyn Daily Eagle*, May 20, 1907.

81 *An act of the Legislature:* "Jamaica's Old Firemen Mourn Their Passing," *Brooklyn Daily Eagle*, June 22, 1907.

81 *Several other companies joined:* "Jamaica's Old Firemen Mourn Their Passing."

81 *Horse-drawn apparatus:* "Foreman Kaiser's Horse," *Brooklyn Daily Eagle*, March 13, 1903; "Ben V, Old Fire Horse, Dies," *Brooklyn Daily Eagle*, May 5, 1913.

81 *a real horse materialized:* "A Fire Horse at Jamaica," *Brooklyn Times Union*, March 20, 1903; "Equipped with New Trucks, New Wagons, Horses and Harness," *Brooklyn Times Union*, June 29, 1903.

82 *"The rapid growth of Jamaica":* "Jamaica's Old Firemen Mourn Their Passing."

82 *Five new hose companies:* "Paid Firemen in Queens," *New York Evening Post*, June 12, 1907; Bureau of Municipal Investigation and Statistics, Department of Finance, *Real Estate Owned by the City of New York under the Jurisdiction of the Fire Department* (New York: Martin B. Jones, 1908), 115.

82 *When Ben V died:* "Ben V, Old Fire Horse, Dies."

82 *The last two horses to run:* "Fire Horses Retire on Coming of Motor," *Brooklyn Times Union*, August 13, 1919.

82 *"We are all sorry to lose":* "Motor Driven Vehicle Is Given to Jamaica Hose Co.," *Brooklyn Chat*, August 23, 1919.

82 *Sparks's mother and father:* "'Sparks' of Truck 12 Unusual Fire Dog," *New York Sun*, May 16, 1915.

83 *"Greatly to our surprise":* "'Sparks' of Truck 12 Unusual Fire Dog."

83 *Smoke and Blackie:* "'Sparks' of Truck 12 Unusual Fire Dog." Note that Blackie was not the cat's actual name. Like many all-black animals of the nineteenth and early twentieth centuries, his given name is now an offensive ethnic slur.

83 *"His vigilance has prevented":* "'Sparks' of Truck 12 Unusual Fire Dog."

84 *"were friends worth having":* "Former War Dog Becomes Fire Fighters' Mascot," *New York Herald*, August 10, 1919.

84 *"a marvel at leaping across":* "Former War Dog Becomes Fire Fighters' Mascot."

85 *"Why, all the village is crazy":* "Former War Dog Becomes Fire Fighters' Mascot."

85 *"I am very glad that he rides"; "He is a wise little fellow":* "Former War Dog Becomes Fire Fighters' Mascot."

86 *"junior 'Smoky Joes'":* "Firemen Save Collie and Await Rewards," *New York Times*, December 12, 1922.

86 *"Brown collie pup mascots":* "Firemen Save Collie and Await Rewards."

86 *Nolan retired:* "Bury Trailblazer for Black Firemen," *New York Daily News*, July 7, 1984.

86 *Wesley had been a Red Cap:* "First Black Fire Chief Turns 80," *New York Daily News*, August 27, 1976.

86 *there were only three Black firemen:* "W. A. Williams, 1st Black Fire Lt," *New York Newsday*, July 6, 1984.

86 *The society was reportedly the first:* Find a Grave, "Chief Wesley Augustus Williams," accessed August 1, 2023, https://www.findagrave.com/memorial/144477312/wesley-augustus-williams.

87 *"He was an inspiration":* "Bury Trailblazer for Black Firemen."

87 *"Brooklyn's fattest dog":* "Jiggs, Boro's Fattest Dog, Slain for Growing Vicious," *Brooklyn Daily Eagle,* September 15, 1925.

87 *Jiggs was born:* "Jiggs, Engine 205 Mascot, Refuses Life of Luxury," *Brooklyn Standard Union,* August 25, 1923.

88 *In his first five years:* "Fireman and Company's Mascot," *Brooklyn Daily Times,* December 16, 1922.

88 *Brooklyn's Engine 205 was the last:* "Last of Boro's Fire Horses Retire; 205 Engine Motorized," *Brooklyn Daily Eagle,* December 20, 1922.

88 *Jiggs received treatment:* "Champion Fat Dog Is Gout Sufferer," *Brooklyn Standard Union,* October 12, 1923.

88 *Jiggs got back into his bad ways:* "Jiggs, Fire Dog, Just Won't Reduce; Is Fatter than Ever," *Brooklyn Daily Eagle,* June 21, 1925.

88 *"any such feminine activity as dieting":* "Jiggs, Fire Dog, Just Won't Reduce."

89 *"with the regularity and fervor":* "'Jiggs,' Canine Falstaff, Pet of Engine 205 Boys, Is Executioner's Victim," *Brooklyn Daily Eagle,* June 21, 1925.

89 *The men sent the dog:* "Firedog Muzzled and Sad," *New York Times,* July 11, 1925.

89 *"Put him back on active duty":* "Jiggs, Famous Fire Dog, Glad to Be Free Again," *Brooklyn Standard Union,* July 25, 1925.

89 *New York Alderman James Cowdin Myers introduced:* "Doctors Favor Muzzles," *New-York Tribune,* April 18, 1903.

89 *legislation requiring summertime muzzles:* "A Dog Conference," *New York Herald,* March 14, 1877.

89 *"I don't think the city is a place":* "Doctors Favor Muzzles."

90 *"There is no use talking":* "Dog Muzzle Problem," *New-York Tribune,* April 26, 1903.

90 *"Well, try it on yourself"; "Wonder how she'd like":* "Dog Muzzle Problem."

90 *All they had to do:* "Unmuzzled Dogs Now Shot on Sight," *New York Times,* July 30, 1908; "S.P.C.A. Bitter against City Health Board," *Brooklyn Standard Union,* August 9, 1908.

90 *"It makes no difference":* "Health Board to Slay All Dogs Found Loose," *Brooklyn Daily Eagle,* June 22, 1908.

90 *the men of the FDNY were outraged:* "Fire Mascot Dogs Won't Run Muzzled," *New York Times,* August 9, 1908.

90 *"under the muzzle torture":* "Fire Mascot Dogs Won't Run Muzzled."

90 *its dog was shot:* "'Joke' Wrongly Placed," *New York Times,* September 21, 1908.

91 *"She's a smoke eater":* "Fire Mascot Dogs Won't Run Muzzled."

91 *"We couldn't keep her away":* "Fire Mascot Dogs Won't Run Muzzled."

91 *"God knows what'd happen":* "Fire Mascot Dogs Won't Run Muzzled."

91 *the Board of Health took another:* "Muzzles the Dogs All the Year 'Round," *New York Times,* July 29, 1914.

91 *there was only one death:* "A Year's Record of the Dog Muzzle Law," *Brooklyn Standard Union,* January 23, 1916.

91 *"chunky little Irish terrier":* "Fire Company's Dog Mascot Goes with Men to All Fires," *New York Times,* November 18, 1928.

91 *"The little terrier seems immune"*: "Fire Company's Dog Mascot Goes with Men to All Fires."

91 *New York's Board of Health modified*: "Dog-Muzzling Law Modified by City," *New York Times*, December 12, 1934.

92 *For two weeks, as Murphy recuperated*: "His Boss Is Ill, Pooch Won't Eat; Firemen Grieve," *New York Daily News*, June 15, 1931.

92 *"But not even orange lollypops"*: Marjorie Colahan, "Sad Pooch Visits Fireman in Hospital—She's Happy," *New York Daily News*, June 20, 1931.

92 *"big shot politician"*: "How 12 Dogs Won Their Honor Medals," *Omaha (NE) Sunday Bee-News*, March 6, 1932.

93 *"a fat, waddling Dalmatian"*: "Heroic Canines Have Day and So Does Just a Dog," *New York Daily News*, November 1, 1931.

93 *"the spotted black and white barrel"*: "Decorate Big St. Bernard for Saving Family at Fire," *Brooklyn Times Union*, November 1, 1931.

93 *Cappy found his way*: "Firemen Lose Pet, Gift of Bergenite," *Bergen (NJ) Record*, March 3, 1939.

93 *he not only carried a cat*: Paul W. Kearney, "Dogs to the Rescue!," *Los Angeles Times*, February 7, 1943.

93 *They may have gotten their idea*: "Smoke Eater," *New York Daily News*, September 5, 1943.

94 *"He could sell anything"; "We used to let him"*: "Last Alarm Rings for Old Fire Dog; Engine Company 65 Mourns Cappy," *New York Times*, May 10, 1950; "Smoke-Eaters' Pal Rides Last Mile," *New York Newsday*, May 12, 1950.

94 *Cappy spent a few days*: "Fire Dog Starts Storage Reform," *New York Times*, October 19, 1938.

94 *one of the sandhogs working*: "Missing Mascot Back in Fire House," *New York Times*, March 5, 1939.

94 *"well fed and quite his old self"*: "Missing Mascot Back in Fire House."

94 *Although the press surmised*: Mary O'Flaherty, "Firehouse Dalmatians Return to Dog's Life," *New York Daily News*, February 19, 1941; "Streamlined Dog Show Catches Public's Fancy," *Lansing (MI) State Journal*, February 11, 1941.

95 *a news photographer captured Henry*: "Pole Cat," *Lansing (MI) State Journal*, January 30, 1941.

95 *Henry disappeared in 1942*: "Precious Puss," *Spokane (WA) Spokesman-Review*, November 8, 1942.

95 *he brooded over his retirement*: George Hamilton, "Big Town," *Cincinnati (OH) Enquirer*, May 18, 1950.

96 *"To look at his rheumy eyes"*: "Firehouse Dogs Will Vie in Show," *New York Times*, November 24, 1949.

96 *"but they brought with them the grief"*: "Smoke-Eaters' Pal Rides Last Mile."

96 *"We'll be out every so often"*: "Smoke-Eaters' Pal Rides Last Mile."

96 *On the front door*: Freeman, "Last Alarm Rings for Old Fire Dog; Engine Company 65 Mourns Cappy."

96 *"Yes, Cappy died"*: Freeman.

96 *"Sure will miss that dog"*: Freeman.

97 *she presented her firemen friends:* "Blooded Fire Mascot Rivaled by Daughter," *New York Daily News*, July 13, 1936.

97 *he'd never go out if only the truck:* "This Firehound Used to Know Every Brewery."

97 *"the daddy of most of the fire dogs":* "This Firehound Used to Know Every Brewery."

97 *"laid away among the tall pines":* "Firemen Mourn Dalmatian Pal, Mascot 8 Years," *Brooklyn Daily Eagle*, October 4, 1939.

98 *Not only did she earn:* "Susie, the Fire Dog, Barks Alarm as Flames Menace Engine House," *New York Times*, August 10, 1936; "Mascot Spots a Fire and Barks Two-Alarm," *New York Daily News*, August 10, 1936.

99 *"He just got that name"; "Everybody likes it":* "Butts, Firemen's Dog, Is Winning Friends," *New York Daily News*, September 28, 1941.

99 *"Boy, what a dog he's going to be":* "Butts, Firemen's Dog, Is Winning Friends."

99 *"We want to keep him in the house":* "Butts, Firemen's Dog, Is Winning Friends."

3. FIRE CATS

Page

101 *"white-fleeced feline fire fighter":* "This Dog Dressed in Army Blue, and This Cat Goes to Fires," *New York Press*, March 29, 1896.

101 *The long runs:* "Firemen Lose Cat Mascots," *New York Sun*, August 8, 1915.

102 *"It is a curious feature":* "The Unofficial Members of the Fire Department," *New York Press*, July 19, 1903.

103 *"where he'd put away":* "Personals of Brooklyn's Fire Fighters," *Brooklyn Times Union*, April 7, 1923.

103 *"more value than that":* Brooklyn Fire Department, *Our Firemen: The Official History of the Brooklyn Fire Department, from the First Volunteer to the Latest Appointee* (Brooklyn: author, 1892), 208.

104 *Ladder 10 responded to calls:* Brooklyn Fire Department, 229.

104 *"who wore a fur coat":* Brooklyn Fire Department, 229.

105 *the first team in Manhattan to receive:* Brooklyn Fire Department, 128; Paul Hashagen, *Fire Department, City of New York: The Bravest: An Illustrated History 1865–2002* (Paducah, KY: Turner, 2002), 44.

105 *More than four hundred people:* Dan Valle, "The Blizzards of 1888," National Weather Service Heritage, accessed May 23, 2023, https://vlab .noaa.gov/web/nws-heritage/-/the-children-s-blizzard.

105 *During the first night:* Hashagen, *Fire Department, City of New York*, 44.

105 *every one of the twenty-two:* "Three-Horse Fire Teams," *New York Sun*, April 22, 1894.

106 *Chief Hugh Bonner told the press:* John Kenlon, *Fires and Fire-Fighters: A History of Modern Fire-Fighting with a Review of Its Development from Earliest Times* (New York: George H. Doran, 1913), 278.

107 *"One now rarely or never hears":* "Three-Horse Fire Teams."

107 *the entire team often had to retire:* Fran Jurga, "New York's Fire Horses," Equus, accessed May 23, 2023, https://equusmagazine.com/horse-world/eqfirehors535/.

108 *"The gong ranged and clanged":* "Dan's Tribulations," *New York World,* January 5, 1894.

109 *"It's a ghost!":* "Dan's Tribulations."

109 *"Yes, it was Dan":* "Dan's Tribulations."

109 *Dan had a relapse:* "Dan, the Cat, Has a Relapse," *New York World,* January 20, 1894.

109 *"Saved again!":* "Dan, the Cat, Has a Relapse."

110 *"There's a baby up there!":* "Sought a Baby, Found a Kitten," *New York Evening World,* March 20, 1903.

110 *Hero and about a dozen other stray cats:* "A Car Stable Destroyed," *New York Times,* June 13, 1886.

110 *all the employees on site:* "The Ruined Car Stables," *New York Times,* June 14, 1886.

111 *"a forlorn-looking cat":* "Ruined Car Stables."

111 *"as gracefully as any member":* Alfred Michael Downes, *Fire Fighters and Their Pets* (New York: Harper Brothers, 1907), 134.

112 *"still as ardent in answering an alarm":* Edward A. Lane, "A Fire Cat," *New-York Tribune,* February 6, 1910.

112 *"with the agility of a veteran":* "Horses, Dogs and Cats Make Good Firemen," *Brooklyn Daily Eagle,* July 20, 1913.

113 *his eyes had not yet opened:* "Firemen Boast Pole-Sliding Cat, Dog Mascot That Counts Signals," *Brooklyn Daily Eagle,* July 17, 1932.

113 *firefighters were required to live:* Barbara Campbell, "Era of Poleless Firehouse Due in '76," *New York Times,* February 24, 1974; New York City Fire Museum, *F.D.N.Y.: An Illustrated History of the Fire Department of New York on Its 150th Anniversary* (New York: author, 2015), 31.

114 *fire horses would sometimes ascend:* Jonathan V. Levin, *Where Have All the Horses Gone? How Advancing Technology Swept American Horses from the Road, the Range and the Battlefield* (Jefferson, NC: McFarland, 2017), 98; Alex Potter, "How an Ingenious Fireman Brought a Pole into the Firehouse," *Smithsonian Magazine,* July 2020, https://www.smithsonianmag.com/innovation/invention-firemans-pole-180975206/.

114 *Spiral staircases prevented:* Hashagen, *Fire Department, City of New York,* 21.

114 *It took more than a dozen men:* "A Fire Horse's Antics," *Brooklyn Daily Eagle,* October 21, 1902.

114 *a polished wood pole:* "Capt. Daniel Lawler Crushed to 'L' Pillar by Friend's Car," *Fire Engineering,* November 16, 1927, 1167.

114 *Fireman Charles H. Morris:* "A Leap Almost to Death," *New York Evening World,* December 31, 1889; "Going to a Fire in Sleep," *New York Evening World,* June 11, 1891.

114 *press reported several similar accidents:* "Going to a Fire in Sleep"; "Deadly Dreams, *Buffalo (NY) Courier,* August 30, 1890; "Fireman Potter's Tumble,"

New York Evening World, July 19, 1890; "A Dreamland Alarm," *New York Evening World*, June 22, 1894.

115 *four firemen were killed*: "Overwrought Firemen Go to Their Deaths, Asleep," *New York Evening World*, March 26, 1902.

115 *"the direct result from use of brass"*: "Doctors against Brass Sliding Pole," *Fire Engineering*, October 31, 1928, 1014.

115 *"were a menace to firemen"*: "Doctors against Brass Sliding Pole."

115 *"We've had a lot of pole-hole injuries"*: Campbell, "Era of Poleless Firehouse Due in '76."

116 *There was simply no way*: Michelle O'Donnell, "In Firehouse, Fastest Way Down Is on Its Way Out," *New York Times*, July 13, 2005.

116 *the humble brass conveyance system*: O'Donnell.

116 *it must have a landing mat*: "Slides Slowly Replace Traditional Firehouse Poles," *Firefighter Nation*, March 4, 2013, https://www.firefighternation .com/leadership/slides-slowly-replace-traditional-firehouse-poles/.

116 *Mac the Dalmatian held a monopoly*: "Mac, the Firemen's Mascot," *Brooklyn Daily Eagle*, September 29, 1911; "Animal Mascots of Police and Firemen Aid to Arrest Thieves and Save Lives," *New York Evening Tele-gram*, December 3, 1911.

117 *"Mac let out a howl"*: "Mac, the Firemen's Mascot."

117 *ran over Mac with his vehicle*: "Fire Dog 'Mac' Is Pensioned; Retires to Staten Island Farm," *Brooklyn Daily Eagle*, May 6, 1912.

117 *Fireman Warren Schneider*: "Old Dog Is Pensioned," *Ansley (NE) Herald*, September 5, 1912.

118 *"vigorously denied and resented"*: "Fire Dog 'Mac' Is Pensioned."

118 *"If it were not for the absence"*: "Firemen Lose Cat Mascots," *New York Sun*, August 8, 1915.

118 *Patrolmen were private civilians*: New York City Fire Museum, "Early Sal-vage Organizations," accessed May 23, 2023, https://www.nycfiremuseum .org/new-york-fire-patrol.

118 *Fire Patrol 3 moved into*: "A New Fire Patrol House," *New-York Tribune*, September 11, 1895.

119 *the black kitten Nellie*: Nellie was not the cat's actual name. Like many all-black animals of the nineteenth and early twentieth centuries, her given name is now an offensive ethnic slur.

119 *"a well-aimed spring"*: "A Station House Cat," *Brooklyn Citizen*, January 14, 1906.

119 *"as gently as an autumn leaf"*: "Firemen Lose Cat Mascots."

119 *he'd shout, "Bouncer!"*: Alberta Platt, "Pets Kept by Firemen in Their Engine Houses," *Brooklyn Citizen*, January 13, 1907.

120 *"No one had been seriously injured"*: "Pet Goat Excites Fifth-Ave," *New-York Tribune*, February 21, 1903.

120 *"Patrol 3. Commander Officer"*: "Firemen Lose Cat Mascots."

120 *"The Finest Firehouse in the World"*: Richard Peck, "Old Firehouses Clang in the Past," *New York Times*, March 2, 1975.

120 *large enough for seventeen horses*: Peck.

121 *"she had returned from there":* "One-Eye Horace Is Sought by Cops," *Stevens Point (WI) Journal*, October 13, 1924.

121 *she continued her hunger strike:* "Smoke, Famous Firemen's Cat, Starves Himself to Death," *New York Times*, August 28, 1924.

121 *Perhaps she was a sympathizer:* "Cat Dies as Result of Hunger Strike," *Kingsport (TN) Times*, September 2, 1924.

122 *for more than eighteen years:* "Patsy, Fire Station Cat in Jamaica, Was Friend of Old Jiggs," *Brooklyn Standard Union*, August 1, 1930.

122 *"the most human cat":* "Firemen's New Home Minus Old Mascot," *Brooklyn Daily Eagle*, February 20, 1931.

122 *the men agreed to search:* "Mascot Missed by 303 Firemen," *Brooklyn Times Union*, February 21, 1931.

123 *a "rascal" and "an old terror":* "Blackie Takes Kittens for Nice Ride to Fire," *Brooklyn Daily Eagle*, June 10, 1945.

123 *"saucily sailing down the brass":* "Blackie Takes Kittens for Nice Ride to Fire."

123 *One of the stations selected:* "City Fuel Chief Plans to Set Up 100 Coal Dumps," *Brooklyn Daily Eagle*, January 22, 1944.

124 *"a big bruiser who hangs out":* "Blackie Takes Kittens for Nice Ride to Fire."

124 *Corporal Gussie may have been born:* "6-Toed Cat Goes into High Society," *New York Sun*, December 1, 1944.

124 *this cat lived at the home station:* John Chapman, "Mainly about Manhattan," *New York Daily News*, July 6, 1932.

125 *"for meritorious service":* "6-Toed Cat Goes into High Society."

125 *the Army Service Forces was abolished:* National Archives, "Records of Headquarters Army Service Forces [ASF]," National Archives Guide to Federal Records, assessed May 23, 2023, https://www.archives.gov/research/guide-fed-records/groups/160.html.

125 *more than one hundred new structures:* Harbor Defense Museum, Facebook, November 4, 2021, https://www.facebook.com/profile/100057155572470/search/?q=theater.

126 *installed in December 1941:* Jane Corby, "Ft. Hamilton's Fire Chief Proud of Efficient Force," *Brooklyn Daily Eagle*, September 21, 1947.

127 *"That's why he hasn't hardly"; "He'll tackle any dog":* Corby.

4. MONKEY MASCOTS

Page

128 *Under the state's Environmental Protection Law:* Hanna Coate, "Overview New York Great Ape Laws," Michigan State University Animal Legal and Historical Center, 2011, https://www.animallaw.info/article/overview-new-york-great-ape-laws.

128 *traders regularly took thousands:* "1,000 Monkeys Coming," *New York Times*, April 19, 1909.

128 *also purchased numerous monkeys:* "The Importation of Monkeys," *New York Sun*, August 20, 1899.

128 *"conveniently carried about in a muff"*: "Monkeys Petted by Women," *New York Sun*, March 31, 1907.
130 *the only "volunteer firewoman"*: "Mrs. Herman Is Back and No. 31 Rejoices," *New York Times*, June 11, 1905.
130 *"with a propriety and a solemnity"*: "Miss Hermann Back to Duty," *New York Sun*, June 5, 1905.
130 *One of the many firehouse pets:* Alfred Michael Downes, *Fire Fighters and Their Pets* (New York: Harper Brothers, 1907), 156–157.
131 *the center offered:* Educational Alliance, "Our History," accessed May 23, 2023, https://edalliance.org/about-ea/history/.
131 *She even got a taste:* "Fire Monkey on the Stage," *Boston Globe*, November 7, 1904.
131 *they made her a sailor suit:* "Miss Hermann Back to Duty."
131 *Captain McAuliffe transferred:* "Monkey Stole $62," *Brooklyn Daily Eagle*, September 21, 1905.
132 *one of five companies established:* "Paid Firemen for Queens," *Brooklyn Times Union*, July 11, 1905.
132 *"like a little lady"*: "Volunteer Firewoman," *Baltimore Sun*, June 7, 1906.
132 *Munn was about to take a nap:* "Monkey Stole $62."
133 *Soon after Betsy and Bob arrived:* "Animal Pets of New York's Fire Fighters," *New-York Daily Tribune*, November 17, 1907; Downes, *Fire Fighters and Their Pets*, 149–152.
133 *one of the firemen happened to be:* Downes, 151.
134 *"second-story thieves"*: Downes, 151.
134 *"the firemen always attributed"*: Downes, 152.
134 *"peculiar fires of doubtful origin"*: Andrew Coe, *F.D.N.Y.: An Illustrated History of the Fire Department of New York on Its 150th Anniversary* (New York: New York City Fire Museum, 2015), 69.
135 *"long practical experience"*: "Domestic News," *New Orleans Daily Delta*, June 25, 1854.
135 *Baker didn't receive a salary:* "A Fire Marshal," *Buffalo (NY) Courier*, May 16, 1854.
135 *who had lived in a basement apartment:* "Arrest for Arson-Investigation before the Fire Marshal," *New-York Tribune*, July 7, 1854.
135 *"some interesting suggestions"*: "The Latest News, Telegraphic by the Morse Line," *Charleston (SC) Daily Courier*, February 4, 1856.
135 *"gangs of idlers"*: "Fires and Their Causes—Incendiarism and Negligence," *Brooklyn Daily Eagle*, March 5, 1858.
135 *He worked as a portrait painter:* "Lonely Death of an Artist," *Pittston (PA) Evening Gazette*, February 27, 1889.
135 *Not only must they first serve:* Coe, *F.D.N.Y.*, 69.
135 *Joann Jacobs and Margaret Moffatt:* "Herstory: Women in Firefighting," United Women Firefighters, accessed May 23, 2023, https://www.united womenfirefighters.org/herstory.
136 *"a desirable acquaintance"*: "Monkey Volunteer Fireman," *New York Times*, February 18, 1910.

136 *He also figured out how to climb:* "Monkey in a Fire House," *Brooklyn Daily Eagle,* February 17, 1910.

137 *"the recapture of Congressman Fitzgerald's gift":* "Fitzgerald's Monk Routs Out Firemen," *Brooklyn Daily Eagle,* February 1, 1914.

137 *"a sinister black cloth":* "Fitzgerald's Monk Routs Out Firemen."

137 *"began a correspondence course":* "Fitzgerald's Monk Routs Out Firemen."

138 *"malicious, vicious, ferocious":* "Monkey Bit Woman, Husband to Rescue; She Sues Fitzgerald," *Brooklyn Daily Eagle,* December 23, 1915.

138 *"even a window screen":* "Monkey Bit Woman, Husband to Rescue."

138 *the FDNY didn't purchase:* Paul Hashagen, "End of an Era," *Firehouse,* June 1, 1997, https://www.firehouse.com/home/news/10544909/end-of-an-era.

139 *"The shouts of the firemen":* "Calamitous Fire," *New York Times,* February 3, 1860.

139 *During a coroner's inquest:* "The Late Catastrophes," *New York Times,* February 7, 1860.

139 *"Such ladders would render":* Anonymous, letter to the editor, *New York Times,* February 24, 1860.

140 *"iron ladders could be constructed":* B. B. Lewis, letter to the editor, *New York Times,* March 10, 1860.

140 *Their "pompier ladder":* "Fire Escapes," *New York Times,* July 11, 1860.

140 *C. D. Brown and W. J. Bunce:* "Improved Fire Escape," *New York Times,* March 17, 1860.

140 *The conductor would then enter:* "London Fire Escapes," *New-York Tribune,* March 17, 1860.

140 *"seemed most capable of being":* "Improved Fire Escape."

140 *It wasn't until twenty years later:* Hashagen, "End of an Era"; Firefly's Fire Service Information, "Christ Hoell & the Pompier Life-Saving Service," accessed May 23, 2023, http://www.fireserviceinfo.com/hoellmanual.html.

140 *The first rescue using these ladders:* "City and Suburban News," *New York Times,* April 11, 1884.

140 *Under Section 25 of this law:* Clerk of the Board of Councilmen, *A Compilation of the Laws of the State of New York* (New York: Edmund Jones, 1860), 508.

140 *This law was updated in 1862:* "An Act to Provide for the Regulation and Inspection of Buildings, the More Effectual Prevention of Fires, and the Better Preservation of Life and Property in the City of New York," *New York Times,* April 30, 1862.

141 *there were close to twenty thousand tenements:* "Tenement-Houses and Fire-Escapes," *New York Times,* February 28, 1868.

141 *three men were resigned:* "Flames in a Death-Trap," *New York Times,* February 1, 1882.

141 *An 1897 law requiring rope:* "Ropes for Hotels," *New York Times,* June 18, 1887.

141 *numerous people fell or slid:* "Fire Destroys Windsor Hotel," *New York World,* March 18, 1899.

141 *"To hang a hotel all around"*: "A Silly Proposal," *New York Times*, March 21, 1899.

142 *The law also established strict rules:* William J. Fryer, *The Tenement House Law of the City of New York* (New York: Record and Guide, 1901), 508.

142 *"Fire escapes are going the way"*: Amber Jamieson, "Safety Concerns Could Make NYC's Fire Escapes a Thing of the Past," *New York Post*, April 12, 2015, https://nypost.com/2015/04/12/fire-escapes-could-be-a-thing-of-the -past-due-to-safety-concerns/.

142 *The firemen named him Jack Johnson:* "Monkey Chase Ties Up Traffic on Sixth Avenue," *New York Evening World*, February 13, 1909.

143 *Jennie briefly shared mascot duties:* "Two Mascot Monkeys," *New-York Tribune*, August 11, 1901.

143 *she was so sympathetic:* "Firemen's Pet Monkey Dead," *New York Press*, September 8, 1907.

143 *one time she bit:* "Truck 20's Pet," *New York Sun*, August 2, 1903.

144 *the men had just returned:* "Animal Pets of New York's Fire Fighters."

145 *In the official report of the incident:* Downes, *Fire Fighters and Their Pets*, 155.

145 *she slipped from her blanket:* "Firemen's Mascot Gone," *Brooklyn Daily Eagle*, September 8, 1907.

146 *"physically satisfactory Tarzan"*: Marguerite Dean, "Tarzan, the Man Ape in the Movies, Was until Recently a New York Fireman," *New York Evening World*, July 8, 1920.

146 *"Who sent you over here"*: Dean.

147 *"Being a 'Smoky Joe' is about as thrilling"*: Dean.

147 *Universal Pictures offered Pohler:* Ed Stephan, "Gene Pollar Biography," IMDB, accessed May 23, 2023, https://www.imdb.com/name/nm0689443/ bio?ref_=nm_ov_bio_sm.

5. HAPPY FAMILIES AND BEST FRIENDS

Page

148 *"perfectly good temper"*: William Chambers and Robert Chambers, *Chambers's Miscellany of Useful and Entertaining Tracts*, vol. 1 (Edinburgh: authors, 1844), 14.

148 *One of the most popular happy family exhibits:* Barnum's American Museum, *Catalogue or Guide Book of Barnum's American Museum, New York: Containing Descriptions and Illustrations of the Various Wonders and Curiosities of the Immense Establishment, Which Have Been Collected during the Last Half Century from Every Quarter of the Globe* (New York: author, 1860), 102.

149 *all these animals and many others:* "Great Fire in New York," *Brooklyn Daily Eagle*, July 13, 1865.

149 *"happy family of six animals"*: "Watson's Jokes Killed Billy," *Brooklyn Daily Eagle*, April 15, 1895.

150 *Billy was the pet:* "Watson's Jokes Killed Billy."

150 *Ben joined the fire department:* "Firedog Ben Is Dead," *Brooklyn Daily Eagle*, April 2, 1895.

150 *If ever Remson was away:* "'Spot' Was Killed," *Brooklyn Times Union*, April 2, 1895.

150 *"You will go down town on charges":* "Firedog Ben Is Dead."

151 *"Billy had a remarkable digestive system":* "Watson's Jokes Killed Billy."

152 *even winning a first-place blue ribbon:* "Blue Ribbons All Awarded," *Brooklyn Daily Eagle*, May 12, 1895; "Brooklyn's Horse Show Over," *Brooklyn Daily Eagle*, May 10, 1896; "Horse Show Closes," *Brooklyn Citizen*, May 10, 1896; "Horse Show's Glories Ended," *Brooklyn Daily Eagle*, May 2, 1897.

152 *"with great force":* "Fire Engine in Collision," *New York Times*, June 25, 1902.

152 *"a big black cat":* "Cat Imperils Human Lives," *New York Times*, August 27, 1902.

153 *"That was the fourteenth floor"; "That thirteen is feared":* "Superstition Holds Sway among City Builders," *New York Sun*, January 11, 1914.

153 *as many as 10 percent:* Shirley Li, "Skipping the 13th Floor," *The Atlantic*, February 13, 2015, https://www.theatlantic.com/technology/archive/2015/02/skipping-the-13th-floor/385448/.

153 *of 629 condo buildings:* Li.

153 *"If our Continental forefathers:* "'13'—Is It Lucky or Unlucky?," *New-York Tribune*, September 5, 1920.

154 *jumped from her room:* "Rich Woman Dives from 13th Floor of St. Regis Hotel," *New York Evening World*, January 17, 1908.

154 *leaped from his office:* "Took 11-Story Death Leap," *New York Times*, May 19, 1909.

154 *leaped or fell to his death:* "Lawyer's Fall to Death a Mystery," *New-York Tribune*, October 7, 1914; "Mystery in Death Fall at Woolworth," *New York Herald*, February 8, 1919.

154 *"his hand-shaking was"; "was fond of him":* Alfred Michael Downes, *Fire Fighters and Their Pets* (New York: Harper Brothers, 1907), 115.

155 *"that a wound upon the lower part":* Downes, 116.

155 *they had considered getting a goat:* "Firemen to Move, Mascots and All," *Brooklyn Standard Union*, December 18, 1904.

155 *"with an occasional mixture":* "Green Parrot Has Missed Few Fires," *New York Herald*, October 31, 1909.

156 *"And be damn quick":* "Green Parrot Has Missed Few Fires."

156 *"Now, even the birds":* "Fire Company Has Parrot for Mascot," *Brooklyn Times Union*, October 2, 1909.

156 *"a soft spot in his heart":* "'Rocks' Is Dead," *Brooklyn Times Union*, December 23, 1907.

156 *A few days before Christmas:* "Firemen's Dog Run Over and Killed," *Brooklyn Standard Union*, December 23, 1907.

157 *"There was nothing to do"; "went through a siege":* "Engine Co. Couldn't Lose Little Mascot," *Brooklyn Times Union*, August 24, 1908.

157 *"Let her alone, boys":* "Engine Co. Couldn't Lose Little Mascot."

158 *The men allowed Abie:* "Engine Kills Firemen's Pet," *New York Times*, March 21, 1910.

158 *the company received a report:* "Mother Saves Child," *Brooklyn Times Union,* March 21, 1910.

158 *Rags arrived at the firehouse:* Downes, *Fire Fighters and Their Pets,* 131–132.

159 *Six months after the new hose wagon:* "Adventures of Fire House Dogs and Cats," *New York Sun,* March 17, 1912.

160 *of little use for great fires:* John Kenlon, *Fires and Fire-Fighters: A History of Modern Fire-Fighting with a Review of Its Development from Earliest Times* (New York: George H. Doran, 1913), 197.

160 *The wooden pipes:* Andrew Coe, *F.D.N.Y.: An Illustrated History of the Fire Department of New York on Its 150th Anniversary* (New York: New York City Fire Museum, 2015), 12.

160 *"to contract for as many pine logs":* Richard G. Schaefer, *East River Waterfront Esplanade and Piers—Inboard Resources Whitehall Street to North of the Brooklyn Bridge Phase 1A Archaeological Assessment* (Westport, CT: Historical Perspectives, 2007), 25.

160 *first primitive street hydrant:* Kenneth Holcomb Dunshee, *As You Pass By* (New York: Hastings House, 1952), 101.

160 *first modern hydrant:* George William Sheldon, *The Story of the Volunteer Fire Department of the City of New York* (New York: Harper and Brothers, 1882), 94.

160 *"practically useless":* "Father of the hydrant": Sheldon, 94.

160 *Cast-iron pipes and hydrants:* Schaefer, *East River Waterfront Esplanade and Piers,* 25; Dunshee, *As You Pass By,* 101; Sheldon, *Story of the Volunteer Fire Department,* 63.

161 *four new high-pressure pumping stations:* Marybeth Kavanagh, *New York's Bravest: Firefighting in NYC, circa 1900,* New-York Historical Society, May 12, 2015, https://www.nyhistory.org/blogs/what-the-business-requires-images.

162 *capacity of more than thirty thousand gallons:* "New York Fire High Pressure System," *Fire and Water Engineering* 46 (July 7, 1909): 186.

162 *Manhattan had 2,066 hydrants:* Kenlon, *Fires and Fire-Fighters,* 198–199.

162 *the FDNY conducted its first practical test:* "Motorizing the Fire Department—The Horse Must Go," *New York Times,* February 19, 1911.

162 *Ten men could ride:* "Superseding Fire Horses," *New York Sun,* September 19, 1911.

163 *it cost only $50 a year:* "Motor Driven Fire Apparatus," *New-York Tribune,* August 6, 1910.

163 *The company's beloved fire dog:* "Mike, an Engine House Dog," *New York Sun,* October 21, 1909.

163 *"He wasn't mad at all"; "He was only bluffing":* "Mike, an Engine House Dog."

164 *"You ought to have seen him"; "Mike would bristle all up":* "Mike, an Engine House Dog."

164 *"Papa is captain and goes ahead":* "Mike, an Engine House Dog."

164 *"The men in the house called Mike"; "He really sang":* "Mike, an Engine House Dog."

165 *"Papa hasn't made up his mind yet"*: "Mike, an Engine House Dog."
165 *the company got another dog:* "Firemen Honor Woman," *Indianapolis Star,* December 25, 1910.
165 *"long and faithful service decoration"*: "Firemen Honor Woman."
166 *"sing a solo or join in a duet"*: "Firemen Possess a Real 'Singing' Dog," *Brooklyn Times Union,* December 4, 1909.
166 *described as an "old-timer"*: "Firemen Possess a Real 'Singing' Dog."
166 *"greatest thing in the United States"*: "Canine 'Sings' at Fire Alarm and Climbs Ladders," *New York Evening World,* March 25, 1909.
166 *Spot was best friends:* "How a Fire Dog Became a Hero," *Brooklyn Citizen,* October 11, 1908.
167 *"He looks as if he didn't amount"*: "How a Fire Dog Became a Hero."
167 *Spot's crowning glory:* "Coach Dog Hero Saves Two Lives," *Sacramento (CA) Star,* October 10, 1908; "Fire Dog Saves Lives of Woman and Child," *Muncie (IN) Evening News,* October 3, 1908.
167 *"Spot did it"*: "How a Fire Dog Became a Hero."
168 *The company was this size:* "Brooklyn's Fire Fighters: Good Record of Engine Company No. 107," *Brooklyn Citizen,* May 19, 1911.
168 *"an old but a substantial"*: Brooklyn Fire Department, *Our Firemen: The Official History of the Brooklyn Fire Department, from the First Volunteer to the Latest Appointee* (Brooklyn, NY: author, 1892), 242.
169 *"was her pride, her joy, her all"*: "Brooklyn's Fire Fighters."
169 *"tearfully watched the last rites"*: "Brooklyn's Fire Fighters."
169 *Whiskers's life ended:* "Mascot Whiskers Killed," *Brooklyn Times Union,* December 29, 1915.
169 *Another popular fire cat and dog duo:* "Firemen Seek Hit-Runner Who Crippled Dog Mascot," *New York Daily News,* May 21, 1933; "Dog, Saved from Execution, Back on Job as Fire Mascot," *Brooklyn Times Union,* April 16, 1934.
169 *"chubby, weak-kneed puppy"*: "All but Tommy, the Fire Cat, Sad over Jack's Broken Paws," *Brooklyn Daily Eagle,* May 21, 1933.
170 *The press described Jack:* "Firemen Boast Pole-Sliding Cat, Dog Mascot That Counts Signals," *Brooklyn Daily Eagle,* July 17, 1932.
170 *he was credited with twenty-two rescues:* "Dog, Saved from Execution."
170 *"probably would have been bowled over"*: "Dog, Saved from Execution."
170 *a hit-and-run driver struck Jack:* "Jack's Back on the Job, So Tommy's Happy Again," *New York Daily News,* June 26, 1933.
170 *"The guy who did that"*: "Firemen Seek Hit-Runner Who Crippled Dog Mascot."
171 *"Jack is a Lothario"*: "Dog, Saved from Execution."
171 *"Believe it or not"*: "Firemen's Dog Mascot Retires, Goes to Blazes," *New York Daily News,* May 23, 1934.
171 *Not only did he take home:* "Mike, Fireman's Dog, Gets Prize at Show," *New York Times,* February 11, 1910; "Prize Dogs Attract Attention at the Bench Show," *Brooklyn Daily Eagle,* February 11, 1910.
171 *Mike partnered with Driver David M. Lynx:* "Dog with a Street Car Pass," *New York Times,* February 3, 1910.

171 *"just like a politician"*: "Dog with a Street Car Pass."

172 *"It's the only pass of the kind"*: "Dog with a Street Car Pass."

172 *Sometimes he'd also catch a streetcar:* "Tom, Mike and Jerry, the Firemen's Clever Pets," *Brooklyn Standard Union*, December 19, 1911.

172 *the family comprised a large gray horse:* "Tom and Jerry and Mike Star Trio of Engine House," *New York Evening Telegram*, August 1, 1910.

173 *Tom was dozing under the engine:* "Mique Saved the Cat," *New-York Tribune*, June 8, 1913.

173 *Mike came to the rescue:* "Jerry the Fire Horse Cured of Bad Habit by Mike the Mascot," *New York Evening Telegram*, December 3, 1912.

173 *Nosey, the oldest and largest:* Kate Sanborn, *Educated Dogs of To-Day* (Boston: McGrath-Sherril, 1916), 33.

174 *"gave the old shell-backed veteran"*: Sanborn, 33.

174 *Mike's best canine friend:* "Jerry and Mike," *New York Sun*, July 11, 1909.

174 *"Any son of Bessie and Oakie"*: "Bessie, Mascot of the Fire Fighters, Pines in the Suburbs for Good Old Days before Motors Replaced Fiery Steeds," *New York Evening World*, March 16, 1914.

175 *His hind legs were crushed:* "Firemen Try to Save Mike, Their Mascot," *New York Evening World*, December 5, 1914.

175 *There were only two other FDNY dogs:* "Yelps Fill Garden," *New York Times*, February 11, 1910; "Firemen to Show Dogs," *Brooklyn Daily Eagle*, January 17, 1909.

175 *"those who are not so much interested"*: "Westminster Dog Show Adds Two Special Events," *Brooklyn Daily Eagle*, January 18, 1941.

175 *These choice dogs had been selected:* "This Firehound Used to Know Every Brewery," *New York Daily News*, September 4, 1949.

175 *"The black-and-white bow-wows"*: Mary O'Flaherty, "Firehouse Dalmatians Return to Dog's Life," *New York Daily News*, February 19, 1941.

176 *"not a bad looking dog"*: O'Flaherty.

176 *Fire Commissioner Patrick Walsh organized:* "'Spot' to Have His Day at Fire Department Show," *Brooklyn Daily Eagle*, February 10, 1942; Frank Keyes, "Speaking of Dogs," *Hartford (CT) Courant*, February 7, 1942.

176 *"probably most of the other"*: Joe Trimble, "Maridor, 'Best' in '38, Upset at Dog Show," *New York Daily News*, February 13, 1942.

176 *The Brooklyn Kennel Club:* "Firehouse Dogs Will Vie in Show," *New York Times*, November 24, 1949; "Fire Dept. Dogs in Brooklyn Show," *Brooklyn Daily Eagle*, December 1, 1950.

6. LIFESAVING HORSES AND MASCOTS

Page

177 *"just good common sense"*: "Horse Leaps over a Boy," *New York Times*, September 24, 1905.

178 *dogs were especially suited:* "Animals Have Caused Serious Fire Losses," *Brooklyn Daily Eagle*, August 13, 1911.

178 *Black Beauty of Engine 131:* "Fire Horse Saves Boy," *New York Sun*, October 1, 1912.

179 *Chief, the veteran fire dog:* Chief was not the dog's real name. This is the name the New York City Fire Museum has assigned to the dog, whose taxidermized body is on display for public viewing.

179 *"heroism, intelligence and loyalty":* "To Honor Hero Fire Dog with Silver Medal Award," *Brooklyn Citizen,* November 10, 1936.

179 *Chief received all these accolades:* New York City Fire Museum, "Object Record: Mount, Specimen," accessed May 24, 2023, https://nycFire museum.pastperfectonline.com/webobject/D3750C48-A472-4CA3-A324 -640615123003; Victor Weingarten, "Firemen's Mascot Takes Honor Just Like a Real Smoke-Eater—Hates Cats, but Rescues Them, Anyway," *Brooklyn Daily Eagle,* May 15, 1936.

179 *"unparalleled in canine history":* From the actual *Dog World Magazine* certificate on display at the New York City Fire Museum.

179 *"part hound, part Flatbush terrier":* "Firemen's Dog Saves 2 Kittens in Blaze," *New York Daily News,* February 2, 1935.

179 *he was even run over:* "Hit-Run Driver Kills Boro Fire Dog Hero," *Brooklyn Daily Eagle,* November 10, 1939.

180 *Chief spent a month:* "Hit-Run Driver Kills Boro Fire Dog Hero."

180 *Chief was able to save two:* "Hit-Run Driver Kills Boro Fire Dog Hero."

180 *"He's the greatest bit of dog-flesh":* "Dog Mascot of Firemen Saves 2 Kittens in Blaze," *Brooklyn Times Union,* February 2, 1935.

180 *He spent more than a week:* "Cat for Which Boy Died in Fire Was Just a Homeless Stray," *Brooklyn Daily Eagle,* November 11, 1936.

181 *Our cat-saving hero came through:* "Fire Dog Rescues Cat as Boy Dies in Vain Attempt to Do So," *Brooklyn Daily Eagle,* November 10, 1936.

182 *"You won't believe it":* "Youth Gives Life for Cat in Blaze," *New York Daily News,* November 11, 1936.

182 *"It was no one's particular pet":* "Cat for Which Boy Died in Fire Was Just a Homeless Stray."

182 *While playing in front of the firehouse:* "Fire Dog Hero Killed by Hit-and-Run Driver," *New York Times,* September 10, 1939.

183 *"When there are more and better rescues":* "Firemen's Mascot Gets Free License," *New York Daily News,* May 3, 1931.

183 *Another cat-saving hero was Happy:* "Did Dog Rescue Cat?," *Brooklyn Daily Eagle,* February 27, 1910.

183 *he performed a dramatic rescue:* "Fire Dog Saves Three," *New York Evening Sun,* December 21, 1911; "Three Cheers for the Dog 'Happy,'" *Kennebec (ME) Journal,* December 21, 1911.

183 *"stopped to marvel at the dog's agility":* "Fire Dog Saves Three."

184 *"stout and short of breath"; "after some difficulty":* "Cat Raised a Big Rumpus," *New York Sun,* May 30, 1897.

184 *"The only other damage":* "Cats Set a House Afire," *New York Times,* May 30, 1897.

184 *Animals occupied a prominent place:* "Animals Have Caused Serious Fire Losses," *Brooklyn Daily Eagle,* August 13, 1911.

184 *Arsonists also used cats and dogs:* Alfred Michael Downes, *Fire Fighters and Their Pets* (New York: Harper and Brothers, 1907), 84.

185 *the FDNY had to commandeer:* John Kenlon, *Fires and Fire-Fighters: A History of Modern Fire-Fighting with a Review of Its Development from Earliest Times* (New York: George H. Doran, 1913), 43.

185 *the law required all civilian horses:* "New York's Volunteer Firemen Make Last Stand on Staten Island," *New York Sun,* October 12, 1913.

186 *"a bit too fat for fire horses":* "New York's Volunteer Firemen Make Last Stand on Staten Island."

186 *The most petted and praised horses:* "Fire Horses Save Driver," *New York Times,* January 20, 1899.

186 *"where he can dream":* "Horses, Dogs and Cats Make Good Firemen," *Brooklyn Daily Eagle,* July 20, 1913.

187 *Baby was killed in the line of duty:* "Big Fire Horse Killed," *Brooklyn Daily Eagle,* February 27, 1914.

187 *another fire dog who was a knight:* "Fireman's Mascot Dog Saves Kitten at Fire in L.I. City," *Brooklyn Times Union,* August 12, 1926.

187 *Long Island City was chartered:* Greater Astoria Society, Thomas Jackson, and Richard Melnick, *Images of America: Long Island City* (Charleston, SC: Arcadia, 2004), 10; "The New Long Island City—Provisions of the Proposed Charter," *New York Times,* February 20, 1870.

188 *even after the city established:* "Queens Veteran Firemen," *Brooklyn Times Union,* January 31, 1903.

188 *the department had comprised:* "Queens Veteran Firemen."

188 *The new paid department could afford:* "Long Island City's Volunteer Fire Department," *Brooklyn Daily Eagle,* December 12, 1890.

188 *the department had just six steam engines:* "Poor Long Island City," *New York Sun,* May 2, 1897.

188 *The solution came on November 1, 1899:* Fire Department City of New York, Chief of Department Edward F. Croker, General Order No. 2, October 31, 1899; Mike Boucher, "Ladder Company 115 Queens," accessed May 24, 2023, https://nyfd.com/queens_ladders/ladder_115.html?msclkid =fa251feabccd11ec9cb5b50a9fb2701a.

189 *"The famous fire horse":* "Autos Replace Fire Horses," *Brooklyn Times Union,* November 28, 1921.

190 *"When the gong tapped that night":* "Maggie of Truck 29," *New York Sun,* May 4, 1908.

190 *"Well, that's just the kind of a dog"; "She seemed to know":* "Maggie of Truck 29."

190 *Perhaps the balloonist William Ivy Baldwin:* "Professor Baldwin's Tour," *Brooklyn Daily Eagle,* January 14, 1896.

191 *Rover ran to the child:* "A Favorite of the Firemen," *Brooklyn Daily Eagle,* March 24, 1895.

191 *Paddy, a large iron-gray horse:* Brooklyn Fire Department, *Our Firemen: The Official History of the Brooklyn Fire Department, from the First Volunteer to the Latest Appointee* (Brooklyn, NY: author, 1892), 189.

192 *the men had been called out:* "Firemen Rescued by a Dog Mascot," *New York Times,* August 17, 1915.

192 *"Gyp, coughing at every bound"*: "Firemen's Mascot Rescues Captain," *New-York Tribune*, August 17, 1915.

193 *"By hen be danged!"*; *"Here I've started"*; *"by the grace"*: "Firemen Knit for the Rainbow Boys," *New York Sun*, January 28, 1918.

193 *"red wagon needle workers"*: "Firemen Knit for the Rainbow Boys."

194 *"You know those men"*: "Firemen Knit for the Rainbow Boys."

194 *"almost human intelligence"*: "Some Well-Known Fire Dogs," *New York Times*, October 17, 1897.

194 *Barney was born:* "Barney, the Fire Dog, Is Dead," *New York Sun*, July 21, 1899.

194 *but it was no doubt:* "Barney, the Fire Dog, Is Dead"; "Where Yesterday's Fires Were," *New York Sun*, November 12, 1896.

195 *Barney lost one of his eyes:* "Barney, the Fire Dog, Is Dead."

195 *"A merrier, happier colony"*: "New York's Real Winter 'Floating Population,'" *New York Times*, February 19, 1905.

195 *a fleet of thirty to forty coal barges:* "2 Dogs Save Eighty on Barges Drifting into Hell Gate's Tides," *New York Daily News*, December 27, 1926; "Three Dogs Sounding Alarm Save 60 from Certain Death," *Brooklyn Times-Union*, December 27, 1926.

196 *"So suddenly and without sudden motion"*: "Three Dogs Sounding Alarm Save 60 from Certain Death."

197 *"choice dainties from their galley cupboards"*: "Three Dogs Sounding Alarm Save 60 from Certain Death."

197 *a cast of firefighters in full uniform:* "Fighting the Flames, Dreamland," IMDB, accessed May 24, 2023, https://www.imdb.com/title/tt0231582/plotsummary?ref_=tt_ov_pl.

198 *the show also featured elephants:* "Elephants Help in Fire-Fighting Show," *New York Times*, August 9, 1904.

198 *The attraction was a huge crowd-pleaser:* "Dreamland by the Ocean," *New York Sun*, May 8, 1904.

198 *"The fire features are thrilling"*: "Orphans Were Guests at Dreamland," *Brooklyn Standard Union*, August 2, 1904. Note that in 1904, American Mutoscope and Biograph produced a four-minute film of the attraction, directed by G. W. Bitzer, which features Harry and two other white fire horses. The film, titled "Fighting the Flames, Dreamland," is currently available for viewing on YouTube.

198 *"Boys, you did well"*: "Good Crowd at Island; Croker Sees Fire Show," *Brooklyn Daily Eagle*, July 10, 1904.

199 *"Fighting the Flames" was so popular:* "Great New Dreamland at Coney This Year," *New York Times*, April 23, 1905; Gary R. Urbanowicz, *Badges of the Bravest: A Pictorial History of Fire Departments in New York City* (Paducah, KY: Turner, 2002), 245.

199 *the 1905 show featured:* "Town Theatres Reopening," *Brooklyn Daily Times*, August 19, 1905.

199 *It was Harry:* "Real 'Horse Sense' at Dreamland," *New-York Tribune*, June 19, 1905.

200 *Only three weeks earlier:* "Killed at Coney Fire Show," *New York Times,* May 28, 1905.

200 *"was not part of the programme":* "Fire Horse Saved Little Girl's Life," *Buffalo (NY) Sunday Morning News,* June 25, 1905.

200 *died only two months later:* "Mimic Fire Horse Is Dead," *New York Times,* August 4, 1905; "Fire Horse Hero Dead," *Brooklyn Citizen,* August 4, 1905.

200 *which simulated the great earthquake:* "The Quake to Be a Coney Spectacle," *New York Times,* May 21, 1906.

200 *this was only the second time:* "Fire Loss Put as High as $5,000,000," *New-York Tribune,* May 28, 1911.

200 *largely due to the failure:* Rich Calder, "On 100th Anniversary, Coney Island Remembers Dreamland Park Fire," *New York Daily News,* May 27, 2011, https://nyPost.com/2011/05/27/on-100th-anniversary-coney-island -remembers-dreamland-park-Fire/.

201 *One extremely popular attraction:* Claire Prentice, "The Weirdest Attractions from Coney Island's Heyday," *Huffington Post,* updated December 6, 2017, https://www.huffpost.com/entry/coney-island-book_b_6004298; David A. Sullivan, "Coney Island History: The Story of William Reynolds and Dreamland," Heart of Coney Island, accessed May 24, 2023, https:// www.heartofconeyisland.com/dreamland-coney-island.html; "A New Coney Island Rises from the Ashes of the Old," *New York Times,* May 8, 1904.

201 *While the park burned:* Rem Koolhaas, *Delirious New York: A Retroactive Manifesto for Manhattan* (New York: Oxford University Press, 1978), 76.

202 *It was in this firehouse:* "William Marcy Tweed," *New York Sun,* April 13, 1878.

202 *His greatest achievement:* "Some Well-Known Fire Dogs."

203 *"a professional tramp":* "Some Well-Known Fire Dogs."

203 *"much larger and fatter":* "A Fire-Fighting Dog," *Rochester (NY) Democrat and Chronicle,* December 28, 1895.

203 *"and slink into his home":* "Some Well-Known Fire Dogs."

203 *"stocky-built dog":* "Jack Is Now a Life Saver," *New York World,* December 20, 1895.

203 *One of the most prominent:* "Lyons Picturesque Figure in Days of the Old Bowery," *Brooklyn Standard Union,* September 18, 1921.

204 *Policeman Farley of the Eldridge Street station:* "Jack Is Now a Life Saver."

204 *"Right on top of me":* "A Fire-Fighting Dog."

205 *"a luxurious dinner":* "Jack Is Now a Life Saver."

205 *Jack met his death:* "Killed by a Ladder Truck," *Brooklyn Standard Union,* August 19, 1899.

205 *"Well, he's a veteran":* "Jack the Bum," *Buffalo (NY) Commercial,* August 19, 1899,

205 *One New Yorker who was especially touched:* "The Social Season in Town and Country," *New York Times,* October 15, 1899.

206 *father and son Dalmatians:* "Fritz and Wag His Son," *New-York Tribune,* June 30, 1907.

206 *"he just up and died":* "Fritz and Wag His Son."

207 *Fireman John Eagan found him:* "Fireman's Coat Shroud of Engine Company Mascot," *New York Evening Telegram*, March 17, 1913.

207 *With special permission:* "Engine Company's Mascot, Veteran of Many Fires, Is Dead," *New York Evening World*, March 17, 1913.

207 *"a lean dog with black and tan markings":* "Fire Dog Longs to See Harlem," *New York Evening World*, August 30, 1905.

208 *it had a mascot dog by the name of Smoke:* "Smoke, the 69th's Mascot," *New York Sun*, September 2, 1917.

208 *The famous regiment:* "The Fighting 69th (The Irish Brigade)," Yale Macmillan Center, accessed May 24, 2023, https://glc.yale.edu/fighting-69th -irish-brigade.

208 *"a Dalmatian veteran with no more pedigree":* "Smoke Wouldn't Look," *Salt Lake (UT) Telegram*, September 12, 1917.

209 *Before diphtheria toxoid became:* Anna M. Acosta, Pedro L. Moro, Susan Hariri, and Tejpratap S. P. Tiwari, "Diphtheria," in *Epidemiology and Prevention of Vaccine-Preventable Diseases*, 14th ed., ed. Elisha Hall, A. Patricia Wodi, Jennifer Hambrosky, Valerie Morelli, and Sarah Schillie (Washington, DC: Public Health Foundation, 2021), https://www.cdc.gov/ vaccines/pubs/pinkbook/index.html; Howard Markel, "Long Ago against Diphtheria, the Heroes Were Horses," *New York Times*, July 10, 2007.

209 *The acute bacterial disease:* Mallory Warner, "How Horses Helped Cure Diphtheria," National Museum of American History, August 15, 2013, https://americanhistory.si.edu/blog/2013/08/how-horses-helped-cure -diphtheria.html.

209 *serum made from the blood:* Warner; "Dr. Loeffler Tells How He Found Diphtheria Cure," *New York Evening World*, September 19, 1912.

209 *the New York City Health Department:* Markel, "Long Ago against Diphtheria, the Heroes Were Horses."

209 *One of the horses who took part:* "Ex-Fire Horse Saves Many Lives," *Daily Long Island Farmer*, January 11, 1917.

209 *"a lockjaw serum plant":* "Ex-Fire Horse Saves Many Lives."

210 *"suffered almost nothing"; "The example of the horses at Otisville":* "Ex-Fire Horse Saves Many Lives."

210 *the farm had about one hundred horses:* "Proud Horses Save City Babies from Diphtheria Death," *Brooklyn Daily Eagle*, April 7, 1929.

211 *A biotech company purchased:* Markel, "Long Ago against Diphtheria, the Heroes Were Horses."

211 *When a reckless boy:* "Broom Was Blazing," *Brooklyn Times Union*, January 11, 1898.

211 *"remarkable intelligence"; "Neither scarcely moved"; "who whinnied a response":* "Broom Was Blazing."

212 *News accounts varied:* "Injured Firemen Better," *Brooklyn Daily Eagle*, January 11, 1898; "Judge Will Not Die," *Brooklyn Citizen*, January 11, 1898.

212 *Sadly, one of the horses:* "Triple Accidents; Two Men Crushed," *New York World*, January 11, 1898.

212 *"the privilege of decorating with flowers":* "To Honor Dead Fire Dog," *New-York Tribune*, May 20, 1907.

212 *The loyal fire dog had lost:* "Dog's Memory Honored," *Brooklyn Daily Eagle*, May 21, 1907; "Flowers for Dog's Grave," *New York Times*, May 20, 1907; "Faithful 'Fly' Mourned by Many," *New York Evening World*, April 23, 1907.
213 *"Here Lies the Body of TIP":* "Dog's Memory Honored."

7. LINE-OF-DUTY DEATHS

Page
214 *The memorial, designed in 1912:* "Children Unveil the Firemen's Memorial," *New York Sun*, September 6, 1913.
214 *"is even more graphic":* Arnold D. Prince, "The Fire Horse, First Aid to Melodrama, Will Soon Respond to His Last Alarm," *New-York Tribune*, January 4, 1920.
215 *"to our brave citizens":* New York City Department of Parks and Recreation, "Firemen's Memorial," accessed May 24, 2023, https://www.nycgov parks.org/parks/riverside-park/monuments/482.
216 *"Many a good man laid down":* "Old Fire Horses as Wise as Serpents," *New York Sun*, January 4, 1930.
216 *shattered the horse's nerve:* "Injured Fire Horses Sold," *New-York Tribune*, July 11, 1906.
216 *Engine 21 tried in vain:* "Explosion and Fire," *Memphis (TN) Commercial Appeal*, February 1, 1901; "Fire Devastates a Big Area," *New-York Tribune*, February 1, 1901.
217 *"That is the way most fire dogs"; "It is impossible to keep":* "Clever Dogs Are Cherished Pets of New York Firemen," *Washington Post*, June 27, 1912.
218 *"A false step in front of":* "Firemen's Pets," *Buffalo (NY) Commercial*, July 23, 1903.
218 *Chappie came of the best blue blood:* "He Met Death at His Post," *New York Sun*, April 3, 1892; "Fire Dog Chappy Is Dead," *New York Evening World*, March 24, 1892.
219 *"ferocious looks utterly belied him":* "He Met Death at His Post."
219 *"an absurd energy":* "He Met Death at His Post."
220 *"was a Catholic cat":* "Chops and Peter Dead," *New York Times*, August 26, 1896.
221 *"until someone appeared":* "Chops and Peter Dead."
221 *"death spasms":* "Chops and Peter Dead."
221 *"He turned a somersault":* "Chops and Peter Dead."
221 *"were entered in sorrow"; "July 22, 1896, 5:00 a.m.":* "Chops and Peter Dead."
221 *"The members of the company":* "Chops and Peter Dead."
222 *they had lost six dogs:* "Wallabout Firemen Mascots," *Brooklyn Times Union*, July 15, 1898.
222 *the company finally adopted a feline:* "Mascot Animals Strangely Killed," *Brooklyn Citizen*, February 20, 1901.
223 *after a kerosene lamp exploded:* "Mascot Animals Strangely Killed."
223 *a fire of suspicious origin:* "Firemen's Pet Horse Killed," *New York Times*, November 21, 1901.

224 *"He died like many"*: "Firemen's Pet Horse Killed."

224 *was struck by a fallen body*: Stephanie Gaskell, "'Bodies Came from the Sky': Anguished WTC Heroes Tell of Haywire Signals and Last Farewells," *New York Post*, August 13, 2005.

224 *When Socks first joined*: "Socks, the Fire Dog, Is Dead," *New York Sun*, December 18, 1902.

225 *Policeman Wilkesman dispatched*: "Fire Dog Meets Untimely End," *New-York Tribune*, December 18, 1902.

225 *"with all the honor due"*: "Socks, the Fire Dog, Is Dead."

225 *Finger made the ultimate sacrifice*: "Brave Fireman Buried," *New York Times*, December 29, 1906.

225 *Mrs. Seligman's coachman*: "Socks, the Fire Dog, Is Dead"; "New $600 Fire Mascot," *New York Evening World*, October 28, 1901.

225 *Seligman was one of eight brothers*: "Death of Jesse Seligman," *New-York Daily Tribune*, April 24, 1894.

226 *"Whenever a fire company"*: "Firemen's Pets."

226 *Engine 39 received a Dalmatian*: "Fire Dog for 'Number 39,'" *New-York Tribune*, July 3, 1900.

226 *a Dalmatian named Swipes*: "The Social Season in Town and Country," *New York Times*, October 15, 1899.

226 *the men bedecked the dog*: "Firemen Get a New Dog," *New York Times*, April 13, 1900.

226 *who had stolen Jack*: "Stolen Dog Given to Firemen," *New-York Tribune*, April 12, 1900.

226 *"The dogs made good pets"*: "Firemen Get a New Dog."

226 *Mike had only seven months*: "Firemen's Mascot Dead," *Brooklyn Daily Eagle*, April 2, 1903.

227 *He presented the kitten*: "Firemen's Pets Are Poisoned," *New-York Tribune*, August 16, 1904; "Firemen's Pets Poisoned," *New York Sun*, August 16, 1904.

227 *"Spot was on his feet"*: "Fire Truck Went On," *New York Times*, June 18, 1908.

227 *"Tenements. Lose no time"; "whirling and circling"*: "Fire Truck Went On."

227 *"howled a not pretty"*: "Fire Truck Went On."

228 *"And this a damn cellar"; "Damage fifteen cents"*: "Fire Truck Went On."

228 *an explosion of illuminating gas*: "Jerry Dies; Girls Safe," *New-York Tribune*, October 18, 1904.

228 *A split-second decision*: "Saved by Horse's Leap," *New-York Tribune*, December 7, 1904.

229 *Engine 76 was a new company*: Mike Boucher, "Fire Company Locations of New York City," New York Fire Department, accessed May 24, 2023, https://nyfd.com/cityhist.pdf.

229 *his long career ended*: "Horse Dies for Child," *New-York Tribune*, July 3, 1905.

229 *the SPCA began running*: James J. Walsh, *History of Medicine in New York: Three Centuries of Medical Progress* (New York: National Americana Society, 1919), 286; ASPCA, "History of the ASPCA," accessed May 24, 2023, https://www.aspca.org/about-us/history-of-the-aspca.

230 *the FDNY now had its own:* "Ambulance for Fire Horses," *New York Times,* April 29, 1906.

230 *This three-story brick building:* "Huge Fire Headquarters to Occupy an Entire Block," *New York Times,* June 16, 1912.

230 *"died in discharge of duty":* "Making a Brain for a Gallant Fire Horse," *New York Times,* March 6, 1904.

230 *"to end his days in front":* "Making a Brain for a Gallant Fire Horse."

230 *In addition to the main hospital:* "A New Fire Engine," *New-York Tribune,* September 7, 1860.

230 *"You see they run"; "It's hard on the horses":* "Breaking in Fire Horses," *New York Sun,* July 24, 1881.

230 *The large complex occupied:* "Training Stable," *Brooklyn Standard Union,* January 2, 1897.

231 *the two old sheds:* "New Training Stable," *Brooklyn Times Union,* January 2, 1897.

231 *"thoroughly equipped engine house":* "Engine Company No. 156 Covers a Dangerous District," *Brooklyn Citizen,* August 2, 1911.

232 *surrendered to the Sinking Fund Commission:* "Smothering One-Alarm Fires by Motor's Reach," *New York Times,* January 2, 1916.

232 *The city's Department of Street Cleaning:* City of New York, *City Record* 44, no. 12993 (February 1916): 1152; "Department of Street Cleaning," *New-York Tribune,* February 21, 1920; "New Training Stable."

232 *The Brooklyn facility served:* "Auxiliary Fire Fighters Will Have Headquarters," *Brooklyn Standard Union,* February 22, 1919; "$8,200,000 Memorial Gifts Pledged in Diocesan Expansion Program," *The Tablet,* April 2, 1960.

232 *The building survived demolition:* "Slum Area to Give Way to Fine Homes, L.I.U. Campus," *Brooklyn Daily Eagle,* August 15, 1954.

232 *Rocks, a Brooklyn brindle bulldog:* "Fire Dog Dies Martyr to Duty," *New-York Tribune,* December 23, 1907.

233 *Bang was poisoned:* "Fire Laddies Mourn Mascot," *Brooklyn Daily Eagle,* August 15, 1907.

233 *Whiskers slid under the wheels:* "Mascot Whiskers Killed," *Brooklyn Times Union,* December 29, 1915.

233 *he would "make trouble":* "Christian, Fire Dog, Killed," *New York Sun,* September 1, 1908.

233 *His action saved the children:* "Fire Horse Killed by Fall," *New-York Tribune,* April 12, 1909.

234 *Putting all his weight on the right rein:* "Fire Horse Killed on Run," *New York Times,* September 29, 1909.

234 *accompanied by the Reverend Joseph Ives:* "Fire Company's Mascot Goes to Death in Chair," *Burlington (VT) Daily News,* May 11, 1921.

234 *"with military honors":* "Martial Honors for Dog Mascot, Dead from Duty," *New York Daily News,* May 12, 1921.

235 *He joined the company in 1904:* "Injured Man Aids Horse," *New-York Tribune,* November 13, 1909. Note that Nick was not the horse's real name. Like many all-black animals of the nineteenth and early twentieth centuries, his given name is now an offensive ethnic slur.

235 *"Killed in the Performance":* "Spot Died at Duty's Post," *New York Times,* August 14, 1904.

235 *may have been a little dog:* "Sport, Fire Dog, Dead," *Brooklyn Citizen,* October 14, 1909.

236 *Engine 166 responded:* "Veteran Fireman Killed by Smoke," *Brooklyn Standard Union,* January 24, 1907; "Fire at Rockaway Beach," *Brooklyn Times Union,* January 24, 1907.

236 *he accompanied one of the firemen:* "Firemen Happy Again," *Brooklyn Daily Eagle,* March 18, 1909. Note that this newspaper called the dog "Chief."

237 *"He died a hero"; "We brought him":* "Fire Dog Died a Hero," *New York Sun,* May 9, 1912.

237 *That was the day Mrs. Deslys died:* "Gaby Deslys Dies after Operation," *New York Times,* February 12, 1920.

237 *Gaby walked outside:* "Dog of Gaby Deslys Ends Grief in Death," *New York Daily News,* March 28, 1921.

237 *"a bull with heavy jowls":* "Well Known Fire Dog Dies," *Richford (VT) Journal and Gazette,* July 12, 1912.

238 *"with all the honors":* "Well Known Fire Dog Dies."

238 *Jimmie was curled up asleep:* "Adventures of Fire House Dogs and Cats," *New York Sun,* March 17, 1912.

239 *"And the toughest part of all":* "Firemen's Pet Killed by Auto," *New York Sun,* May 6, 1913.

239 *They both went to St. Catherine's:* "Last Rites Given to Dying Firemen in Burning Ruins," *New York Evening World,* November 24, 1913; Paul Hashagen, *Fire Department, City of New York: The Bravest: An Illustrated History 1865–2002* (Paducah, KY: Turner, 2002), 7.

240 *"I have reported":* "Throngs at Funeral of Father M'Gronen," *Brooklyn Tablet,* October 10, 1914.

240 *The two Manhattan-based chaplains:* "Fire Department Chaplains," *Brooklyn Citizen,* March 29, 1899; "Fire Chaplains Appointed," *Brooklyn Standard Union,* March 29, 1899.

240 *"The new chaplains will furnish":* "Gold Badges for Chaplains," *Brooklyn Daily Eagle,* March 30, 1899.

241 *As he observed:* "Gold Badges for Chaplains."

242 *"theaters, race tracks":* "Gold Badges for Chaplains."

242 *"small token":* "Gold Badges for Chaplains."

242 *The two chaplains received:* "Chaplains' First Fire," *New York Sun,* March 31, 1899.

242 *A. H. Meter Pabst Harlem Music Hall:* "The Legendary Pabst Harlem in Harlem, NY, 1900–1917," *Harlem World Magazine,* accessed May 24, 2023, https://www.harlemworldmagazine.com/pabst-harlem-harlem-1900-1917/.

242 *He was still a young pup:* "Sport, Firemen's Pet, Dead," *Brooklyn Daily Eagle,* April 8, 1914.

243 *"and a tongue that seemed":* "Heroic Fire Dog to Pay with His Life," *New York Sun,* April 24, 1917.

243 *"could smell his way":* "Will Honor Smoke Who Saved Lives of Many Firemen," *Buffalo (NY) Courier,* May 6, 1917.

243 *"by taking risks that ordinarily"*: "Firemen Get Back Luck with Smoke," *New York Sun*, January 13, 1917.

243 *he was possibly chased out of town*: "Supertom Leads Submarine Cats," *New York Sun*, March 5, 1917.

243 *"a series of staccato barks"*: "Firemen Get Back Luck with Smoke."

244 *"only six of the countless number"*: "Supertom Leads Submarine Cats."

244 *When the valiant dog left*: "Smoke, Fire Dog, Chloroformed To-Day," *New York Evening World*, April 24, 1917.

244 *The firemen thought it fitting*: Warren MacAllen, "Fire Dog Who Made Good Dias as Four-4s Sound," *New York Daily News*, October 15, 1929; "Puppy, Firehouse Pet, Killed Answering Alarm; Dog Hit by Taxi as It Dashes to Post on Engine," *New York Times*, October 15, 1929.

245 *She eventually retired*: "Bessie, Mascot of the Fire Fighters, Pines in the Suburbs for Good Old Days before Motors Replaced Fiery Steeds," *New York Evening World*, March 16, 1914.

245 *A photo of him grabbing*: "Betting on the Dog," *New York Daily News*, September 26, 1929.

245 *Rex was chosen*: "Rex Is King," *New York Daily News*, May 25, 1935.

245 *He died from pneumonia*: "Fire Fighters Mourn Death of Mascot," *New York Daily News*, November 20, 1936.

245 *Rex II followed*: "Fire Engine Is Dog's Hearse as Rex II Gets a Hero's Burial," *Brooklyn Daily Eagle*, July 25, 1938.

246 *Rex III joined the company*: "Fire Mascot Dies Trying to Hitch Ride to Blaze," *New York Daily News*, August 4, 1941.

246 *two sisters from Huntington*: Alice Cogan, "Firemen's Pet Slain, Hurled from Roof," *Brooklyn Daily Eagle*, July 28, 1939.

247 *"The firemen loved him"*: "Clown, Firemen's Mascot, Slain by Supposed Friend," *Asbury Park (NJ) Press*, November 19, 1939.

247 *"Someone just threw Clown"*: "Clown, Firemen's Mascot, Slain by Supposed Friend."

248 *"depraved mentality"*: "Clown, Firemen's Mascot, Slain by Supposed Friend."

248 *"If the killer had"*: "Clown, Firemen's Mascot, Slain by Supposed Friend."

248 *The men named him Clown II*: "Dog 'Clown' Dead, Firemen Get No. 2," *New York Daily News*, August 9, 1939.

EPILOGUE

Page

249 *"The eighth alarm has rung"*: "Fire Engine Is Dog's Hearse as Rex II Gets a Hero's Burial," *Brooklyn Daily Eagle*, July 25, 1938.

INDEX

ABOUT THE AUTHOR

Peggy Gavan is a senior editor, New York City tour guide, and volunteer firefighter with thirty years of service in Warwick, New York. She is the author of the *The Cat Men of Gotham: Tales of Feline Friendships in Old New York* (Rutgers University Press, 2019) and the winner of the 2019 Certificate of Excellence and MUSE Medallion from the Cat Writers Association.